Zohar Segev
The World Jewish Congress during the Holocaust

New Perspectives on Modern Jewish History

Edited by Cornelia Wilhelm

Volume 7

Zohar Segev

The World Jewish Congress during the Holocaust

Between Activism and Restraint

DE GRUYTER
OLDENBOURG

ISBN 978-3-11-055402-1
e-ISBN 978-3-11-032026-8
ISSN 2192-9645

The e-book of this title is freely available on www.degruyter.com.

Library of Congress Cataloging-in-Publication Data
A CIP catalog record for this book has been applied for at the Library of Congress.

Bibliographic information published by the Deutsche Nationalbibliothek
The Deutsche Nationalbibliothek lists this publication in the Deutsche Nationalbibliografie; detailed bibliographic data are available in the Internet at http://dnb.dnb.de.

© 2017 Walter de Gruyter GmbH, Berlin/Boston
This volume is text- and page-identical with the hardback published in 2014.
Typesetting: Michael Peschke, Berlin
Printing: CPI books GmbH, Leck
♾ Printed on acid free paper
Printed in Germany

www.degruyter.com

Preface

One way that historical research differs from other fields of academic inquiry is in the isolation of the scholar. We generally sit alone reading documents in archives and write our articles and books without co-authors. But, this book could not have been written without material and moral assistance from colleagues, family and friends.

Archival documents constitute the basis for the historical research that has led to the writing of this book. This research could not have been carried out without the devoted help and professional skill of archive workers in the United States and in Israel. My deepest thanks to those in the Central Zionist Archive in Jerusalem, in the Archive of the American Jewish Historical Society in New York, in the Yad Vashem Archive in Jerusalem and in the American Jewish Joint Distribution Committee (JDC) in New York and Jerusalem.

A special debt of gratitude is due to Professor Gary Zola, head of the Jacob Rader Marcus American Jewish Archives in Cincinnati, Ohio and to his staff, who managed to combine a homelike environment with consummate professional skills. The preservation and maintenance of World Jewish Congress documents in the Cincinnati Archives is a shining example of archival work. The generous scholarships received from the Cincinnati archive, together with the outstanding physical surroundings I enjoyed at the archive and on the Hebrew Union College campus in Cincinnati were central to the possibility of completing this research.

Heartfelt thanks are extended as well to research workers and colleagues whom I consulted in the course of my writing: Anita Shapira, Mark A. Raider, Daniel Gutwein, Lee Shai Weissbach, Hasia Diner, Ronald W. Zweig, David Myers, Aviva Halamish, Ofer Schiff and Jonathan D. Sarna. Conversations with them opened up new research perspectives; their comments removed obstacles, clarified difficulties and brought research issues into sharper focus. The research forum at the Chaim Weizmann Institute for the Study of Zionism and Israel at Tel Aviv University, headed by Prof. Shapira, afforded significant historical insights for my research in general and for this book in particular.

The Jewish History Department and the Faculty of Humanities at the University of Haifa were my home in the full sense of the word while I wrote the book. I thank them for their support over the years.

Last but certainly not least is De Gruyter Publishers that brought the project to its conclusion. Fortunate is the author who has a publisher with such a dedicated and courteous professional staff. Special thanks are due to the manuscript editor Marcia D. Rothschild, to the publisher's editor Dr. Julia Brauch and to Prof. Cornelia Wilhelm, editor of the series New Perspectives in Modern Jewish History.

As the book was being written, our family life was going through far-reaching changes. Facing the Mediterranean from Mount Carmel, a wonderfully supportive new family arose. To my life partner Naama, to her children and to mine, this book is dedicated.

Contents

Preface —— v

List of figures —— ix

Introduction: The Founding of the World Jewish Congress —— 1

Chapter 1
World Jewish Congress Activity in the United States during World War II —— 23
    The World Jewish Congress and Reports of the Holocaust of
    European Jewry —— 23
    The World Jewish Congress Leadership and the Jewish Public in the United
    States at the Time of the Holocaust —— 35

Chapter 2
**Stephen Wise, Nahum Goldmann, and the Question of Palestine
in 1940s America —— 43**
    The Episode of the Pro-Zionist Proposals in Congress —— 43
    The Party Platforms —— 76
    Moderation and Restraint: The Response by American Jews to the Holocaust
    and the Struggle for the Establishment of the State of Israel —— 91

Chapter 3
The World Jewish Congress's Rescue Effort —— 115
    The "Soul Searching" Conference in Atlantic City —— 115
    Philanthropy and Politics: The World Jewish Congress and the Jews of Europe
    1936–1942 —— 124
    The Untold Story: The Operation to Rescue Children in Portugal —— 134
    From Denmark to Bulgaria: The Involvement of the World Jewish Congress in
    Further Rescue Operations in Europe —— 158

Chapter 4
**Diaspora Nationalism, The World Jewish Congress, American Jewry,
and the Post-War Rehabilitation of Europe's Jews —— 168**
    The Rehabilitation of Europe's Jews —— 168
    The Institute of Jewish Affairs —— 184
    Diaspora Nationalism —— 201

Summary —— 217

Afterword —— 224

Bibliography —— 227
    Archives —— 227
    Published Documents —— 228

Index —— 233

List of figures

Figure 1: A poster advertising the Foster Parents Plan for European Jewish Children. AJA, 361 J11/5 —— **105**
Figure 2: Photographs of children hidden with peasant families in the Foster Parents Plan for European Jewish Children. AJA, 361 J11/5 —— **106**
Figure 3: World Jewish Congress Children Division, 1946. AJA, 361 J11/5 —— **107**
Figure 4: Nahum Goldmann. AJA, 361 J13/24 —— **108**
Figure 5: Stephen Wise. AJA, 361 J14/23 —— **109**
Figure 6: Program cover of the War Emergency Conference, Atlantic City, N.J., 26-30 November 1944. AJA, 361 J17/1 —— **110**
Figure 7: Participant tags of the War Emergency Conference, Atlantic City, N.J., 26-30 November, 1944. AJA, 361 J17/1 —— **111**
Figure 8: Poster of the American Committee for the Rehabilitation of European Jewish Children. AJA, 361 J18/1 —— **112**
Figure 9: War Emergency Conference at the St. Charles Hotel, Atlantic City, N.J., 26-30 November 1944 —— **113**

Introduction:
The Founding of the World Jewish Congress

The inaugural convention of the World Jewish Congress (WJC), which was attended by 280 delegates from 32 countries, took place in Geneva in August 1936. While the organization itself was new, its ideological roots lay in the transformations experienced by the Jewish communities in the United States and Europe in the wake of World War I, and in the Balfour Declaration. The purpose of the WJC was twofold: to continue in the tradition of the American Jewish Congress (founded in 1918) and the Committee of Jewish Delegations (founded in 1919) to operate as a voluntary organization representing Jewish communities and organizations worldwide vis-à-vis government authorities and international bodies, and to foster the development of social and cultural life in Jewish communities around the world.

The establishment of the Congress, as well as the organizational and political activity of its institutions, was the outcome of an ideological view manifested in a wide range of speeches, journal articles, and minutes of meetings dating back to the beginning of the organization's creation. In 1933, the American Founding Committee, in conjunction with the American Jewish Congress, distributed an open letter informing the Jewish public in the United States of the intention to found the organization, and explaining the ideological position that had driven the initiative.[1] Its lead founder and first president was the Reform rabbi Stephen S. Wise, among the foremost Zionist leaders in the United States and an active supporter of the Democratic Party.[2] The founders proceeded upon the assumption that the condition of world Jewry in 1933 unequivocally demonstrated to Jews

---

[1] Letter of the Founding Committee of the World Jewish Congress, October 26, 1933, documents of the World Jewish Congress at the Jacob Rader Marcus Center of the American Jewish Archives, Cincinnati, OH. Manuscript collection 361, box A40, folder 4 (hereafter AJA, 361 A40/4).

[2] For a general account of the WJC see Leon A. Kubowizki, *Unity In Dispersion: A History of the World Jewish Congress* (New York, 1948); and Isaac I. Schwarzbart, *25 Years In the Service of the Jewish People: A Chronicle of Activities of the World Jewish Congress August 1932–February 1957* (New York, 1957). Among the other leading figures who actively participated in the founding of the organization were the Zionist leader Leo Motzkin, and Louis Lipsky, the former chairman of the American Zionist Organization. For an appreciation of the dominance of the United States, see letter from Nahum Goldmann to Eliezer Kaplan, Treasurer of the Jewish Agency at the time, January 11, 1943, Central Zionist Archive in Jerusalem, record group Z-6, file 2755 (hereafter CZA, Z-6/2755). On the organization's total financial dependence on the United States, see letter from Nahum Goldmann to Stephen Wise, December 17, 1936, AJA, 361 A1/1. For an example of the voluminous works on Wise, see Melvin I. Urofsky, *A Voice That Spoke for Justice: The Life and Times of Stephen S. Wise* (Albany, 1982).

and non-Jews alike that the Jewish Diaspora was a distinct entity that shared a single destiny. The drafters of the letter believed that the signing of the Balfour Declaration made it possible for international recognition of the need for the establishment of a national home in Palestine to go hand in hand with recognition of the existence of a Jewish entity in the Diaspora—that the national home in Palestine and the Jewish Diaspora were two sides of the same coin. In their view, these constituted two parallel lines of development of Jewish nationality, which coexisted and nourished each other.[3]

The issue of Palestine resurfaced later in the letter. While the WJC leadership was well aware of the importance of Palestine in absorbing Jewish immigration, it emphasized its belief that Jewish migration from Europe to Palestine was ideologically driven, and that the new organization should therefore not engage with it, since the mission of the WJC was to find a comprehensive solution for the masses of Eastern and Central European Jews. Palestine could not, so they believed, provide an answer to the distress being suffered by Eastern European Jewry.[4]

The founders of the WJC were aware that the need for establishing an international Jewish organization in the mid-1930s was not self-evident, particularly in light of the existence of the Zionist movement and other philanthropic Jewish bodies that were operating in the international arena. This realization was expressed in a booklet distributed among the Jewish public in the United States in 1934. The document took the form of questions and answers and was intended both to introduce the WJC to the Jewish public and to address concerns regarding its singularity and necessity.[5] The first question addressed in the booklet was "What is the World Jewish Congress?" The authors' response emphasized the democratic nature of the organization, adding that its structure would facilitate addressing the severe problems besetting the Jewish people in the 1930s. Subsequent questions referred to the uniqueness of the WJC vis-à-vis existing Jewish organizations engaged in defending the rights of Jews and in attempting to improve their economic condition. The authors asserted that the existing organizations represented only a relatively small number of Jews within the entirety of world Jewry and that, because of their undemocratic nature, they had sometimes failed to adequately represent the interests of the Jews as a whole. Furthermore, activities directed at improving the economic circumstances of the Jews had been primarily philanthropic in character, whereas the WJC would seek to radically transform the global Jewish economic structure.[6]

---

3 Letter of the Founding Committee, October 26, 1933, AJA, 361 A40/4.
4 Ibid.
5 Questions and Answers Booklet, 1934 (no precise date given), AJA, 361 A40/4.
6 Ibid.

The uniqueness of the WJC in relation to existing bodies was likewise highlighted in the question that presented issues the organization planned to tackle in future. The answer covered a wide range of issues—from Jewish migration, through the rehabilitation and amelioration of the condition of Jews unable to migrate, to the struggle against anti-Semitism and for the Jews' basic human rights. The authors noted that the issue of migration to Palestine was the responsibility of the Jewish Agency, and that the WJC would engage in this area only in order to support and assist the activity of that body. The authors thus laid out a singular world view (that would be spelled out more clearly later in the document), in which the Congress was not opposed to the Zionist enterprise in Palestine, but did not regard this as its overriding concern.[7]

The objectives presented by the founders to the WJC were far-reaching and ambitious—and likely to raise doubts as to its ability to achieve them. In their response to questions along these lines, the authors stated that, unlike the Jewish bodies that had operated thus far, the institutions of the WJC would prepare a comprehensive collection of data and information relating to world Jewry in order to facilitate correct and effective action in relation to the global political system. The founders believed that the attack on the rights of European Jewry and Nazi propaganda directed against the Jews would serve to intensify the pressure on the League of Nations to find appropriate solutions to the distress of the Jews. Given the current crisis of European Jewry, the efforts of the public relations campaign that the WJC intended to wage, combined with the joint action undertaken by all the Jewish organizations and with the activity within the League of Nations, were likely to produce a future solution and to improve the situation of the Jews worldwide.[8]

The renowned philosopher and sociologist Professor Horace M. Kallen affirmed the necessity of founding the World Jewish Congress when he addressed its preparatory convention in Geneva in 1934. Kallen argued that the processes of globalization and democratization had destroyed the Jewish solidarity of the Middle Ages, and that it was essential to establish the WJC in order to rebuild it. The vital need for the organization was underscored, he believed, by the anti-Jewish propaganda emanating from Germany as well as world-wide trends toward racism and totalitarian regimes. It was the Jews who were suffering most from these trends; consequently, it was the duty of Jews worldwide to oppose them with renewed vigor. A democratic Jewish congress was, therefore, the essential response. Kallen stressed that the Jewish philanthropic organizations that had arisen in the wake of the emancipation were not confronting the problems facing

---

7 Ibid.
8 Ibid.

world Jewry. Ad hoc solutions that provided a temporary material response to the hardships experienced by Jews could not resolve the Jewish problem and in a certain sense exacerbated it, since they offered local, short-term measures, thereby postponing more comprehensive solutions.[9]

The tendencies manifested in the letter of 1933 and in Kallen's address were reinforced in a memorandum submitted by the directorate of the WJC to the institutions of the League of Nations in 1936.[10] The memorandum reviews the traditional Jewish support for peace and international cooperation, and underscores the organization's contribution to the struggle for these ideals. The memorandum was intended to secure the League of Nations' support for the rights of minorities in general and of the Jews in Europe in particular, and to position the Congress as the exclusive representative of the Jewish people in the Diaspora. For this reason, the members of the Executive Committee of the WJC, who authored the document, stressed that the organization represented the Jews of the Diaspora and was fighting for minority rights, but likewise supported the Jewish community in Palestine and was working to stabilize the mandated government there.[11] Thus they clarified their world view: advocating a complex Jewish reality that combined a Jewish national existence in the Diaspora with the founding of a national home in Palestine. The WJC was the ultimate manifestation of the dual reality they presented, and through its very existence and modus operandi could address the complex nationalism encompassing both the Jewish Diaspora and the Land of Israel. Stephen Wise, president of the WJC, developed the argument that the organization was fulfilling an essential purpose. According to Wise, the establishment of a democratic Jewish organization prepared to take robust action on behalf of world Jewry was a vital matter because of the situation of European Jewry. He maintained that the founding of the WJC constituted a historic turning point, the full significance of which lay in the establishment of a democratic Jewish organization precisely at a time of deep crisis.[12] Wise went on to describe the democratic voting process whereby each Jewish home in the United States would receive a voter card for the price of ten cents. The election was to be super-

---

9 Horace Kallen at the preparatory convention of the WJC, August 20–23, 1934 (no precise date), AJA, 361 A40/5.
10 Memorandum of the Executive Committee of the WJC submitted to the League of Nations on December 16, 1936, AJA, 361 A1/2.
11 Memorandum of the Directorate of the World Jewish Congress to the League of Nations, AJA, 361 A1/2.
12 Open letter from Wise to the Jews of America in the context of elections to the World Jewish Congress, March 1938 (no precise date given), AJA, 361 A9/4. For an address in a similar vein, see the public declaration by Louis Lipsky, May 9, 1938, ibid. See also letter from Wise to Rabbi Joseph Rantz of Louisville, Kentucky, December 1, 1941, AJA, 361 C68/13.

vised by a national election committee that would determine the number of delegates that each community would elect to the Congress's institutions. Later in the letter Wise underscored in large print that the appropriate response to the attack on millions of Jews around the world by anti-democratic forces was the mass participation in this democratic process by Jews in the United States, which would signify the commitment on the part of America's Jews both to the struggle for democracy and on behalf of the Jews of the world.[13]

It should be noted here that the WJC defined itself as an international organization, although, in fact, it operated as an American Jewish organization. Its headquarters were located in the United States and its European and South American offices were financed by American sources and reported on their activities to the Congress Directorate in the New York. In 1939, Nahum Goldmann, co-founder of the WJC, believing that the only monetary source for the organization's activity in Europe was to be found in the United States, stressed that the initiative for founding the Congress had emanated from America, therefore placing greater responsibility on American Jewish leaders, and on Wise in particular, to muster the resources required to ensure the organization's continued functioning in light of the grave situation of European Jewry.[14] This state of affairs had prevailed prior to World War II and naturally took a turn for the worse following its outbreak. Indeed, an official announcement by the WJC explained that the organization's headquarters had been relocated to New York in the wake of the outbreak of war.[15] This announcement divulged that, unlike in the past, the branches of the Congress in London and Geneva would become departments whose sole function would be to take care of the Jews of Europe. The European offices would report to headquarters in New York, and the organization's policy would be determined in New York alone. It was clearly stated that any significant activity by the branches in Europe required prior authorization from New York, and that prominent European functionaries would move from Europe to the United States as part of the organizational transformation. The authors of the document explained that the organizational change was essential, given that the United States was a democratic country and because of the relative power wielded by its Jewish community, which made the American arena the only location in which significant Jewish activity could be conducted in the early 1940s.[16]

---

[13] Wise, open letter, March 1938, AJA, 361 A9/4.
[14] Letter from Goldmann to Wise, May 30, 1939 (sent from Paris), AJA, 361 A9/6.
[15] Official announcement of the directorate of the World Jewish Congress in New York, August 1, 1940, AJA, 361 A5/2.
[16] Announcement of the Directorate of the World Jewish Congress, August 1, 1940, ibid.

A significant factor that facilitated the activity of the WJC in the United States and enhanced its capacity to operate in the American sphere was the fact that it was virtually identical to the American Jewish Congress. Stephen Wise served both as president of the American Jewish Congress and as chairman of the Executive Committee of the WJC, a situation that symbolized the organizational similarity of the two bodies, as well as the fact that the American Jewish Congress was the dominant body within the WJC, providing it with financial support and political backing.[17] In this vein, Arieh Tartakower, who served as chairman of the organization's Welfare and Relief Committee during World War II and subsequently became Professor of Sociology at the Hebrew University, defined the WJC as an American organization. Describing the power of the American Jewish community, he wrote: "This element determined, as mentioned, the status and modus operandi of the Congress, which itself now became to no small degree an American institution with the head office to New York, and once the best of the leadership had assembled there, included a large section of the former European leadership".[18]

Studies of the American Jewish leadership of the 1930s and '40s deal extensively with top WJC executives, whose activities are closely examined and often severely criticized.[19] Such criticism primarily addresses the issue of assistance to the persecuted Jews of Europe. There exists a huge volume of scholarly literature on the inability of the American Jewish leadership to effect the rescue of Jews during the Holocaust.[20] The complexity of this topic is well expressed by Henry

---

17 See the memorandum of the directorate of the World Jewish Congress regarding the Congress's activity since the outbreak of war, no author given, May 31, 1940, AJA, 361 A5/1.

18 A native of Galicia, Arieh Tartakower immigrated to the United States in 1939 and served as Chairman of the Congress's Welfare and Relief Committee as well as Deputy Director of the Institute of Jewish Affairs. He immigrated to Palestine in 1946, was appointed Professor of Jewish Sociology at the Hebrew University and continued to function within the World Jewish Congress. Among other roles, he headed the organization's cultural department and served as Chairman of the Congress's Israel wing. See Arieh Tartakower, Manuscript on the World Jewish Congress (which did not appear in book form), undated, CZA, C-6/352 Tartakower furthermore emphasized the structural unity of the World Jewish Congress and the American Jewish Congress: "With the transfer of the Congress's head office to New York, it began in any case to cooperate with the American Jewish Congress. The two principal institutions of the Congress at that time, the Relief Committee for Jewish War Victims and the Institute of Jewish Affairs were in effect run jointly, the former de facto and the latter also formally . . . [deletion by the author]. Dr. Wise directed both of these institutions." See Tartakower, ibid., 7.

19 For a prominent example of these, see David S. Wyman and Rafael Medoff, *A Race Against Death: Peter Bergson, America, and the Holocaust* (New York, 2002), 29–30, 230–231.

20 See, for example, David S. Wyman, *The Abandonment of the Jews: America and the Holocaust, 1941–1945* (New York, 1984); Rafael Medoff, *The Deafening Silence* (New York, 1987). For

Feingold, who stressed that discussion of American Jewry and the Holocaust should take into account the broad context of these leaders' exceptional awareness of the fate of Jews in other cases, as well as the constraints and difficulties they faced during World War II.[21]

Indeed, one cannot ignore the sense of uneasiness and the questions that emerge from the study of American Jewish leadership at the time of the Holocaust.[22] Nevertheless, letters and documents of the period that address the activity of this leadership enable us to add a further layer to the study of the American Jewish elite (including the WJC leadership) at the time of the Holocaust, thereby enhancing our understanding of the array of factors that influenced the activity of the WJC leadership at this most critical juncture for world Jewry. This book addresses the similarities between the World Jewish Congress and the Zionist movement. The fact that the WJC was an organization that identified with the ideology and actions of Zionist movement during the 1930s and '40s raises serious questions about the motives of its founders, most of whom were members of the World Zionist Movement, in establishing a separate Jewish organization. Initial findings suggested that there was no need to found the Congress in 1936, yet a number of underlying motives subsequently emerged. These are linked to the manner in which the Jews functioned as a minority group in the United States during World War II, and to their desire to engage in ethnic politics (which represent the narrow interests of a minority group), thereby exerting influence at the national political level.

The letters and speeches of WJC leaders presented here reveal the tremendous hardships encountered by the American Jewish community and the representative bodies of the Jewish people during and after World War II as they strove as a minority within American society to rescue Jews, care for the refugees, and realize the objectives of the Zionist movement—namely the founding of a Jewish state after the war. These difficulties were among the factors that led them to moderate their political demands, curtail overt protests, and engage instead in covert activities of which the broad Jewish community remained unaware.

---

an extensive list of like-minded studies, see Gulie Ne'eman Arad, "Cooptation of Elites: American Jewish Reactions to the Nazi Menace, 1933," *Yad Vashem Studies* 25 (1996): 32–33. See also Allan J. Lichtman, *FDR and the Jews* (Cambridge and London, 2013; hereafter: Breitman and Lichtman, *FDR*).

21 Henry L. Feingold, *Bearing Witness: How America and Its Jews Responded to the Holocaust* (New York, 1995), 14–16, 205–76; Henry L. Feingold, "Was there Communal Failure? Some Thoughts on the American Jewish Response to the Holocaust," *American Jewish History* 81 (1993): 60–80.

22 Robert D. Shapiro, *A Reform Rabbi in the Progressive Era: The Early Career of Stephen S. Wise* (New York, 1988), 422–423.

Ostensibly, the founders of the WJC were seeking to promote democratization of Jewish life and to step up activity designed to rescue Jews and to oppose Nazi Germany. In fact, however, they cooperated with other Jewish elites and with the U.S. administration with a view to *moderating* the American Jewish reaction to the Holocaust, although they were fully aware of the dimensions of the persecution. Such patterns of activity generated an essential disparity and intrinsic tension between the overt political activity of the WJC leadership during the war years in the United States and its covert activity, which, under the circumstances, was confined to rendering local assistance to persecuted Jews and failed to exert a meaningful influence on the United States Administration. This book serves to show that the wish of the heads of the WJC to soften the outward reaction of the American Jewish public to the Holocaust can be understood in light of the changes that had occurred in the socio-economic status of Jewish Americans, as well as changes in the public and individual status of the WJC leaders within the overall political and social system the United States during the 1940s.

This by no means indicates a wish to detract from the real difficulties and the serious failings of the World Jewish Congress during the thirties and forties. Yet despite these failings, it should be stressed that the heads of the organization, particularly Executive Chairman Stephen Wise and Executive Committee Chair Nahum Goldmann, played an important role in the overt and covert contacts with the administration concerning various issues related to world Jewry and the Zionist movement, and acted on behalf of the Jewish Congress to shape the reaction of the American Jewish public to the Holocaust according to their outlook.

Wise and Goldmann's activity in the United States during the 1930s and '40s may be fully appreciated by considering Wise's status within the Democratic Party and the impressive web of contacts with key figures in American politics that Goldmann wove after arriving in the country as a refugee in the early 1940s. It was Stephen Wise, a Reform rabbi, among the founders of the American Zionist movement and one of its most influential leaders until the mid-1940s, who in fact initiated the establishment of the WJC. He worked tirelessly toward this objective beginning in 1932, and was elected president of the organization at its inaugural convention in 1936. In addition to this activity, Wise was the president of the American Zionist Organization from 1936 to 1938, and chairman of the Zionist Emergency Committee in the United States from 1943 to 1945. This book does not aspire to be a biography of Wise, but rather to demonstrate the key role he played in the founding of the WJC and in its activity.

Wise (1874–1949) was born in Budapest, Hungary, and grew up in New York. He belonged to a family of Orthodox rabbis, but his religious outlook differed from theirs. He joined the Reform movement and turned the Reform rabbi's sermon into a veritable cult in his community. His political power was focused in

New York, where he engaged in his public activity at the Free Synagogue, which he himself founded in 1907 after turning down the position of rabbi at the prestigious Reform synagogue Temple Emanu-El because he objected to the demand of the community leadership that they be allowed to censor his sermons. One factor that made Wise an outsider in the Reform movement was his disagreement with the anti-Zionist attitude that reigned within it. The control exercised by the non-Zionists at the Hebrew Union College (HUC) in Cincinnati was among the central factors that in 1920 led Wise to found an independent rabbinical seminar, the Jewish Institute of Religion (JIR), alongside his New York synagogue.[23] Wise was deeply involved in American life and politics. Social and political events played a large part in his sermons as a Reform rabbi as well as in the articles he wrote for the journal *Opinion*, which he founded in 1931. Among other issues, he campaigned for improved conditions for industrial workers, against corruption in New York's city hall, and for the rights of African Americans. Wise's public activity in the national arena was not confined to social issues. At the outset of his career he supported the Democrat Woodrow Wilson. Wise was a respected member of the national Democratic Party and of the Democratic establishment of New York, and remained a party faithful throughout his life. His connections to President Franklin Delano Roosevelt—forged when he supported Roosevelt's successful candidacy for the office of governor of New York in 1928—were of great importance. Wise declined to support Roosevelt's first attempt to win the Democratic nomination for president because he believed that as governor, Roosevelt had not combated corruption in New York, but he consistently supported him from 1936 onward, primarily because of the president's New Deal policy.[24] Between 1944 and 1946, Wise's position of eminence in the American Zionist leadership was gradually eroded because of the struggle he waged against Abba Hillel Silver, a Reform rabbi and the most prominent American Zionist leader in the late 1940s. Roosevelt's death in 1945 further weakened Wise's political stature; he lost his close connection with the White House and was unable to establish a similar relationship with President Harry S. Truman. As he was edged out of the American Zionist leadership, Wise devoted himself increasingly to activity on behalf of the WJC.

---

23 The American Zionist Emergency Council was composed of representatives of the Zionist organizations in the USA and conducted Zionist activity there during World War II. The Council was founded in 1939 according to a resolution adopted by the Zionist Congress, and was initially named the Emergency Committee for Zionist Affairs. On the Emergency Council, see Doreen Bierbrier, "The American Zionist Emergency Council: An Analysis of a Pressure Group," *American Jewish Historical Quarterly* 1 (1970): 82–105.
24 For a general information about Wise, see Stephen Samuel Wise, *Challenging Years: The Autobiography of Stephen Wise*, 1874–1949 (London 1951).

At the time that Wise was actively promoting the founding of the WJC, Nahum Goldmann's stature in the World Zionist Organization was growing. He came to particular prominence following the 17th Zionist Congress held at Basle, Switzerland, in 1931, where he acted to remove Haim Weizmann from the presidency of the Zionist organization.[25] Goldmann's involvement in Zionist circles in the United States (to which he paid his first extended visit after the 17th Zionist Congress) played an important role in his becoming a leading Zionist activist. One of the noteworthy aspects of his activity in America was the particularly close political and personal connection that he forged with Wise.[26] Goldmann identified with Wise's objectives in both the American and the Zionist arenas, and worked alongside him as one of his longstanding associates.[27] Since Goldmann, while still in Europe, acceded to the rank of Zionist leader just as his connection with Wise was growing closer, he participated in the founding of the World Jewish Congress. As part of his extensive activity in this cause, he set out to persuade the representatives of Jewish communities in Europe and in South America to join the enterprise, and took part in preparing the inaugural convention of the new body, at which he delivered one of the principal speeches. He rapidly became a leading figure in the WJC, initially in Europe and then in the United States, to which he immigrated in June 1940. Goldmann's entry to the United States was facilitated by Wise, who officially invited him to take part in the Congress's activity in New York. In his letter, Wise explained that Goldmann's presence in the country was vital to the effort on behalf of European Jewry and to the undertaking of preparations for presenting the Jewish issue to the peace conference that would convene upon the ending of the war. Wise clarified that Goldmann was expected to remain in the United States for some time; therefore, his wife and children were included in the invitation.[28] Goldmann succeeded Wise as president of the World Jewish Congress in 1949, remaining in the position until his resignation in 1977. The role constituted an important anchor for his overall political and public activity.[29]

---

25 Nahum Goldmann, *The Autobiography of Nahum Goldmann: Sixty Years of Jewish Life* (New York, 1969), 115–118.
26 Nahum Goldmann, "Dr. Stephen Wise," in *On the Paths of My People* [in Hebrew] (Jerusalem, 1968), 217–229. For a further example of the close bonds between Wise and Goldmann during the 1940s, see Wise's energetic support of Goldmann among United States Zionist circles in a letter from Wise to Goldmann, November 18, 1946, CZA, Z-6/98.
27 See, for example, the letter from Goldmann to Wise, August 10, 1944, CZA, Z-6/2759.
28 Goldmann, *The Autobiography*, 192–193. See also Wise's letter to Goldmann, February 5, 1940, AJA, 361 A27/2.
29 Nahum Goldmann, "The Congress at Work," in *The Jewish Paradox* (London, 1978), 54–55.

The World Jewish Congress, the Zionist Movement, and their Parallel Paths

During the years he spent in the United States, Goldmann held a wide range of positions in Zionist and Jewish organizations simultaneously. While a number of senior Zionist figures engaged in similar public activity, the multiple functions performed by Goldmann and his associates in the WJC leadership endowed them with singular power.[30] An anecdote that reflects this state of affairs relates to a request Goldmann submitted to the New York Telephone Company in the summer 1943 that they must immediately install a main phone line and two extensions in his new apartment in Manhattan. In support of his application Goldmann reviewed his various roles, among them that of chairman of the WJC's administrative committee, his membership on the Executive Committee of the Zionist Organization, and the position of chairman of the Jewish Agency office in Washington, all of which he occupied at the same time. Goldmann claimed that in order to fulfill these functions he had to maintain ongoing and reliable contact with senior administration officials, with the media, and with Zionist representatives worldwide, and that this entitled him to an additional phone line.[31]

As mentioned previously, it was not only Goldmann and Wise who occupied multiple posts at the same time in the Zionist movement and in the WJC, but other central figures in the WJC as well. Most of those elected to key positions at the inaugural convention of the organization were leading Zionist activists. Louis Lipsky, for example, ex-chairman of the American Zionist Organization and its current president, was elected chairman of the Jewish Congress alongside his position as member of the Zionist Executive Committee and Judge Julian Mack, honorary president of the WJC in 1936, had been president of the American Zionist Organization in 1918. Examination of the curriculum vitae of deceased founders of the Congress who were eulogized and commemorated in speeches delivered at WJC conventions reveals that many of the organization's broad circle of activists likewise operated in parallel in the Zionist movement.[32] These data

---

30 On this phenomenon, see Tuvia Friling, *An Arrow in the Dark: Ben Gurion, The Yishuv Leadership, and Attempts at Rescue During the Holocaust* (Jerusalem, 1998), 8–9 (Hebrew; hereafter: Friling, *Ben Gurion*).
31 Goldmann's letter to the New York Telephone Company, June 3, 1943, CZA, Z-6/18.
32 Nahum Goldmann, memorial speeches at the Preparatory Council and the Inaugural Convention of the World Jewish Congress [in Hebrew], August 23, 1934 and August 10, 1936, CZA, Z-6/2273. For general background on this issue, see Mordechay Figowitz, "The American Jewish Background to the Founding of the World Jewish Congress: Shaping Policy and Organizational Patterns Between the Zurich Convention in 1927 and the Geneva Convention in 1932" [in Hebrew] (M.A. dissertation, Haifa University, 1977), 91.

raise the above-mentioned question about the considerations that led Stephen Wise, Nahum Goldmann and their associates to found the World Jewish Congress alongside their activity in the Zionist movement.

This question becomes more pertinent upon considering certain further facts that reinforce the impression that the new organization focused on precisely the same issues with which the existing organization was already engaged. For example, one of the WJC's fundamental objectives was to care for Jewry worldwide, but especially for the Jews of Eastern Europe. Perusal of the ideology and the actions of the Zionist movement during the 1930s reveals that it had already taken upon itself the task for which the new organization was established. The founders of the WJC, who were also leading Zionist activists, were well aware of this duplication of effort, and of the existence of other non-Zionist bodies that were primarily concerned with caring for Jews in countries around the world.[33] Goldmann himself noted that the Zionist movement was the driving force in the organization of Jewish communities in the Diaspora and in reviving Jewish culture. He stressed that the Zionist movement was engaging in the rescue of Jews in distress more than any other Jewish body.[34] As early as 1933, as the initial steps were being taken to found the WJC, Stephen Wise remarked that many within the Zionist movement, particularly those in the Labor Zionist movement, opposed the establishment of the organization because they believed that the Congress's future activity on behalf of world Jewry would harm the Zionist movement and erode its status as the movement that represented all Jews worldwide and which had made caring for Jews in the Diaspora one of its fundamental objectives.[35] The heads of the WJC, however, countered with an array of arguments designed to justify the existence of the Congress alongside the Zionist movement. They maintained that although the Zionist movement had decided at the Helsinki Conference of 1906 to engage in "present-day work among the Jews in the Diaspora," it had been unable to undertake this task, most of its effort being devoted to activity in Palestine. They believed that there was a need for an international Jewish organization that would complement the activity of the Zionist movement, receive its support, and promote its aims.[36]

---

[33] See, for example, Yehuda Bauer, *My Brother's Keeper: A History of the American Jewish Joint Distribution Committeee, 1929–1939* (Philadelphia, 1974).
[34] Lecture delivered by Nahum Goldmann at a convention of the World Jewish Congress in Atlantic City in November 1944 (precise date not given), CZA, Z-6/2248.
[35] Wise's oral report on his visit to Europe, submitted to the Executive Committee of the World Jewish Congress, September 23, 1933, AJA, 361 A1/9.
[36] Kubowizki, *World Jewish Congress*, 67, 14–17.

This explanation does not dispel the questions regarding the separate existence of the World Jewish Congress, which are sustained by the words of Wise's biographer Melvin Urofsky. Defining the WJC as an organization with a pro-Zionist orientation, Urofsky explicitly addressed the problematic issue of its existence alongside the Zionist movement.[37] In his assessment, the WJC did not turn into an alternative to the Zionist movement, and its leaders continued to serve in parallel with central positions in the Zionist movement in the United States and worldwide. Their ideological manifesto and political programs were founded on support for the establishment of a Jewish state in Palestine, and they publicly declared their close cooperation with the Jewish Agency.[38] These statements throw some doubt on the assertion that the WJC had been established as an international Jewish organization that would be able to operate on behalf of world Jewry while adapting its activity to American conditions. In fact, however, the continuing membership of the heads of the WJC in the Zionist movement was more likely to reinforce rather than mitigate such allegations of dual loyalty.

While the heads and founders of the WJC did indeed underscore their intention to cooperate with the Zionist movement, it may have been assumed that the founding of an organizational body alongside the Zionist movement and in competition with it would lead to friction between the two organizations. Such tension did, indeed, occur as can be seen in a 1941 correspondence between Nahum Goldmann and Arthur Hantke, director of the head office of Keren Ha-Yesod in Jerusalem (one of the Zionist movement's principal institutions), concerning which organization's fundraising appeals controlled donations from South America.

In this correspondence and in response to a memorandum that Hantke sent to the agency executive in Jerusalem, Nahum Goldmann explained that the Zionist movement had no jurisdiction over the activity of WJC since the congress was, he claimed, an independent body. Nevertheless, Goldmann stressed that, despite the Congress's "independence" and despite the financial loss it incurred because of this, the organization had allocated most of the money it had collected toward Zionist and pioneering causes, and that there was thus no justification for the struggle being waged by the Zionist bodies against the fundraising activities of the Jewish Congress.[39] Hantke responded by tracing the lack of clarity and the difficulties generated by the independent existence of the WJC, and noted that it was absurd for Goldmann to be a Zionist activist and not be subject to the authority

---

37 Urofsky, *Wise*, 298–299. Regarding the Congress's pro-Zionist orientation, see also Wyman, *The Abandonment of the Jews*, 76–77.
38 Lecture by Nahum Goldmann at a World Jewish Congress convention, September 23, 1933, AJA, 361 A1/9.
39 Letter from Goldmann to Hantke, November 6, 1941, CZA, Z-6/2755.

of the Zionist institutions. This state of affairs, he asserted, hindered cooperation between the two movements, harmed Zionist interests, and enabled Goldmann and his associates to conduct an independent policy through the Congress that was not necessarily compatible with the interests of the Zionist movement.[40]

The difficulties raised by the very existence of the WJC alongside the Zionist movement constituted the main topic of a secret letter sent to Goldmann and Wise in June 1943 by Dr. Jacob Robinson, founder of the WJC's research institute (the Institute of Jewish Affairs), the Jewish Agency's legal advisor, and subsequently the WJC's representative at UN discussions.[41] Robinson's letter notes that he was writing to them precisely because they were prominent officeholders both in the Zionist movement and in the WJC, and describes the relationship between the two movements as a grave conflict. In his view, the WJC's attempt to separate its engagement with the issue of the fate of European Jewry from the issue of Palestine in order to determine an agenda separate from that of the Zionist movement had generated serious ideological and practical difficulties for the organization.[42] Goldmann himself was aware of these difficulties, as he disclosed in a summation following his retirement as president of the WJC in which he wrote of the considerable constraints on cooperation between the two organizations during the entire period of their coexistence, even though the Zionist movement had officially supported the Jewish Congress. He demonstrated the intrinsic lack of clarity created by the existence of these two organizations by remarking that he himself had for many years served simultaneously as president of the World Jewish Congress and president of the Zionist movement. When the need arose to settle disagreements between the organizations, he added, he found himself talking to himself, or in his words: "Goldmann is negotiating with Goldmann."[43] This situation humorously underscores the misgivings raised by the existence of the WJC as a separate organization.

In his speech at the inaugural convention of the WJC in August 1936, Wise felt compelled to explain the need to establish the organization.[44] He underscored the importance of Jewish settlement in Palestine, which had proved to skeptics that the Jews were able to live as a nation in the modern day. Yet, he continued, Zionist work in the Palestinian context and traditional philanthropic activity had

---

40 Letter from Hantke to Goldmann, December 3, 1941, CZA, Z-6/2755. Tuvia Frilling underscored the fact that the WJC was not subject to the authority of the Jewish Agency's institutions. See Frilling, Ben Gurion, part 1, 8–9.
41 Letter from Robinson to Goldmann, March 25, 1943, CZA, A-243/73.
42 Ibid.
43 Goldmann, *The Congress*, 58–59.
44 Wise's speech at the inaugural convention of the World Jewish Congress, August 8, 1936, AJA, 361 A40/8.

failed to provide adequate answers to the fundamental problems encountered by world Jewry, particularly following the Nazis' rise to power, and there was thus a need for international Jewish action along political lines. Wise asked his audience why the non-Jewish world should show interest in and fight for Jewish issues when the Jews themselves refrained from doing so. He asserted that the lack of organization among world Jewry was playing into the hands of the enemies of the Jewish people. Anticipating criticism of the patterns of action to be adopted by the Jewish Congress as an international Jewish organization, Wise stressed that the anti-Jewish campaign was an international one, and that this called for a Jewish response that would span individual states and continents. He emphasized further that the organization would not be a Jewish super-state, and that it would be a serious mistake to think of it as a Jewish parliament. A parliament, he explained, was a juridical concept, something that constituted part of the existence of a state, whereas the Congress was not a state.[45]

The ideas presented by Wise in his speech to the inaugural convention of the Congress found practical political expression in the report that the WJC's economic committee prepared for submission to the economic forum of the League of Nations.[46] In the spirit of Wise's outlook, the authors of the document regarded themselves as representatives of the entire Jewish nation, and sought to conduct a comprehensive study of the Jews in all their locations of residence. They examined a wide variety of topics, ranging from the effect of the Nazi party's policy on the economic situation of European Jewry to a survey of the effect of World War I on the economic condition of Jews in various countries. The document was not designed to create a file of information to be used for future philanthropic activity, but rather as the beginning of a political effort to transform the economic condition of the Jews with the assistance of the League of Nations and its institutions.[47] The continuous deterioration in the condition of European Jewry reinforced the conviction of the WJC leadership that the traditional philanthropic modes of activity were no longer relevant. This outlook was demonstrated at a press conference held by Nahum Goldmann at a meeting of the League of Nations Council in January 1939.[48] Goldmann reviewed the plight of the Jews of Romania,

---

45 Ibid.
46 Memorandum of the Economic Committee of the World Jewish Congress, March 14, 1937, AJA, 361 A9/3.
47 Ibid.
48 The press conference was held on January 19, 1939 at the WJC offices in Geneva. See secret memorandum on the activity at the League of Nations Council, January 24, 1939, AJA, 361 A1/1. For a further example along similar lines, see Letter from Goldmann to Wise following the Evian Conference, July 16, 1938, AJA, 361 A27/1; and a WJC memorandum on the refugee problem, no author attributed, February 28, 1939, AJA, 361 A5/1.

Hungary, Czechoslovakia, Poland and Germany, asserting that a problem of this magnitude could not be solved through local measures but only by means of an overall international effort. This would have to include an international program of migration supported by world-wide funding, based on recognition of Jews' civil rights. In parallel, the heads of the WJC would initiate steps within the United States to enhance the political aspects of the activity of the various Jewish organizations and create a unified political front in which the Congress would play a major role.

Louis Lipsky, one of the founders of the Congress, wrote a clandestine personal letter in this vein to Henry Monsky, president of B'nai Brith.[49] Lipsky sought to set up a federation of all the Jewish organizations in the United States on the basis of democratic principles with protecting the rights of Jews as its objective. From this letter it emerges that Lipsky's overture was part of a broad political campaign that comprised the preparation of memoranda and the holding of individual meetings with a view to promoting the idea of, in the wording of the letter, a "united Jewish front."[50] Lipsky approached Monsky in person in the wake of B'nai Brith representatives' previous opposition to contacts designed to form a united Jewish front initiated by the WJC. Lipsky notes in the letter that he was approaching Monsky in the belief that good will would facilitate close cooperation among the various Jewish organizations in the United States. He drew parallels between Zionism and the activity of the WJC on behalf of protection of the rights of Jews around the world. He felt that Zionism had become an intrinsic and legitimate part of Jewish life everywhere, and that a similar process should take place regarding the struggle for equal rights for world Jewry.[51]

Lipsky's political activity was not conducted in a vacuum; it should be understood against the backdrop of the continual deterioration in the condition of European Jewry, as manifested in the letter written by the historian and

---

49 Letter from Lipsky to Monsky, June 3, 1938, AJA, 361 A9/4. For further sources addressing this issue, see a speech delivered by Lipsky in which he calls on additional Jewish organizations in the United States to join the WJC front, Lipsky speech, May 9, 1938, no location given, AJA, 361 A9/4. At the Evian Conference the Congress likewise maintained that a single Jewish body should be established to address the issue. See Congress memorandum on the topic of the Jewish Refugees, February 28, 1939, unspecified author, AJA, 361 A5/1. Monsky would subsequently become involved in steps to form a Jewish alliance in the United States, manifested in the founding of the American Jewish Conference in 1943. See Hasia R. Diner, *The Jews of the United States* (Berkeley 2004), 216–217.
50 Lipsky letter, June 3, 1938.
51 Ibid.

thinker Shimon Dubnov to the heads of the WJC.[52] Reviewing the terrible plight of Europe's Jews, Dubnov related how hundreds of thousands had been deprived of their civil and human rights. Dubnov believed that since they had no realistic chances of migrating, large swathes of European Jewry were left with but two options: the bottom of the sea or the purgatory of the lands of pogroms, which included not only Germany and Italy, but also other large areas of the continent. Dubnov stressed that, unlike other groups in Europe that were subject to Nazi aggression, the Jews had no state that could protect them. He therefore called for the formation of an international Jewish defense front under the slogan "an end to silence" in order to combat the aggression and violence. In his estimation, through its delegations in Paris, Geneva and the United States, the WJC was the appropriate organization to lead this move.[53]

Wise's lecture and the memorandum submitted to the League of Nations provide some evidence of the objectives of the founders of the WJC in 1936. Contemporaries and scholars alike have questioned the motivation for establishing the organization. While most of its founders regarded themselves as Zionists and some held senior positions in Zionist bodies, they believed that their Zionism was entirely compatible with their activity in the WJC. They certainly did not think that the organization was superfluous. On the contrary, they were proud to be Zionists and worked tirelessly toward the establishment of a Jewish state, while at the same time seeking to strengthen the ethnic identity of Jews in the Diaspora, in which Zionism constituted a major component. When attempting to understand the world view of Wise, Goldmann, and their colleagues in the WJC leadership, it is important to appreciate that while the WJC was defined as an international organization, it in fact operated as an American Jewish body. It is noteworthy that American Zionism developed along different lines than its European counterpart. American Zionists refrained from emphasizing migration to Palestine as a central component of their ideology and practice, and shaped their Zionism into an important element of their fabric of life within American society rather than a means toward the practical realization of migration to the Land of Israel.[54] Successive generations of American Zionist leaders created an ideological and organizational foundation that enabled any American Jew who chose to be a Zionist to bridge the gap between the largely European oriented Zionist ideology and the reality of life in the United States. They actively engaged in creating

---

52 Letter by Simon Dubnov to the Heads of the World Jewish Congress. Declared classified and translated into English, June 14, 1939, AJA, 361 A9/6.
53 Ibid.
54 Ofer Shiff, "The Integrative Function of Early American Zionism," *The Journal of Israeli History* 15, no. 1 (1994): 1–16.

a Jewish nationalism that downplayed the elements of territorial concentration and political sovereignty, opposed the concept of "rejection of the Diaspora," and underscored the moral dimensions of Judaism [55] The founders of the WJC accordingly saw no contradiction between their efforts to reinforce the ethnic and national identity of Jews in the Diaspora in the wake of the Holocaust and support for the establishment of a Jewish state. On the contrary, they regarded Zionism as a political and social movement that accords fresh legitimacy and meaning to Jewish life in the Diaspora and in the United States. Zionism enables Jews to live in the modern world while maintaining their singular ethnic and cultural identity, which is of utmost importance to humanity in general and to Jews in particular. The importance of Zionism to Jewish history derives not merely from its success in founding a sovereign Jewish state, but also from the creation of new patterns of Jewish life all over the world. The shaping of a world-wide Jewish community acting as a political force with common goals and vibrant institutions was a by-product of the supreme effort on the part of world Jewry to build a national home.[56]

As will become evident in the forthcoming chapters, apart from the ideological dimension, the founding of the WJC enabled its leaders, especially Stephen Wise and Nahum Goldmann, to conduct political and community activity within the United States independent of the Zionist institutions worldwide. This was something of considerable importance particularly in view of the growing political and public power of the American Zionist leader Abba Hillel Silver during the 1940s, with whom Wise and Goldmann engaged in a prolonged political, public and personal struggle.[57]

---

55 For an example of such an approach, see the work of Richard Gottheil, Professor of Semitic languages at Columbia University and President of the American Federation of Zionists from 1898 to 1904, Richard J. Gottheil, *Zionism* (Philadelphia, 1914).
56 Lecture on Herzl delivered by Stephen Wise at a memorial assembly in memory of Herzl, New York, July 18, 1929, CZA, A-246/164. For a further lecture in similar vein, see Wise's address, The Epochal Herzl (undated, location unspecified), CZA, A-243/163.
57 For an extensive discussion of various aspects of this issue, see the articles in a volume on Goldmann, Mark A. Raider, "Idealism, Vision, and Pragmatism: Stephen S. Wise, Nahum Goldmann, and Abba Hillel Silver in the United States," in Mark A. Raider, ed., *Nahum Goldmann, Statesman Without a State* (Albany, 2009), 139–168; Zohar Segev, "Nahum Goldmann and the First Two Decades of the World Jewish Congress," in Raider, *Goldmann*, 107–124. The status of the WJC as an organization that adopted an independent political position which differed from that of the Zionist movement is manifested in the affair of the anti-German boycott in the United States. The WJC supported the boycott and opposed the "transfer" agreement concluded by the Zionist movement with the Nazi regime in the 1930s. For an extensive discussion of this issue, see Yfaat Weiss, "The Transfer Agreement and the Boycott Movement – A Jewish Dilemma on the Eve of the Holocaust," *Yad Vashem, Collection of Studies* 26 (1998): 129–171.

This outlook advocating the leverage of the Jewish community in the United States and throughout the world as a political force sharing common objectives became manifest in the launching of the World Jewish Congress in 1936. The timing of the inauguration was not coincidental. The accession of the Nazis to power in 1933 had accentuated the need for a Jewish organization devoted both to the struggle for the rights of Jews in their countries of residence and to institutional philanthropic activity on their behalf. Meanwhile, the plight of Central and Eastern European Jewry and the anti-Jewish propaganda emanating from Germany was enhancing the sense of Jewish solidarity and gradually motivating American Jews to act as an organized ethnic group in promoting Jewish goals. These developments generated a convenient platform for the operation of the Congress in the American arena, which was, at that time, the only sphere in which significant and politically powerful Jewish activity could be conducted.

The founders of the WJC noted on numerous occasions that the deterioration in the situation of European Jewry had served as a catalyst for the establishment of the organization. They referred to the imperative of countering the burgeoning Nazi propaganda, stressing that past solutions such as migration were no longer feasible. The reality of the thirties required organized, unified Jewish action of a political nature to an unprecedented extent. Those who formulated the founding position paper believed that international recognition of the necessity of a Jewish national home in Palestine as manifested in the Balfour Declaration and in resolutions of the League of Nations indicated a fundamental willingness to recognize the rights of the Jewish minority, and therefore in no way weakened—but even reinforced—international willingness to recognize the rights of Jews as a minority in Europe as well. The drafters of the paper pointed out the similarity of the processes whereby Jews were excluded in the various countries. They believed that this phenomenon demonstrated not a fundamentally nationalistic process, but rather an international phenomenon that necessitated an international Jewish response and a solution that transcended national borders.[58] During a prepara-

---

58 See position paper of the Preparatory Committee of the World Jewish Congress in the United States, October 26, 1933, AJA, 361 A40/4, and a declaration of support by Louis Lipsky. Lipsky links the need for the organization to events in Europe. Lipsky's declaration, May 9, 1938, AJA, 361 A9/4. On the Congress's European activity during the 1930s, including its public activity against Germany, demonstrations in the United States, and meetings with the foreign ministers of Poland, Romania, Italy, and Czechoslovakia, see the classified survey of the WJC Executive's Political Activity, 1937, no specific date, AJA, 361 A5/1; memorandum on the topic of East European Jews submitted to the League of Nations, March 14, 1937, AJA, 361 A9/3. Regarding links with and support of the Polish opposition, see Goldmann's letter to Wise, May 1937 (no precise date), AJA, 361 A27/1. See also, Minutes of Meeting between Nahum Goldmann and the Polish Ambassador to Washington (which includes threats of anti-Polish activity in the United States if

tory gathering of the WJC in the summer of 1934 in Geneva, Nahum Goldmann described the seriousness of the condition of German Jewry following the Nazis' accession to power, the wave of anti-Semitism washing over the world, and the grave plight of the Jews in Soviet Russia. He portrayed these developments as a dramatic series of events unprecedented in the annals of the Jews in modern times that called for an appropriate Jewish response, in which the establishment of the WJC would form the primary stratum.[59] The heads of the WJC contended that the deep crisis in which European Jewry found itself made it imperative to set up a broad organization with an extensive, independent bureaucratic infrastructure. The WJC would open delegations in the main European capitals alongside the offices in the United States. Goldmann's and Wise's experience in the Zionist movement had taught them that in order to ensure its effectiveness, the new body would need to set up an administrative structure staffed by qualified people who drew a full salary. They believed that the failings of the Zionist movement to operate on behalf of the Jews of Europe stemmed in part from the fact that the organization was managed by volunteers, causing patterns of activity undertaken by some of the Zionist activists to be unsuited to Europe's changing reality in the mid-1930s.[60]

Rogers Brubaker has written about the complex challenges facing a voluntary organization that represents an ethnic minority dispersed among numerous countries. Such an organization strives to operate in a practical manner and to project itself to its surroundings as the exclusive representative of the majority of individuals who belong to the ethnic minority. According to Brubaker, such a situation cannot exist in reality for two reasons. First, the great variety that generally exists within the ethnic group precludes uniform representation; and second, members of ethnic groups dispersed throughout various lands are primarily concerned with existential problems that are not necessarily related to their groups' minority status. Even if the existential problems are linked to the reality of life within an ethnic minority, those needs differ significantly from country to country. Such varying needs may even be found among the members of the ethnic minority living in the same country, in accordance with their varied socio-eco-

---

its anti-Jewish policy were to continue), January 19, 1939, AJA, 361 A1/1; a description of activity in Europe, including meetings with various leaders in the United States, Britain, and with the Polish Government in Exile, cooperation with the Red Cross and other non-governmental organizations regarding the dispatch of provisions to Polish Jews; Classified Minutes of Meeting of Congress Functionaries in Europe, December 6, 1939, AJA, 361 A7/1.

59 See minutes of the opening meeting of the Congress's preparatory committee, August 8, 1936, AJA, 361 A40/5.

60 Letter from Goldmann to Wise, May 30, 1939, AJA, 361 A9/6.

nomic status.[61] The founders of the WJC were unfamiliar with Brubaker's thesis, but they had discerned that the story of 1930s European Jewry was a singular one, which enabled their organization to contend with the challenges confronting a representative international ethnic body. Their view was that the crisis of European Jewry resulting from its exclusion from all political, economic, cultural and social spheres of life had generated a different reality in which all Jews were confronting similar problems. This was a general phenomenon, which, unlike the circumstances of other minorities, called for a response that was ethnic in nature and that transcended national borders. German, Polish, and Romanian Jews were not subject to economic, political and social tribulations specific to their places of residence, but rather were confronting a pan-European phenomenon. Therefore, by contrast to other ethnic groups, the formation of an international Jewish body was an organizational and ideological response that was relevant to the Jewish condition in the latter half of the thirties.

The outbreak of World War II reinforced the WJC leadership's conviction that the organization was of vital importance to world Jewry. Nahum Goldmann referred to this in a lecture entitled "The Need for a World Jewish Congress," in which he asserted that those who refuted the need for an inter-Jewish international organization were blind to the events of the past decade and had learned nothing from them. He continued by maintaining that the idea of founding a world Jewish congress in the reality of the thirties was so obvious that it required no explanation. He strongly condemned those who argued that Jewish activity of an international nature was liable to raise doubts as to Jewish citizens' loyalty to their countries. Goldmann believed that these were groundless assertions that ran contrary to the patterns of international activity conducted by numerous bodies, from Socialists to Catholics. In his opinion, the fact that a significant part of the activity carried out by American Jews on behalf of their brethren was philanthropic in nature and involved primarily financial support, had transformed the Jewish issue from a political problem with which the world had to engage into an insignificant matter of welfare; but because of European Jewry's ghastly situation and despite the policy of philanthropy, the Jewish problem had become a major topic on the agenda of the world's leaders during the latter half of the 1930s. The problem of Europe's Jews was exceptionally serious since, unlike what was occurring in the Zionist context in Palestine, there was no entity representing the Jews of the world with which gainful contacts could have been established. This state of affairs had made it impossible to take effective action on behalf of

---

61 Rogers Brubaker, *Ethnicity without Groups* (Cambridge MA. and London, 2004), 22–24.

the Jews. The WJC was designed to correct this failing and to constitute a representative body that would operate along the lines of the Zionist movement.[62]

Reports of the bitter fate of European Jewry under German occupation merely served to reinforce Goldmann's conviction regarding the necessity of the WJC.[63] Although at this point he had not yet received reliable information about the Final Solution, Goldmann explained that whereas in the past only some of the Jewish communities in Europe had been subject to pogroms and the survivors had been able to rehabilitate themselves in a different community, this time the destruction was absolute and was occurring throughout Europe. The conclusion to be drawn from the terrible plight of European Jewry, he observed, was the need to turn the Jewish issue into a major European concern, and to explain that its solution must involve the entire world. The WJC was the sole Jewish organization able to lead the effort toward a solution of the Jewish problem at the international level.[64] The subsequent information on the final solution and the methods of mass murder of the Jews of Europe served to bolster the Congress leaders' belief in the necessity for the WJC. Speaking to Jews in the United States in 1943, Wise proclaimed that Jews had responded to the Nazi challenge by closing ranks throughout the world. He stressed that American Jewry could not confront the Nazi challenge alone. Jewish unity in the United States was not sufficient, and it was now imperative to generate international cooperation and Jewish unity along the lines proposed by the WJC.[65]

The descendants of Jewish migrants from Eastern Europe, most of whom were Zionists, allied themselves with those of German and Central European origin who supported Jewish activity on a democratic basis. They were joined by European Jewish leaders who recognized the dominance of the American Jewish community on the eve of World War II, most of whom had immigrated to the United States in the second half of the 1930s and the early 1940s. These different groups formed a singular ethnic Jewish mix whose leaders supported the establishment of a Jewish state in Palestine, but did not regard it as the be all and end all. They saw themselves as the representatives of the Jewish world on the eve of World War II, during the hostilities, and thereafter, and as such they promoted the founding of a Jewish state as well as the rehabilitation of Jewish life in the Diaspora as two complementary objectives.

---

62 Goldmann lecture, The Need for a Jewish Congress (no location given), November 1941, no precise date, AJA, 361 A5/3.
63 Goldmann's lecture in New York, April 6, 1942, AJA, 361 A28/14.
64 Ibid.
65 Wise's address at the Council of American Jewry, New York, August 29, 1943, AJA, 361 A2/3.

Chapter 1
World Jewish Congress Activity in the United States during World War II

The World Jewish Congress and Reports of the Holocaust of European Jewry

In justifying the founding of the organization to the broad public, the "World Jewish Congress leadership cited the need for Jewish unity in circumstances of extreme crisis. Yet upon perusing speeches delivered at intimate forums and confidential documents written by WJC leaders in the latter half of the 1930s and the early 1940s, a number of additional reasons leading to the decision to establish the organization emerge. The WJC leadership's clandestine activity during the war years is quite different from its overt rhetoric; from it we learn that an additional motive for founding the Congress was the desire of the elite to maintain control over Jewish political activity rather than "abandoning" it to those liable to harm the interests of American Jewry.

Whereas broad sections of the American Jewish public appeared eager to exert overt and intensive pressure on the United States administration, the initiators of the WJC feared that such direct mass activity might adversely influence the status and interests of American Jews, and sought to respond to the public's demand for "ethnic politics" in a manner that would satisfy, but not harm it.

The intensive correspondence among WJC leaders in the United States reveals their views on the political and public means whereby they hoped to persuade the wielders of political power in Europe and the United States to take action on behalf of European Jews, while protecting the interests of the American Jewish public. They believed that it would be dangerous to allow those unfamiliar with the ways of world politics to lead the Jewish struggle since they were apt to damage these interests. They thus opposed, for example, the public campaign waged by American Jews in 1938 for the imposition of an American embargo on trade with Romania in the wake of the deteriorating situation of the Jews in that country. This had come about because of the anti-Jewish policy pursued by the Goga-Cuza regime, which took the form of discriminatory legislation, rescinding the citizenship of hundreds of thousands of Romanian Jews, and depriving them of their livelihoods in villages and cities.[66] Wise and Goldmann were aware of

---

[66] Jean Encel, *The Annals of the Holocaust: Romania* [in Hebrew] (Jerusalem, 2002), vol. 1, 51–82.

the plight of Romania's Jews, but felt that the call for an embargo was illogical and irresponsible, since those waging the campaign were largely ignorant of the workings of international politics and knew little about the facts on the ground. They were unaware, for instance, of the small volume of Romanian imports to the United States, which meant that the embargo would not constitute a substantial threat to the Romanian regime, and that calls for its imposition were seriously jeopardizing efforts to reach an understanding with the Romanian government aimed at improving the conditions of its Jewish citizens.[67] Wise was convinced that the League of Nations was the appropriate forum in which to engage in activity on behalf of Romanian Jewry. Furthermore, he believed that this activity should focus on applying international political pressure on the Romanian regime through individual diplomatic meetings with its leaders, such as Nahum Goldmann's encounter with the Romanian foreign minister, which he would describe in a report to Wise in September of that year.[68]

Several factors exacerbated the dilemma facing the WJC functionaries regarding the appropriate approach to use on behalf of European Jews: the outbreak of World War II, the United States' entry to the war, and reports of the murder of European Jews by the Nazis. The actions of the WJC leaders reflected the fact that they possessed reliable and current information on the murder of European Jewry. The most well-known evidence of this is the telegram dispatched by Gerhart M. Riegner, director of the Congress's Geneva bureau, to Stephen Wise in New York. The message contained dramatic information, furnished by the German industrialist Eduard Schulte, about Hitler's decision to exterminate European Jewry in its entirety using industrialized killing machines operated by gas. The telegram reached New York via a circuitous route on August 28, 1942, twenty days after it had been dispatched. The communication was dubbed "the Riegner Telegram" and the information it contained is considered to be the first reliable source of information on the Final Solution. Upon receipt of the telegram, Wise immediately contacted the U.S. State Department to convey the terrible news and request authorization to make it public. The response from Under-Secretary of State Sumner Welles was to ask Wise to delay publication be until the information was verified. Wise agreed—a decision that would later draw fierce criticism from

---

[67] Wise's letter to Goldmann, January 18, 1938, CZA, Z-6/2765.
[68] On the WJC leadership's prior activity on behalf of Romanian Jewry, see Schwarzbart, *25 Years*, 9–10; Encel, *Annals of the Romanian Holocaust*, 69–74. On Goldmann's meeting with the Romanian foreign minister, see Goldmann's letter to Wise, September 22, 1938, CZA, Z-6/2765. Wise also proceeded with great caution with regard to efforts to impose an embargo on German products. See Urofsky, *Wise*, 297–298. On the Holocaust of Romanian Jews, see Loanid Radu, *The Holocaust in Romania – The Destruction of Jews and Gypsies Under the Antonescu Regime, 1940–1944* (Chicago, 2000).

scholars and non-academics alike. Authorization from the State Department was not received until November 24, 1942, at which time Wise announced to the press that the Nazis intended to annihilate European Jewry and that two million Jews had already been murdered.[69]

While Riegner's telegram is widely cited, it is but one example of evidence obtained through an elaborate information-gathering network that the WJC operated in neutral European countries.[70] The WJC leadership not only had the foresight to continue running its offices in the neutral countries, they also developed clandestine modes of operation more quickly than did other Jewish organizations, enabling them to obtain information about the fate of the Jews in Nazi-occupied countries in real time. The heads of the Congress were thus able to gain knowledge on topics ranging from information on individual Jews, to the layout of the Treblinka extermination camp, to the situation of Jewish children in hiding in France and Belgium. The reports and testimonies that reached the offices of the WJC during 1942 and 1943 reveal that the organization's leaders were indeed aware of the plight of European Jewry. Therefore, we can stipulate that efforts by the WJC in the United States to rescue Jews during the Holocaust should be examined in light of the extensive information at their disposal.

Specific information on current events in Poland also reached WJC offices in the United States and in Europe, and was collated into a comprehensive report. The authors of the report, submitted in October 1942, stressed that part of the information had arrived directly from the Warsaw Ghetto, while other parts had been sent by a circuitous route, and in some cases were based on oral testimony alone.[71] Nevertheless, since the numerous sources provided similar or identical information, they were assumed to be reliable. Reporting in their introduction that hundreds of thousands of Jews had been murdered in Warsaw, the authors comment that "The horror defies belief." Other reports told of the systematic gassing of many Warsaw Jews who were removed from the ghetto and transported to an unknown location. Upon assembling the testimonies, the report's authors concluded that the Germans' campaign of murder of the Jews had commenced with the Jews from Western and Central Europe to work camps in the East. The majority of those arriving in the camps soon died of hunger and disease.[72]

---

69 Jonathan Sarna, *American Judaism* [in Hebrew] (Jerusalem, 2005), 252–253. The matter of the delayed revelation is discussed here in the chapter on the topic of rescue.
70 See, for example, Friling, Ben Gurion, 84–85.
71 Report from the Congress office in Geneva titled "The Situation of the Jews in the General Government," October 8, 1942, AJA, 361 H287/12.
72 Ibid.

The report went on to describe the deportation and murder of Jews in various locations in Poland, as well as the reaction of the non-Jewish public to the Nazis' treatment of the Jews. Anonymous sources within the Polish government-in-exile reported that in many areas the Poles had participated in massacres of Jews, termed pogroms by the report's authors. In Warsaw, however, the city's Polish population had not taken part in the anti-Jewish activity for the simple reason that the total separation of the ghetto prevented them from participating in the massacres.[73]

Additional testimony regarding events in occupied Europe reached the Congress office in Geneva shortly after the Riegner telegram was dispatched. This information was passed on to a Congress functionary, the jurist Prof. Paul Guggenheim, by a senior official in the Swiss administration, whose name had been deleted for obvious reasons.[74] The witness had learned from key figures in the Nazi regime of an order by Hitler to exterminate (this term appears in the original testimony!) all the Jews of Germany and occupied Europe by the end of December 1942. The informer related that S.S. Commander Himmler and Governor of Poland Frank opposed the immediate implementation of the order. This did not stem from humanitarian considerations, but rather from a desire to continue to exploit the Jews for forced labor. Professor Guggenheim emphasized that the information pertaining to the extermination order was supported by two further sources: a German Foreign Ministry official posted in Bern, and an official in the German War Ministry. Additional information was passed to Guggenheim by a Swiss national resident in Belgrade. This source related that German officials with whom he was in contact had informed him that the Jewish issue was of the utmost importance to the Nazi leadership and advised him to refrain from any involvement with the matter in light of his prior intervention on behalf of Jews. This Swiss national told of information he had received suggesting that no Jews remained in Serbia. Guggenheim stressed that the information he had obtained lent support to the facts contained in Riegner's telegram.[75]

Jewish refugees who had managed to escape from Nazi-occupied countries supplied important information about events in occupied Europe. The WJC office in Switzerland actively sought to locate refugees who had arrived there. The office assisted them financially and handled bureaucratic issues in order to prevent the

---

[73] The report includes a comprehensive survey of information pertaining to Jewish issues appearing in the German press and in newspapers in the occupied lands. See Geneva Report, October 8, 1942, AJA, 361 H28/12.
[74] The information is contained in Guggenheim's official testimony to the American consul in Geneva, October 29, 1942, AJA, 361 A8/11.
[75] Guggenheim, ibid.

refugees' deportation from Switzerland; meanwhile the Congress functionaries interrogated them thoroughly. The full importance of this process emerges in light of the fact that the Swiss authorities made no effort to debrief these Jewish refugees, totally ignoring the information they conveyed. A Jewish refugee of Polish origin residing in Brussels, who eventually moved to Switzerland, told of his arrest in Belgium.[76] Those arrested included women and children, some of whom had received no prior warning. After the arrest the men were separated from the women and children and taken to an unknown destination. The man then told of the horrors of being transported in crowded cattle trucks to the Russian front and put to work in the mines and on fortifications there in conditions of constant hunger. The daily food ration consisted mainly of 225 grams of bread. When one of the German chauffeurs fell ill, the informant was appointed to act as chauffeur to a German officer, with whom he developed a cordial relationship. The officers' two brothers had been killed on the Russian front and he opposed Nazi policy toward the Jews. The officer told him that Jews who were unable to work were either shot dead or murdered by having poison added to their food. The officer had given the survivor an appropriate work permit and clothes and put him on a train to Paris; from there he had escaped to the Vichy-controlled territory and on to Switzerland. The interviewers noted in the document that the 33-year-old informant was highly reliable and that his narrative matched the information conveyed by other refugees.[77]

Further information about the fate of Poland's Jews arrived in a telegram sent from the WJC's London office to New York.[78] Unnamed sources told of the deportations from the Warsaw Ghetto, noting that ten thousand Jews were being sent to their deaths every day. While it does not mention mass murder by means of gas, the cable conveys information on Sobibor, Belzec, and Treblinka—all defined as death camps where mass murders of men, women and children take place and their bodies buried in mass communal graves. The telegram concludes with a heart-rending cry, "Believe the unbelievable!"[79]

Additional testimonies reached the WJC office early in 1943, assembled in a comprehensive report that primarily addressed the Treblinka extermination camp and the Warsaw Ghetto. Of Treblinka the authors wrote: "Treblinka, the concentration camp which absorbed the Warsaw Ghetto dwellers *for all eternity* will

---

[76] Report by the Congress office in Geneva titled "Report of a Jewish Refugee," November 19, 1942, AJA, 361 H287/10. The refugee delivered his testimony on October 10, 1942, but it reached New York only on November 19.
[77] Ibid.
[78] See Telegram, December 1, 1942, AJA, 361 A9/20.
[79] Ibid.

probably be the greatest Jewish mass grave in our history."[80] The information on Treblinka and Warsaw Ghetto was delivered in three separate reports dispatched by official sources close to the Polish government-in-exile. While WJC officials believed that these were entirely reliable non-Jewish sources, they nevertheless maintained that the reports were slightly biased since their authors were gentiles. They felt, for example, that the emphasis placed on the fact that the Jews had not resisted the German actions over a prolonged period stemmed from the wish to absolve the Polish public of blame for cooperation with the Germans, intimating, in other words, that since the Jews themselves had not resisted, Warsaw's Polish residents could hardly have been expected to actively oppose the atrocities.[81]

The authors of the summary document, distributed among a wider group of WJC officials, noted that it was based on the reports of Jewish as well as non-Jewish witnesses, some of whom were still located in Nazi-occupied countries. The testimonies of the witnesses were cited without alteration, apart from essential deletions to preserve their anonymity. The authors mentioned that they had refrained from including the witnesses' conjectures or testimonies that were not substantiated by several sources.[82]

---

[80] Memorandum to the top leadership of the WJC, including Wise, Goldmann and Tartakower, regarding information on events in Poland, June 26, 1943, AJA, 361 B1/5 (emphasis in the original).
[81] Ibid.
[82] Document on Treblinka and the Warsaw Ghetto, presented by the World Jewish Congress and a delegation of Polish Jewry, September 1943 (no precise date or author specified), AJA, 361 H294/2. Shortly prior to the publication of the report, the Congress leaders met with Jan Karski, an emissary of the Polish underground who had visited the Warsaw Ghetto and one of the classification, or transit, camps linked to the Belzec extermination camp, and who had revealed to the Allies and to the WJC leadership what was occurring there. The report does not rely on the information conveyed by Karski, since it addresses the Treblinka extermination camp and the final stages of the existence of Warsaw Ghetto, which were not topics addressed by Karski. On the Congress leaders' meeting with Karski, see minutes of meeting, August 9, 1943, AJA, 361 H287/12. Yitzhak Arad has written that the Polish underground knew what was happening at Treblinka and conveyed information on the camp to the Polish government in exile in London. One may assume that part of the information in the Congress report is based on the material transmitted from occupied Poland to the Polish government in exile. The Congress maintained close links to the Polish government in exile and it is therefore reasonable to assume that the material was conveyed to the WJC rather than to some other Jewish organization. On the reports by the Polish underground on Treblinka, see Yitzhak Arad, *Belzec, Sobibor, Treblinka: The Operation Reinhard Death Camps* (Bloomington and Indianapolis, 1987), 349–359. Arad's descriptions of Treblinka accord with those in the Congress's report. See Arad, *Treblinka*, 81–113. On the links between the WJC and the Polish government in exile, see, for example, Minutes of a Meeting of European Congress functionaries, including Goldmann and Riegner, classified top secret, December 6, 1939, AJA, 361 A7/1.

The first section of the document provides detailed information about the Treblinka extermination camp. The witnesses told of its location in the vicinity of the village of Treblinka, adjacent to the railway station. The camp began operation as a detention center for Poles; the camp known as Treblinka B was erected later. Construction ended in April 1942 when the building of what the witnesses dubbed "Death Chamber No. 1" was completed.[83]

A detailed map describing the security measures and the electrified fence was appended to the document. Particular attention was paid to the description of death chambers Nos. 1 and 2, including detailed information on building materials, dimensions, and technical specifications regarding their means of operation. The witnesses related that a small team of Ukrainians and SS men, led by an SS officer named Saur who held a rank equivalent to major, operated the death chambers. This was followed by an account of the camp's daily routine, including a description of the accommodation blocks housing the Jews who worked in the camp, and an explanation of the role of the *kapos* (prisoners in Nazi concentration camps assigned by the SS to supervise forced labor and/or carry out administrative tasks). According to the report's authors, the testimonies indicated that the majority of Jews who operated the death machine in Treblinka failed to survive beyond two weeks, succumbing to hunger and the cruel treatment meted out to them.[84]

A large part of the report was devoted to a description of the process of murder, from the arrival of the transports, through entry to the gas chambers, to the burial of the corpses. The entire process was termed "The Tragedy of Treblinka." The witnesses reported that two transports arrived daily, one in the morning and another toward evening, but on some days additional transports would arrive. The separation of the men from the women and children was described, as was the subterfuge by which the Germans sought to conceal the true function of the gas chambers from the victims. The document provides detailed data, from a description of the signs welcoming those arriving from the Warsaw Ghetto, to the precise manner in which the corpses were burned. The information contained in the report is extremely comprehensive and corresponds to what is known today. One may thus assume that the details are reliable and are based on first-hand experience.[85]

The second section of the report addresses the Warsaw Ghetto. The testimonies tell of its establishment in October 1940 and of the means of terror employed to herd the Jews inside. Based on the collection and comparison of a variety of

---

83 Report, September 1943.
84 Ibid.
85 Ibid.

data, the authors concluded that the ghetto housed between 450,000 and half a million Jews prior to the deportations. A Jew who succeeded in escaping from the ghetto with the assistance of a Polish friend told of the atmosphere of fear and terror in the ghetto on the eve of the deportations and as they were taking place. The document is replete with details of everyday life: the price of bread, the various plants that employed Jews and the number of workers in each of them, the food given to the workers, the number of those who willingly reported for transportation as opposed to those who went into hiding, tables recording the daily number of deportees, and information on the numbers of those who perished of famine and disease.[86]

In contrast to the detailed descriptions of daily life in the ghetto, the document provides little information about acts of resistance. It is possible that the witnesses and sources available to the document's authors had not actively participated in the fighting and did not belong to resistance organizations.

The resistance that began in January 1943 and the subsequent German offensive on April 19, 1943, are portrayed from the perspective of a bystander who is impressed by the manner in which the Germans were stopped in the initial stages of the uprising and goes on to relate how the resistance petered out beginning on April 23 as the Germans began to burn down the ghetto. The authors surmise that only a small number of ghetto residents had survived by escaping to the Polish section of Warsaw. The rest were either killed during the course of the German offensive, shot by the Germans in the ghetto, or dispatched to the death camps.[87]

The information accumulated by the WJC office during 1942 and the first half of 1943 pertaining to the process of murder of European Jewry was instrumental in making Jewish leaders around the world, the heads of the Zionist movement, and Allied leaders aware of the fact that the Germans were energetically and systematically exterminating the Jews of Europe.[88], as well as graphic descriptions of the killing process: the unbearable crowding in the cattle trucks used to deport the Jews, testimonies on the miniscule portions of food allocated to the Jewish

---

86 Ibid. The information in the report on Warsaw Ghetto likewise accords with the findings of scholars in later years. On Warsaw Ghetto, see Israel Guttman, senior editor, *Encyclopedia of the Holocaust* [in Hebrew], vol. 2 (Tel Aviv, 1990), (459–480).
87 Report, September 1943.
88 Stephen Wise conveyed the information about the process of extermination to other Jewish leaders in the United States and to various arms of the administration, including President Roosevelt. See Urofsky, *Wise*, 321–323. The WJC convened press conferences and initiated radio broadcasts in the United States and Britain on the topic of the extermination of European Jews and also organized mass demonstrations, particularly in New York. See Kubowizki, *World Jewish History*, 160–164. On efforts to arrange a meeting with the Under Secretary of State in the wake of the information from Europe, see Memorandum of November 19, 1942, AJA, 361 H287/10.

laborers, and descriptions of the manner in which the corpses were disposed of to ensure maximum efficiency.

Tuvia Friling has addressed the "leap of consciousness" required of David Ben Gurion, chairman of the Jewish Agency Executive, and of other Jewish leaders in order to internalize and appreciate what was happening in Europe, even after they were exposed to the initial reports on the process of extermination.[89] The information provided by the institutions of the WJC created a factual base that enabled Congress leadership and Jewish leaders in general to make that leap of consciousness and comprehend fully and accurately what was occurring in Europe, and would continue to occur there throughout the German occupation.[90] WJC documentation demonstrates the enormous impact of the information on its leaders' perception of the events in Europe. The Congress leadership had been aware of the process of ghettoization, the famine and the mass killing of Jews in Eastern Europe (pogroms), prior to receiving the information from Europe.[91] Even after the initial reports of the final solution arrived, the modes of its precise implementation remained unclear. The reports told of increasing numbers of Warsaw Jews who had been transported to an unknown destination, and whose fate remained unknown.[92] Receipt of the detailed descriptions of the killing process in the Treblinka extermination camp completely altered the WJC leadership's understanding of events in Europe. The importance of the information collected by WJC offices in Europe was not lost on scholars; nevertheless, one can only appreciate the full significance of this information by perusing the volumes of documents pertaining to the issue, which are preserved in the WJC archive and are cited here.

The attempts on the part of the WJC team of authors to find the appropriate words to describe the extermination process reveal something of the challenge they faced in their efforts to comprehend the information that flowed from Europe. They sought to impress upon their readers that what was happening could not be adequately understood in the same context as previous instances of Jewish persecution throughout European history. Guggenheim was able to write about the Germans' intention to exterminate the Jews of Europe, but the authors of these documents found it all but impossible to portray the events of which they were

---

89 Friling, Ben Gurion, 96–97.
90 For his thoughts on Ben Gurion's exposure to the Riegner telegram, see ibid, 84–6. In the following chapters we trace how some of the Congress leaders' assessments of the scope of the extermination process and of what lay in store for the Jews of Europe were submitted to the Zionist leadership and to bodies in Palestine. See letter from Nahum Goldmann to Yitzhak Gruenbaum, April 5, 1943, CZA Z-6/2755.
91 See Report on the Condition of European Jewry prepared by the Congress's Institute of Jewish Affairs, July 1, 1942, AJA, 361 A1/7.
92 Classified memorandum prepared by Jacob Robinson, January 25, 1943, AJA, 361 D104/6.

now aware.⁹³ Thus, in a telegram describing what was happening to the Jews of Poland, they simply characterized the events of 1942 as "unbelievable!" Similar terminology was employed in other documents reporting the murder of Polish Jews.⁹⁴ The events in Warsaw Ghetto were described as "tragic," while further acts of mass murder in other locations in Poland were designated as "pogroms." A subsequent report defines the German actions as a program designed to exterminate the majority of European Jewry.⁹⁵ The first—and only—reference to the term Holocaust in WJC documents of 1942–43 was made by Stephen Wise in a speech delivered to the American Jewish Convention in New York in August 1943.⁹⁶ On this occasion the concept of Holocaust was not the primary expression used by Wise to describe the bitter fate of Europe's Jews, but was one of a number of terms he used to explain what was occurring in the death camps of Eastern Europe.⁹⁷

The information that flowed to the WJC offices was instrumental in exposing the dimensions of the murder of European Jewry, but its importance went further than that. The factual evidence collected by Congress branches in Europe was new, more detailed, and more extensive than earlier data. Consequently, the raw material and its interpretation by the WJC leadership have been of pivotal importance in shaping Holocaust memory from the 1940s to this day. A prime example of this is the October 1942 report on the condition of Polish Jews, which provides dramatic details of the murder of hundreds of thousands and the use of gas as a means of murder. The authors relate further that the corpses of the murdered Jews provided raw material for the manufacture of soap. This was the first mention of Jewish corpses being used for the manufacture of soap.⁹⁸ We may assume that any report dispatched to the head office in New York from the Congress office in Geneva would come into Stephen Wise's hands. Several weeks later, in the November 26, 1942, edition of the *New York Times*, Wise wrote regarding the use by the Germans of Jewish corpses to manufacture soap. This announcement by Wise marks the beginning of the trans-

---

93 Guggenheim's testimony, October 29, 1942, AJA, 361 A8/11.
94 Telegram on the fate of Polish Jewry, December 1, 1942.
95 The Geneva report, October 8, 1942, AJA, 361 H287/12. Also, Document on Treblinka and Warsaw Ghetto, September, 1943. On the discourse about the concepts of Holocaust and genocide and their presence in history, see Frank Chalk and Kurt Jonassohn, *Genocide Analyses and Case Studies* (New Haven and London, 1990), 323–377.
96 Wise's address to the American Jewish Convention in New York, August 29, 1943, AJA, 361 A2/3.
97 For a comprehensive discussion of the evolution of the concept Holocaust, see Uriel Tal, "On the Study of the Holocaust and Genocide" [in Hebrew], *Yad Vashem, Collection of Studies* 13 (1980): 43–47. For discussion of the concept of Holocaust in the American arena, see Hasia R. Diner, *We Remember With Reverence and Love* (New York, 2009), 21–22, 382–383.
98 The Geneva Report, October 8, 1942, AJA, 361 H287/12.

formation of the report's content into an issue that gained a significant foothold in public memory and has continued to resonate among scholars to this day.[99]

There is general consensus among Holocaust scholars that while isolated attempts to manufacture soap from Jewish corpses may have been made, the Germans did not conduct an industrial manufacturing process of this kind. The soap story constituted but one element of the accurate information collected by WJC functionaries during 1942. It was possibly the difficulty of coming to terms with the tragic condition of Europe's Jews in 1942 that led Wise and later generations to use the topic to bring home to the public the fact that the process of extermination of European Jewry could not be grasped in relation to any familiar human norm.

A further issue that emerged from the reports on events in Europe is the manner in which the documents' authors addressed the topic of Jewish resistance. In their interpretation of the material pertaining to Treblinka extermination camp, the anonymous author or authors expressed surprise at the fact that the young people in the camp, particularly the prison laborers, had utterly failed to resist the Germans' actions. This criticism was voiced in spite of the various editors' above-mentioned caveat that a large part of the testimony had emanated from Polish rather than Jewish sources, and that these sources had deliberately sought to emphasize the passivity of the Jewish response to the horrendous acts perpetrated by the Nazis. Particular attention was drawn to a description of the murder of 500 Jewish prisoners who served in the camp's labor force. The slaughter took place in early September; the victims were shot one after another, the first at seven thirty in the morning and the last at three thirty in the afternoon. The report's authors stressed that although the 500 victims were young and were murdered in succession over a period of many hours—which ostensibly had allowed them the opportunity to resist—not one of them had lifted a hand against the murderers. Despite its critical view, the report makes clear that the prolonged famine and emotional attrition at the hands of the Germans had caused the Jews to lose their capacity for resistance. All they desired was to ensure that their deaths came quickly and smoothly and that they be spared additional suffering.

The report's authors viewed the failure of the thousands of Jews who arrived by train to resist their murder in a similar vein. Here too they underscored the Jews' physical and emotional exhaustion and furnished additional details of the Germans' strategy of deception, including the posting of signs displaying trades such as tailor and shoemaker so as to create the impression that the selection

---

[99] For discussion of the issue of use of Jewish corpses for the manufacture of soap, see Joachim Neander, "The Danzig Soap Case: Facts and Legends around 'Professor Spanner' and the Danzig Anatomic Institute 1944–1945," *German Studies Review* 29, no. 1 (2006): 63–86.

process was intended to form groups that would work for the Germans. It is somewhat ironic that the early criticism of the Jews' behavior in the extermination camps was aimed at the inmates of the Treblinka camp; in the latter stages of the war, a well-organized underground operating there would mount an impressive and heroic uprising that led to the cessation of the camp's extermination process.

In contrast to their criticism of the behavior patterns of the Jews imprisoned at Treblinka, the authors wrote with great admiration of the Jewish uprising in the Warsaw Ghetto. Despite the meager source material at their disposal, the authors devoted considerable space to a description of the revolt, adding their interpretation of the Jewish acts of heroism toward the end of the document: "A Jewish fighting organization led the defense in the ghetto. Their forces were small, they did not have much ammunition. Nevertheless they fought for four weeks with more effort than the Germans in this tragic struggle."[100] Thus, as early as 1943 a singular mix evolved containing criticism of the Jews' acceptance of their fate on the one hand, and glorification of Jewish resistance, particularly in the Warsaw Ghetto, on the other. This emphasis on the significance of the Jewish resistance in Warsaw Ghetto in the 1943 report heralded a concerted effort on the part of the WJC leadership to enhance the role of the Warsaw Ghetto uprising in the Holocaust memory that they sought to shape. As will be revealed in subsequent chapters, the leaders furthered this objective through the organization's publications by preparing study programs on the uprising, and by organizing memorial events in which the uprising played a major role.[101]

The authors of the WJC documents produced in 1942 and 1943 leveled criticism at the manner in which the Jews at Treblinka comported themselves, but refrained from commenting on the *Judenrat* (council of Jews responsible for implementing Nazi policies within their communities) in the Warsaw Ghetto or the kapos at Treblinka. The special status of the kapos in the camp was mentioned, along with the attendant benefits, but no value judgment was made. The activities of the Judenrat in the Warsaw Ghetto were addressed in a similar vein. The authors merely provided a general description of its activity and wrote of its role in the transport of Jews from the Ghetto, without criticizing its members in any way. They underscored the fact that its activity was conducted according to the Germans' demands. This approach differs considerably from the historical and public discourse conducted during the initial post-Holocaust decades, in

---

100 Report, September 1943 (no precise date or author given), AJA, 361 H294/2.
101 See the Congress's collection of documents and publications on the topic of the uprising produced in the 1950s, AJA, 361 H294/2. This issue is extensively addressed in later chapters in the context of the WJC's role in shaping Holocaust memory in the United States.

which trenchant criticism was leveled at the Jewish councils, and occasionally led to indictment of individuals who had acted as kapos.

Discussion of the shaping of Holocaust memory both in general and in the context of collaboration between Jews and Nazis goes beyond the scope of this book. One may assume that the work of scholars and intellectuals such as Hannah Arendt contributed to the emergence of a critical discourse on patterns of cooperation between Jews and Nazis during World War II, at the final stages of the war, and thereafter. The WJC documents clearly show that so such discourse was conducted when the reports from Europe began to arrive.[102]

The World Jewish Congress Leadership and the Jewish Public in the United States at the Time of the Holocaust

The tragic news conveyed by the WJC's European bureaus to the New York headquarters shaped the perception of the organization's leadership with regard to the destiny of Europe's Jews. This new perception stems from an April 1943 letter from Nahum Goldmann to Yitzhak Gruenbaum, a member of the Jewish Agency executive and chairman of the Rescue Committee, who was based in Palestine.[103] This letter, which has not attracted the attention of scholarship until recently, reveals cardinal aspects of the issues under discussion.

Goldmann notes that the purpose of the letter was to report on the situation in the United States with regard to activity pertaining to European Jews, and especially on the WJC's efforts concerning this matter. He describes how the initial reports of the murder of Jews by the Germans had been received from WJC representatives in Europe, how officials at American delegations to neutral countries had verified them, and the manner in which the information had been made public in coordination with the U.S. State Department. Upon receipt of the news, the WJC became the driving force in launching varied and intensive action

---

[102] For a discussion of the role of the concept "Like lambs to the slaughter" in the United States, see Feingold, *Bearing Witness*, 41–53. Among the prominent studies that sparked debate about the Holocaust in general and the patterns of collaboration of Jews with the Germans in particular, see Raul Hilberg, *The Destruction of the European Jews* (Chicago, 1961). For an extensive discussion of similar contexts of Holocaust memory in Israel, see Hanna Yablonka, "The Development of Holocaust Consciousness in Israel: The Nuremberg, Kapos, Kastner and Eichmann Trials," *Israel Studies* 8 (2003): 1–24. For a prime example of critical writing in the United States regarding the behavior of the Jewish public in general and of the Jewish leadership in particular at the time of the Holocaust, see Hannah Arendt, *Eichmann in Jerusalem. A Report on the Banality of Evil* (New York, 1963).
[103] Letter from Goldmann to Gruenbaum, April 5, 1943, CZA, Z-6/2755.

designed to arouse public opinion and to persuade Washington to take more concerted action toward rescuing Jews and assisting those Jewish refugees who had managed to flee from Europe. This activity, according to the letter, had come to a head in a mass rally held in March 1943 at Madison Square Garden in New York. Yet despite this impressive volume of public activity, Goldmann concludes by stating that the practical achievements of the WJC on behalf of European Jewry had been meager. He describes the sympathy expressed by senior state department officials toward the plight of Europe's Jews—in contrast to the apathy exhibited by Britain's Foreign Minister Anthony Eden—but adds that he and the Congress leaders were convinced that the U.S. State Department would take no practical action to assist European Jewry, verbal support of its leaders notwithstanding. Goldmann explains that this state of affairs was manifested when the Bermuda Conference turned out to be a meaningless event. (The conference was convened in April 1943 and was attended by delegates from Great Britain and the United States—ostensibly to discuss the problem of all World War II refugees, but in fact to address the Jewish issue.) He particularly underscored the Allied leaders' unwillingness even to consider implementation of his plan, the principal element of which was the issuing of a formal request by the Allies to Germany to allow Jews to leave the areas under German occupation, together with an offer to provide food for the Jews of Europe on condition that the mass murder ceased.[104]

Goldmann himself was thus well aware that the Congress's efforts to rescue the Jews of Europe would come to nothing; as his letter to Gruenbaum demonstrates, this conclusion did not stem from some transitory frustration at the failure of the rescue effort, but rather from a profound analysis of the American political arena. This is evident from a previous letter that Goldmann sent to Myron Taylor, a State Department official and chairman of the Inter-Governmental Commission on Refugees. In it Goldmann collated detailed information from Europe that had been forwarded to the State Department pertaining to the mass murder of Polish Jews and the expansion of the Germans' murderous deeds to additional areas of Europe. This information had clearly failed to spur the Roosevelt Administration into taking effective action, and Goldmann believed that this state of affairs would not change.[105]

While he was fully aware that they had failed to assist European Jews, Goldmann made it clear to Gruenbaum that this had not incited WJC functionaries to initiate more radical public action, nor to attempt to increase public pressure on President Roosevelt's administration to act. They had adopted this less aggressive approach because they knew that their limited public power in the American

---

104 Ibid. On Goldmann's plan, see Wyman, *Abandonment of the Jews*, 187–188.
105 Goldmann's Letter to Myron Taylor, March 24, 1943, CZA, Z-6/2755.

arena and the obstacles presented by the reality of a world war made it exceedingly difficult for them to influence administration policy concerning the Jewish cause. They believed that the only success that the organization had achieved on behalf of the Jews had come from clandestine diplomatic activity on the margins of events, such as preventing the expulsion of Jewish refugees from Spain, rather than from open public action. Goldmann stressed the futility of dispatching Zionist leaders from Palestine to the United States in order to increase pressure on the administration.[106] He ended the letter on a painful note, saying that one must assume that the majority of Jews living in the areas of Nazi occupation would be exterminated. He was aware of the gravity of his words, stressing that this was a harsh diagnosis but that any other conclusion would be tantamount to disregarding the facts.[107]

Goldmann's words merely serve to exacerbate questions about the tendency of WJC functionaries to moderate their overt public and political activity on behalf of European Jews, and even to take measures to restrain American Jewish activity. They chose this path despite being fully aware of the fate of European Jewry—even though vigorous public action on behalf of Jewish groups throughout the world had formed a major element of their public platform throughout the thirties and forties. The disparity between Goldmann's overt and covert activity became apparent several months later. In August 1943 he delivered one of the main speeches at a conference of the American Jewish Congress, which had assembled at the Waldorf Astoria Hotel in New York. His speech addressed events in Europe, but presented a more optimistic prognosis regarding the fate of European Jewry. While in his classified letter to Gruenbaum he had predicted that the great majority of Europe's Jews would be murdered by the Nazis, in his public speech to the conference he asserted that millions of European Jews would survive the horrors of the war. Goldmann continued in this optimistic tone even so far as to entertain the possibility that a significant number of Jews would be able to return to Warsaw, Cracow, Vilnius and other cities of Eastern Europe after the war. He then enumerated the complications involved in the process of return, and emphasized the social and spiritual aspects associated with rehabilitation.[108]

---

106 A similar survey of the rescue efforts in the United States as well as the conclusion that it was impossible to achieve more and the conviction that there was no need to dispatch Zionist leaders from Palestine to the United States may be found in an earlier and less detailed letter from Goldmann to Eliezer Kaplan, a member of the Zionist executive and Treasurer of the Jewish Agency. See Goldmann's letter to Kaplan, January 11, 1943, CZA, Z-6/2755.
107 Goldmann Letter, to Gruenbaum, April 5, 1943, CZA, Z-6/2755.
108 Goldmann's speech to the American Jewish Congress, New York, August 30, 1943, AJA, 361 A2/3.

A possible explanation of the WJC's restraint is to be found in the relationship between the Congress leadership and that of another body, the American Jewish Committee, which represented the American-Jewish elite of German origin. In his letter to Gruenbaum, Goldmann portrayed the American Jewish Committee and particularly its president, the jurist Joseph Proskauer, as having consistently opposed any attempt to take more radical action on behalf of Europe's Jews, and cited their firm opposition to intensifying the public campaign on this issue.[109] Despite this portrayal, which suggests that WJC functionaries were overtly attempting to lay part of the responsibility for the lack of action on the Committee—going so far as to portray the American Jewish Committee as bearing most of the blame for the failure of the campaign to generate significant public pressure on the administration—we learn from Goldmann that the two organizations had worked in close cooperation and coordination. They both sought to moderate the public activity of the American Jewish community.[110] This matter is particularly noteworthy because in his memoirs, Goldmann goes to great lengths to show that the WJC took political and public action to counteract the Jewish elites of the kind represented by the Committee, emphasizing the need to democratize Jewish life in the United States and to oppose the Jewish philanthropists. He goes on to note that economic struggle against the philanthropic foundations was one of the Congress's objectives, thereby justifying its independent existence, especially its fundraising machinery.[111]

It is worth noting that this disparity between the public stance of the founders of the WJC regarding their objectives in establishing the body and their practical activity also became evident during the preparations for founding the organization and its actual establishment in Europe between 1932 and 1934. The publicly pronounced desire to create a democratic organization in Europe that would not discriminate between Eastern- and Western-European Jews clashed with opposing trends arising from the practical need to mobilize the Jewish elites of Western Europe and North America toward activity within the WJC, because those cohorts possessed the financial and political resources that could provide the WJC public power and financial stability. Stephen Wise, Louis Lipsky and Nahum Goldmann thus made a point of ensuring that the Congress's convention in Geneva in 1936

---

109 Ibid. Discussion of the activities of the American Jewish Committee during World War II goes beyond the scope of this book. I have merely quoted Goldmann on this matter, and have not taken a stand on this complex issue. For an extensive discussion of this topic, see Naomi W. Cohen, *Not Free To Desist: The American Jewish Committee 1906–1966* (Philadelphia, 1972), 227–264 (hereafter: Chen, *The American Jewish Committee*).
110 On the cooperation between Wise and Proskauer, see Cohen, *The American Jewish Committee*, 244–245.
111 Goldmann, *Autobiography*, 195–196.

would be relevant above all to the Jews of the Western world. They regarded this as a supreme goal, citing the need to reinforce the impression of the dominance of Western Jewry in the WJC, and to guard against an Eastern-European atmosphere from prevailing at the convention. In order to achieve this, they meticulously sought to arrange the opening session in such a way that the majority of speakers would be Western Jews. Sessions were, whenever possible, to be conducted in English, and the addresses were to be short and to the point—in keeping with their perception of the American style.[112]

Thus, Goldmann's criticism of the American Jewish Committee appears to contradict the cooperation that he described in the letter. In fact, the two organizations worked together far more closely than can be inferred from the letter to Gruenbaum—and far beyond the extent required either to present a united Jewish front or to leverage the political connections and personal stature of the heads of the Committee.

A desire to conceal the political cooperation between Goldmann and Proskauer, who belonged to manifestly competing organizations, is likewise evident during the latter half of the 1940s. The political coordination between the two men in preparation for Goldmann's mission to Washington in summer 1946 as a representative of the Jewish Agency, which had convened in Paris, was close and ongoing. Nevertheless, Goldmann impressed upon Proskauer the need to keep their relationship a secret and to refrain from mentioning it in public.[113]

There is further evidence of the way in which Wise, Goldmann and Proskauer coordinated their political and public activities. There are records of discussions among the three men regarding a press conference scheduled for April 1943. The hope was that describing the dire plight of Europe's Jews and condemning the Roosevelt administration's inactivity on the issue would spur the administration into more concerted action on their behalf. On April 22, 1943, Wise reported to Goldmann on a conversation he had held with Proskauer some days earlier, in which the two had concluded that the planned press conference should be canceled.[114] Not only did Wise believe that the press conference would be of no

---

112 Louis Lipsky documents, Archive of the American Jewish Historical Society, New York, collection P-672, box 3. File 5 (hereafter P-672 3/5).
113 Goldmann's letter to Proskauer, June 28, 1946, CZA, Z-6/69. On testimonies regarding further clandestine meetings attended by Goldmann and Proskauer, see letter from Emanuel Neumann, an American Zionist functionary and assistant to Abba Hillel Silver, to Louis Lipsky, August 30, 1946, CZA, A-123/120.
114 Wise's letter to Goldmann, April 22, 1943, CZA, Z-6/18. We may surmise that the press conference had been planned following the failure of the Bermuda Conference. In the end no press conference was convened by an official Jewish or Zionist body to protest the failure of the Bermuda Conference.

benefit to the struggle, but he feared that it might undermine it. It would not motivate the United States Congress to exert pressure on Roosevelt. On the contrary, Wise foresaw that in the public debate that the press conference would kindle, the president would for the first time win the support of the generally hostile Congress. He felt that Congress was, on the whole, anti-Semitic, and could thus be expected to support Roosevelt if he were to be accused of failure to support the Jews of Europe. Wise stressed that while a press conference could easily be convened and public meetings held, one must take into account their possible repercussions. He believed that such action would result in the closing of doors that remained open to Jewish activists, and that it was unrealistic to expect any help from Roosevelt in the rescue of Jews. Such public action would, he thought, be counterproductive, since as long as pressure was being exerted clandestinely rather than in the form of public press conferences, Roosevelt, who admittedly had yet to respond adequately to the murder of the Jewish people in Europe, would nevertheless remain a friend who had and would continue to do everything in his power for the sake of rescuing Jews.[115]

The letters reveal the bind in which Wise and Goldmann found themselves. They were both aware that the administration had not made an effort to undertake any rescue activity, but believed that this was due to structural constraints within the American political system in the first half of the 1940s. These constraints, so they thought, necessitated coordination with the administration with regard to the nature of public action taken in the United States to promote the rescue of Jews.[116] Wise and Goldmann thought it advisable to blur Roosevelt's engagement with the Jewish issue in order to minimize his exposure to political pressures from his many adversaries in Congress, whom, as mentioned, they perceived to be anti-Semites who sought to denigrate the president by portraying him as a friend of the Jews—or even as someone who was prosecuting the war in response to Jewish pressure rather than in concern for American interests. Wise and Goldmann further believed that public criticism of Roosevelt's lack of action to save European Jews would harm him in another respect: He and his party's candidates were likely to lose their Jewish support as a result, which could

---

[115] Wise's letter to Goldmann, April 22, 1943, CZA Z-6/18. For a similar opinion expressed by Wise concerning the nature of Roosevelt's activity on the Jewish issue, see a later letter to Goldmann. Wise expected that Roosevelt would not alter his approach to rescuing the Jews of Europe, and that they could do no more to promote the campaign for rescue in the United States. Wise's letter to Goldmann, July 27, 1943, CZA, A-243/24. Roosevelt's close advisor and speech writer has written about the considerable store he set on his stature in Congress and of his apprehension at the difficulties awaiting him in this political arena. See Samuel and Dorothy Rosenman, *Presidential Style* (New York, 1976), 346–347.

[116] See, for example, the letter from Wise to Goldmann, September 4, 1942, CZA, A-243/124.

restrict his political leeway. Goldmann, Wise and Proskauer thought that such a development would endanger the United States as well as world Jewry.[117] Thus, in the official correspondence they conducted with a broad range of people, Wise and Goldmann presented an optimistic view with regard to the president's and the State Department's commitment toward European Jewry. Their predictions that the president would take no more than limited action appeared only in confidential correspondence, with a view to dampening the Jewish campaign against the president.[118]

Wise's view that it was essential to downplay the issue of the fate of European Jewry in the context of World War II, especially his desire to mitigate criticism leveled at the administration's actions regarding rescue, is further manifested in his address to the American Jewish Congress in late August 1943. Wise chose to begin his speech with a declaration that this was an American convention, explaining to his audience that the central component of their identity was their Americanism, and that they could be defined only as Americans rather than according to some other component linked to their religion or race: "This is an American Conference. We are American, first, last and all the time."[119] Wise continued by declaring that American Jews in 1943 shared the common goal of all American citizens, namely victory in the war against fascism. Defeat would mean that there would be no future. Throughout his entire address, Wise interlaced the dominant theme that an American victory in the war was the primary objective of all Jews and particularly of American Jews, thereby creating a clear link between victory in the war and the rescue of European Jews.[120]

---

117 For a clear example of Wise's world view as an American, and of his belief that the American democracy constituted the sole means whereby to rescue the Jews of the world and to defeat Hitler, see Wise's speech to the American Jewish Congress convention, February 11, 1940, CZA, A-243/71.
118 In addition to their critical comments toward the president's policy presented here, Wise and Goldmann uttered positive assessments of his actions and those of the administration. See Wise's report on his contacts with Roosevelt, addressed to Goldmann and to the heads of Jewish organizations, September 14, 1942, CZA, A-243/173; Goldmann's speech to the first assembly of the World Jewish Congress following the outbreak of war, November 1944 (no precise date), CZA, Z-6/2248. The policy of restraint in general, and the cooperation with the Jewish elites are of particular interest in light of Wise's prior propensity to wage bitter campaigns against these same elites. Discussion of this issue is beyond the scope of this book. Suffice it to say that the change in Wise's policy may have been due to a combination of factors linked to the singular circumstances that prevailed during the 1940s and to the fact that he had become a Jewish leader well connected to the Democratic establishment. On Wise's struggle against New York's Jewish elites, see Louis Lipsky, *Zionist Figures* [in Hebrew] (Jerusalem, 1957), 132–140
119 Wise's address to the American Jewish Congress, New York, August 29, 1943, AJA, 361 A2/3.
120 Ibid.

Wise stressed that the goal of the Jewish Congress in August 1943 should be to protect and defend the United States, and as a corollary, also to protect and defend the Jewish people. He portrayed the close connection between victory in the war and the rescue of Europe's Jews as a consequence of President Roosevelt's leadership during World War II. Wise praised Roosevelt's integrity and his humanist outlook, proclaiming that the convention delegates unanimously supported the Commander in Chief (as he referred to Roosevelt in his speech) and his commitment to enhancing efforts at saving Europe's Jews. He went on to bemoan the difficulties that European Jews had encountered as they sought to migrate prior to 1939, emphasizing that unless the rescue efforts gained momentum there would be no one left to save.[121]

By underscoring the "Americanism" of Jews in the United States and equating the issue of the rescue of Jews with an American victory in the war, Wise sought to downplay the presence of the Jewish issue in the public arena. If his theses were accepted, there would be no need to undertake more intensive independent Jewish activity to press for the rescue of European Jews. His underscoring of the expectation that the administration would take more decisive action to rescue Jews was a calculated move and offered the only hint of his dissatisfaction with Roosevelt's insufficiently resolute action to promote the rescue of Jews. By virtue of his status as president of the WJC and his links to senior figures in the Roosevelt administration, Wise was aware of both the dimensions of the murder of Europe's Jews and the administration's feeble efforts with regard to their rescue. He merely alluded to criticism of the administration's activity on this issue and failed to call for concerted action to be taken. This position should be understood in light of his arguments against clashing with the Roosevelt administration, as manifested in the affair of the press conference that failed to convene in April 1943. Yet Wise nevertheless chose to imply criticism of the administration in an attempt to prompt it to take action and in order to respond to criticism on the part of American Jews leveled at the futility of rescue activities.[122]

---

121 Ibid.
122 Wise was well aware of the popularity enjoyed among the American Jewish community by militant associations such as the Bergson group, which sought to intensify public activity in the American arena to promote the rescue of Jews and to protest against the administration's inactivity on this issue. See Urofsky, *Wise*, 333–335.

Chapter 2
Stephen Wise, Nahum Goldmann, and the Question of Palestine in 1940s America

The Episode of the Pro-Zionist Proposals in Congress

The issue of the rescue of European Jews was not the only one to concern the Jewish public in the United States during the Holocaust period and the early postwar years. A political and public campaign was being waged in the American arena on behalf of the establishment of a Jewish state in Palestine as part of the international arrangements to be put in place after World War II. The endeavor to promote the idea of founding the Jewish state was conducted during the war years alongside engagement with the topic of rescue, but Wise, Goldmann and their associates in the WJC leadership in fact cooperated with the administration to restrain American Jews' public activity, not only in the context of the rescue of Europe's Jews, but also with regard to the struggle for the establishment of a Jewish state. Despite the similarity between the two campaigns, Wise and Goldmann were more willing to intensify the campaign for a Jewish state than to step up public activity to press for the rescue of Europe's Jews. The fact that the WJC leadership chose to act similarly in both these contexts—the struggle for a Jewish state and the rescue of the Jews of Europe—with regard to various additional aspects of Jewish public activity in the United States, reinforces the view that this was a matter of deliberate policy aimed at restraining the public campaign on behalf of Jewish and Zionist causes in order to protect the Democratic administration.

A prime example of Wise and Goldmann's desire to dampen Jewish and Zionist agitation in the United States in favor of founding a Jewish state is well-illustrated in the episode of the pro-Zionist resolutions. Late in 1945, both houses of Congress adopted a joint pro-Zionist resolution. The vote in the Senate and in the House of Representatives marked the conclusion of a complex political maneuver that had continued for two years. This was one of the major political processes that shaped the political map of American Zionism and American Jewry and defined their relationship with the U.S. administration and with the world Zionist movement. During the course of the campaign to promote the pro-Zionist resolutions American Jewish leaders maintained a wide range of contacts with elements in the American political system in order to secure the cooperation of members of the Senate Foreign Relations Committee and the House Foreign Affairs Committee, and to ensure that administration officials would not take action to block their adoption. The decision of American Zionist institutions to actively promote the pro-Zionist resolutions forced the administration on its part to maintain ongoing contact with the heads of the Jewish and Zionist establishment in order to impact the content of the resolutions and the timing of their approval, should they be accepted. Examination of the political maneuvering that led to the eventual adoption of the pro-Zionist resolutions in Congress enables one to study major aspects of the reciprocal relationship between the Jewish leadership in the United States and the American political system.

American Jews became far more willing to act as an ethnic group in pursuit of specific political objectives within the country in the wake of the Allies' victory and the flow of information about the Holocaust to the United States. It is important to remember that American Zionism's increasing power and significance during the 1940s was primarily a function of American Jewish identification with the objectives of the Zionist movement and the State of Israel after 1948, rather than a result of their formal membership of the Zionist Organization of America and Hadassah. They were well aware that by actively promoting Zionist goals they were positioning themselves at the most particularistic ethnic pole on the American political scene, and were thereby acting as pioneers and pointing the way for other ethnic groups in the United States.[123]

The nomination of Rabbi Abba Hillel Silver alongside Wise to the position of chairman of the Emergency Council in August 1943 transformed the nature of the Council's public activity, despite Wise's opposition. It also marked Silver's rise to the status of leader of American Jewry in the latter half of the 1940s—replacing Wise. The importance of this development lies in the fact that it was now Silver who shaped the manner in which American Jews would act as a political pressure group in the post-war 1940s. Examination of the complex relationship between Wise and Silver sheds light on the wider aspects of Wise's activity in his capacity as an American Jewish leader during the war years, and on the factors that led to the erosion of his public stature among American Jews, particularly in view of the significant differences between him and Silver that emerge later in this chapter.

Silver arrived at the center of Jewish public activity in the United States in 1917, when he was appointed to the post of Reform rabbi of Tiferet Yisra'el Congregation in Cleveland, Ohio, one of the largest and most important Reform communities at the time. Silver's remarkable success as a rabbi and a public figure is indicated by the fact that he was appointed to the post despite his considerable ideological differences with the Cleveland congregation, which was radically

---

123 On American Jews' choice of Zionism as a central component of their ethnic identity in the context of the Holocaust, see Jonathan D. Sarna, *American Judaism, A History* (Yale University, 2004), 263–264.

reformist, did not use Hebrew in its services and adhered to an anti-Zionist world view. Cleveland became home to Silver and constituted his political power base throughout his public career, although he meticulously performed his duties as community rabbi even during the most intensive periods of his public activity in the United States and in the Zionist movement. During his subsequent political path in the Zionist movement, Silver was among the founders of the United Jewish Appeal and served as its chairman from 1938 to 1943. He also headed the Zionist Emergency Committee and the Emergency Council.[124] The Emergency Committee was formed on September 19, 1939, in response to the fear that the various Zionist centers would lose contact with one another and the desire to concentrate political activity in the United States. In effect, it functioned primarily as a political pressure group with a view to prompting the Roosevelt administration to further Zionist objectives. In July 1943 its title was changed to the Emergency Council. Silver represented the position of the Jewish Agency United Nations forums and served as president of the Zionist Organization of America from 1945 to 1947.[125]

One of the major concerns of Silver and his associates was winning over American public opinion. Upon the suggestion of Emanuel Neumann, Silver's assistant and political colleague, a decision was made to lobby for resolutions declaring support for the founding of a Jewish state to be adopted by both houses of Congress. This was considered a dramatic move, designed to focus the attention of American Jews, and the American public in general, on the struggle for a Jewish state. In addition, it was decided to work toward the inclusion of similar undertakings in the election platforms of both major parties in the run up to the presidential election of 1944. Silver reported to the Executive Committee of the Emergency Council on his contacts with supportive senators who had agreed to submit the resolutions to a vote, informing the committee members of the text of the resolutions he had forwarded to them. In the wake of these moves there followed many months of political endeavor in Washington to attain approval for the resolutions submitted to both houses of Congress.[126]

---

124 On Silver's powerful position within American Zionism, see Robert H. Ferrell, *Harry S. Truman* (Columbia, 1994), 307–308.
125 This survey of Silver relies on Marc Lee Raphael, *Abba Hillel Silver* (New York, 1989) and on the articles in the collection "Abba Hillel Silver and American Zionism" (Special Issue), *The Journal of Israel History* 17, no. 1 (1996). For a recent study on Silver, see Ofer Shiff, *The Defeated Zionist: Abba Hillel Silver and His Attempt to Transcend Jewish Nationalism* [in Hebrew] (Tel Aviv, 2010).
126 For a detailed survey of the political events related to the submission of the pro-Zionist resolutions, see Raphael, *Silver*, 97–134. For a survey of the resolutions issue following Silver's resignation, see "Silver Replaced by Wise as Council Head," *The Jewish Post*, January 5, 1946, 1–2. See also a printout of a proposed declaration by the House Foreign Affairs Committee with regard to

The lobbying for adoption of pro-Zionist resolutions in the House and the Senate was among the most important political moves that Silver undertook. The submission of the resolutions was opposed by Wise, Goldmann, David Ben Gurion and the members of the Jewish Agency Executive in Jerusalem. The resolutions were initially rejected because of the administration's opposition, and were adopted only after Roosevelt's death, during Truman's term as president. Silver was deposed from his position in the wake of the initial failure, whereupon Wise was appointed sole chairman of the Emergency Council.

Following Silver's dismissal, he and Neumann and their supporters prepared themselves for a public campaign designed to restore Silver as soon as possible to the center of Zionist political activity in the United States. He was duly reinstated as chairman of the Emergency Council in July 1945. Silver's reappointment was facilitated by the disappointment felt by American Jews at the results of Roosevelt's meeting with Churchill and Stalin at Yalta, and following his meeting with King Ibn Saud, after which he reported to Congress that he had learned more about the entire problem, the Muslim problem and the Jewish problem, from a five minute conversation with Ibn Saud than he could have learned from two or three dozen letters.[127] The anger and dismay at Roosevelt's actions bolstered Silver's stature, since he was considered to be Roosevelt's main opponent among the American Zionist leadership. Wise, who was considered a Roosevelt supporter, was, on the other hand, left considerably weakened by these moves. Neumann, Silver and their associates exploited this state of affairs and moved to depose Wise from the leadership of the Emergency Council and to reappoint Silver, who was granted extensive executive powers.

A wide-ranging public debate developed among American Jews during and after the episode of the submission of the pro-Zionist resolutions to Congress. During these discussions Stephen Wise and Nahum Goldmann referred to the issue as a failure. They maintained that the resolutions controversy had led to a rift in the relations between American Jewry—especially the American Zionist movement—and President Roosevelt; and that even had the resolutions been passed in the Senate and the House, the process would have been detrimental because of the opposition on the part of the State Department, elements within the army, and the president himself. The debate underscored the struggle between Wise, who had opposed the submission process, and Silver, who had used all his

---

a Jewish national home in Palestine: Declaration on a Jewish National Home in Palestine, House Foreign Affairs Committee, the 78th Congress, Second Session, March 17, 1944, CZA, A-123/349.
127 Zvi Ganin, "The Debate between Activists and Moderates in the US Zionist Leadership during the 1940s: The Stephen Wise and Abba Hillel Silver Dispute" [in Hebrew], *Ha-Tsionut* 9 (1984): 342–343.

political power on behalf of the resolutions, defying Wise and his supporters on the Emergency Council.[128]

The correspondence between Silver and Neumann during 1944 reveals a very different approach to that taken by Wise concerning the pattern of political policy that the Jews should adopt as an ethnic minority during World War II, as manifested in the cancellation of the press conference in April 1943. Neumann and Silver lobbied for the resolutions because they believed that the political reality in the United States demanded it Neumann presented the arguments in favor of the move in a working paper,[129] in which he set out the reasons for submitting the resolutions to Congress despite the fact that they would have no practical influence on U.S. foreign policy and were liable to lead to a rift between the Jews of America and President Roosevelt. He states that the American Zionist movement had tried all possible means to persuade the administration to make a declaration that would clarify its policy on Palestine.[130] This effort continued for five years, beginning with the publication of the White Paper in 1939, but was to no avail. The American Zionist movement responded by appealing to public opinion and activating the Jewish public and American citizens in general in support of the Zionist movement. The success of the public campaign and the broad sympathy toward the Zionist movement against the backdrop of World War II and the Holocaust forced the administration to obfuscate its Palestine policy lest it stir

---

128 A number of documents that present the view of Wise and Goldmann are referred to below. See also the minutes of the Jewish Agency Executive's meetings in Jerusalem, which likewise reflect their views: minutes of meeting of the Jewish Agency Executive, February 4, 1945, CZA, collection S-100 (filed by date; hereafter S-100).
129 Neumann's memorandum concerning submission of the pro-Zionist resolutions to Congress, 1944, CZA, A-123/530.
130 Jehuda Reinharz has elaborated on the inability of the Zionist establishment to influence Roosevelt's policy regarding the Palestine question and efforts to rescue Jews during the war years. He stresses that the extent to which the Amerian Zionist movement and American Jews were misled by President Roosevelt has only recently become known. See Jehuda Reinharz, *Zionism and the Great Powers: A Century of Foreign Policy* (New York, 1994), 12–13. In his doctoral dissertation Mark Raider likewise writes about the inability of the American Jewish public to influence Roosevelt's policy regarding the rescue of European Jewry during World War II. This was due partly to the fear of stirring up anti-Semitism in the United States and worldwide, and partly to the president's ability to persuade the Jewish public that his policy was the right one. Roosevelt maintained that the rescue of Europe's Jews depended primarily on an Allied victory. Zionist leaders such as Stephen Wise and Jewish public figures such as Felix Frankfurter supported Roosevelt's view. See Mark A. Raider, "From the Margins to the Mainstream: Labor Zionism and American Jews, 1919–1945" (Ph.D. Dissertation, Brandeis University, 1996), 307–313. This work was published in book form as Mark A. Raider, *The Emergence of American Zionism* (New York and London, 1998).

up public criticism that could have electoral consequences.[131] Therefore, discussion of the Palestine issue became taboo in Washington; an attempt was made to address the Zionist issue only behind the scenes and by means of classified reports. This state of affairs gave free rein to the opponents of the Zionist enterprise in Palestine, enabling them to act without fear of public discussion and free of the restrictions of public opinion. Thus, the purpose of submitting the resolutions to Congress was to put an end to this situation and to place the Palestine question once again squarely on the public agenda.

Neumann stressed that the timing of the move to submit the resolutions was significant. This was done close to the March 31, 1944, the end of the official period of enforcement of the White Paper, with a view to influencing the new arrangements that would come into force. Further incentives to lobby for the submission of the resolutions were provided by the increasing involvement of the United States in the Middle East and the growing activity of the oil companies in that area. The overall intention was to prevent decisions being made that would affect the future of Palestine without the knowledge of American Jewry, thus rendering them unable to influence events.[132]

Neumann clarified further that Silver and he sought not only to turn the Palestine question into a focus of political debate in the United States, but also to force the administration to reveal, at least partially, the contours of its policy on the Palestine issue. The process of hearings conducted by the House Foreign Affairs and Senate Foreign Relations Committees forced the administration's policy makers to set out their policy on the Palestine question clearly and to divulge their considerations for and against the establishment of a Jewish national home. Such exposure served both men's objectives in two ways. First, exposure of the administration's considerations would reveal its true policy (which presented a severe setback to the Zionist movement and its interests with regard to Palestine) would hinder the administration's attempt to conceal its political moves concerning Palestine, thereby enabling American Jews to campaign more effectively against trends that appeared to them to be dangerous. Second, open opposition to the resolutions by the administration would facilitate the mobilization of both

---

131 On the importance of Jewish votes to the Democratic Party from the presidential election of 1944 onward, see the letter from Bartley Crum, a lawyer close to President Truman and one of the American members of the Anglo-American Committee of Inquiry, to Robert Hannegan, a leading Democrat, Chairman of the Democratic National Committee and President Truman's right-hand man. The letter comprised part of a prolonged discussion between the two concerning the administration's policy on the Palestine question and the effect of this policy in the American arena. Letter from Crum to Hannegan, October 1, 1946, CZA, Z-5/1154.
132 Neumann's memorandum concerning submission of the pro-Zionist resolutions to Congress, 1944, CZA, A-123/530.

the Jewish and general American public against Roosevelt and his administration—in stark contrast to the objectives of Wise, who sought to tone down Jewish agitation on the Palestine issue.[133]

Following the submission of the pro-Zionist resolution to the House Foreign Affairs Committee, Neumann wrote to Silver informing him that the raising of this issue in the House itself had generated significant public resonance. He described the extensive public activity that had prepared the ground for submission of the resolutions. Prior notifications published in the New York Jewish press had put pressure on Committee Chairman Sol Bloom, the Democratic Congressman from New York, who, although he opposed the resolution, could not prevent its submission to the committee. Neumann explained that raising the Zionist issue by means of the resolutions was the last opportunity for American Jews to influence administration policy on the Palestine question prior to the forthcoming discussions on post-war arrangements.[134] Neumann was aware of the tension generated between Silver and Roosevelt by the submission of the resolutions.[135] He believed that Silver would most likely be summoned to the White House to explain his actions. If so, he suggested that Silver tell the president that had the institutions of the Emergency Council not proposed the resolutions, they would have been submitted by irresponsible elements outside the Zionist establishment, such as the Bergson group (which was becoming more active at the time). He proposed that Silver argue further that if Bergson and his associates had raised the issue, the damage to the administration would have been greater.[136] Neumann expected

---

[133] On doubts as to Roosevelt's ostensibly pro-Zionist policy, see Joseph B. Schechtman, *The United States and the Jewish State Movement* (New York, 1969), 93–117.
[134] Letter from Neumann to Silver, January 28, 1944, microfilm edition of the Abba Hillel Silver Archive in Cleveland, Ohio, microfilm roll 2, file number 165 (hereafter: Silver Archive), 2/165.
[135] On Roosevelt's opposition to the resolutions and his efforts to thwart them, see Herbert Parzen, "The Roosevelt Palestine Policy, 1943–1945," *American Jewish Archives* 1 (1974): 40–43.
[136] Neumann's proposal rested on the increased activity of the extremist group known as The American League for a Free Palestine, or the Peter Bergson group. Reports were circulating in the press to the effect that this group was preparing to propose a similar resolution and to have it passed with the help of members of Congress close to them. Peter Bergson (Hillel Kook), a member of the underground *Ha-Irgun Ha-Tsva'i Ha-Leumi* and the group's leader, refused to accept the authority of the Zionist institutions in the United States or to coordinate his activity with the Emergency Council. Bergson had arrived in the United States as a representative of Beitar, but he cut his ties to the party and ceased to take orders from it. Bergson succeeded in gaining the support of a number of well-known figures in political and press circles, and with money, transfer of acquired from benefactors he ran a propaganda campaign while initiating moves such as the opening of a Jewish embassy in Washington. See Raphael, *Silver*, 102–106; Monty Noam Penkower, "In Dramatic Dissent: The Bergson Boys," in Jeffrey Gurock, *American Zionism, Mission and Politics* (American Jewish History, vol. 8), 361–389, (New York 1998).

Silver to come under attack not only by the administration but also by the Emergency Council, and mentioning the potential danger posed by the Bergson group was intended to be a rejoinder to those members of the Emergency Council who argued against submitting the resolutions. However, presenting Bergson as the reason for the move was merely a pretext.[137]

Silver and Neumann believed that the submission of the resolutions was a political necessity, and they intended to proceed with it in any event. They foresaw the political consequences in the form of an expected rift with the administration and a dispute within the Zionist movement, and prepared themselves for these eventualities. They felt that the need to submit the resolutions—and the benefit to the Zionist movement that would accrue from this move—outweighed the likely difficulties. Silver and Neumann assessed that, given the political circumstances that pertained prior to submission of the resolutions, Roosevelt's administration had no intention of acting on behalf of the Zionist movement. Presentation of the resolutions was designed to generate a political chain reaction that would expose Roosevelt's true intentions regarding the founding of a Jewish national home, and would lead to a crisis and struggle against the administration, which would enable them to exert considerable and more effective political pressure in the American arena. They likewise hoped to derive benefit from the resolutions' controversy in the internal Jewish sphere. Exposure of Roosevelt and the Democratic administration as having harmed the Zionist movement would undermine the stature of Roosevelt's supporters among the American Zionist establishment and American Jewry—and in particular the political power of Wise (Silver's political opponent and the partner forced upon him in the leadership of the Emergency Council).

In the wake of the failure to pass the resolutions, Neumann referred to the great harm it had caused to Silver's stature among the Jewish public and to the enhancement of Wise's standing. The sense of failure was, in his opinion, unjustified and Jewish disappointment could be leveraged to intensify anti-administration activity through public pressure, the sending of telegrams and letters, and the submission of a memorandum that would, for example, express the dissatisfaction of New York Jews with the administration's policy. Neumann maintained further that the greatest problem with which he had to contend was the unsatisfactory content of the pro-Zionist declaration released by President Roosevelt, which did not include a substantive commitment to act in favor of Palestine. Since the president was not prepared to disregard the recommendations of the State Department, he refused to include in the declaration elements that may have exerted pressure on Britain to alter its policy on the Palestine question.

---

137 Neumann's letter to Silver, January 28, 1944, Silver Archive, 2/165.

Neumann expressed his apprehension that in the wake of the declaration American Jews were likely to gain the impression that Roosevelt was prepared to take active measures in support of the Zionist movement, which would have deflated the Zionist campaign. Neumann perceived Roosevelt's declaration to be particularly grave against the backdrop of the rift between him and Silver because the appearance of the president to appear to be supportive of Palestine would place Silver, who opposed him, in a ridiculous position.[138]

Neumann added in an additional letter to Silver that the inability to pass the resolutions had come as no surprise to him, insisting that this should not be considered a failure. By virtue of these resolutions American Jewry had succeeded in placing the Palestine question squarely on the country's public agenda. Neumann was aware of the gap between his assessment of political success and the general sense of failure among the Jewish public. He felt that this perception of failure among Jewish activists was unjustified and had breathed new life into Wise's supporters and the opposition to Silver, who was associated with the submission of the resolutions and who bore the brunt of public criticism.[139]

Silver commented on his position vis-à-vis the pro-Zionist resolutions episode in the draft of an autobiography that has remained unpublished.[140] In line with Neumann, Silver relates that the resolutions were submitted despite the realistic prospect that they would not be adopted by the House and the Senate. He explains that the intention was not to have the proposals adopted, but rather to place the Zionist issue at the center of the political agenda both in the United States and in the entire world. On another occasion he observed that his activity in Washington had not been aimed at persuading Roosevelt to agree to adopt the resolutions, but rather to force the administration to respond to the move initiated by the Emergency Council.[141] It is safe to surmise that the perfect scenario from

---

[138] A similar view of President Roosevelt's declaration was expressed by I.F. Stone in an article in the weekly *The Nation*. Stone, the Washington editor of the weekly, was among the first American journalists to visit the camps housing Holocaust survivors in Europe. He also traveled to Palestine aboard a vessel carrying illegal immigrants. The weekly for which he wrote was founded in 1865 and was one of the most important and influential liberal mouthpieces in the United States. Stone compared Roosevelt's pro-Zionist declaration to the testimony given by General Marshall, Chairman of the Joint Chiefs of Staff, before the Senate Foreign Relations Committee. General Marshall had described the damage that public support of Zionism may do to United States foreign policy. His evidence contradicted Roosevelt's declaration and further obfuscated Washington's position. Stone asserted that the discrepancies between the declarations detracted from the president's credibility. See I. F. Stone, "Palestine Run-Around," *The Nation*, March 18, 1944.
[139] Neumann's letter to Silver, March 7, 1944, Silver Archive, 2/165.
[140] Draft of Silver's autobiography, 1963, Silver Archive, 7/3.
[141] Silver was speaking about the modus operandi of the Emergency Council in 1944. See Silver's speech, 1944, Silver Archive, 5/653.

Silver's point of view would have been the adoption of the resolutions despite the administration's opposition, which would have reinforced his political standing among the Jewish public and at the same time achieve his political objectives in Washington. Yet Silver and Neumann knew that the likelihood of overcoming the administration's opposition was slim, and were therefore quick to exploit the political benefit to be gained from the process of submission itself and the exposure of the administration's opposition. Silver stressed that the United States Congress constituted one of the world's most important forums of political discussion and that whatever took place within its walls became an important item of news in the United States and worldwide, making even the discussion of the resolutions of tremendous importance. He maintained that in light of the Roosevelt administration's consistent disregard of the demands of American Zionists and the Zionist movement ever since the publication of the White Paper of 1939, the resolutions were the most effective and perhaps the only political tool with which to penetrate the administration's cloak of silence concerning Palestine.[142]

Silver described the preparations for submission of the resolutions: Hundreds of Zionist activists throughout the United States had lobbied their senators and congressmen to support the resolutions.[143] Backing for the resolutions was likewise promised in declarations by the majority leaders in both houses of Congress. An additional avenue toward ensuring support for the resolutions was opened by the joint submission of a resolution to the Senate Foreign Relations Committee by Republican Senator Robert Alfonso Taft and Democratic Senator from New York Robert Wagner. The resolution had the support of many members from both parties. The data available to Silver indicated that the resolutions would have passed by a large majority had they been put to a vote in the House and the Senate.[144] The fact that Silver and his colleagues succeeded in gaining the support for the resolutions by a majority of Congress may explain why the administration took steps to block them at the committee level. While cessation of the debate in the committees greatly damaged the administration, the harm may have been far greater had the resolutions passed this stage and come to a vote.

---

142 Silver's draft autobiography, 1963, Silver Archive, 7/3. For more on Roosevelt's policy in the Zionist context, see Selig Adler, "Franklin D. Roosevelt and Zionism: The Wartime Record," *American Jewish History*, vol. 8, 209–220.
143 See, in addition, an announcement made by the Zionist Organization of America requesting American. Zionists to call on the senators representing their states to support the resolution proffered by Wagner and Taft, and on their congressmen to support the resolution submitted to the House Foreign Affairs Committee. To ensure that no mistake was made, the numbers of the resolutions were added to the information on the committees. Announcement of the Zionist Organization of America regarding the resolutions, February 15, 1944, Silver Archive, 8/83.
144 Silver's draft autobiography, 1963, Silver Archive, 7/3

The resolutions were submitted in the election year of 1944, a move that forced representatives who depended on the Jewish vote for reelection to take steps to have the resolutions adopted. This state of affairs came to light in a passage written by Silver about Senator Wagner, who required the support of New York's Jews for reelection. In a letter to Herman Salomon, a member of the Emergency Council, Silver maintained that Wagner had not displayed sufficient vigor in promoting the resolution that he himself had proposed. Silver added that Wagner should have been told that New York's Jews had expected him to work more energetically for the pro-Zionist resolution, and that he would be held accountable for the failure to pass the resolution if he did not promote it as required.[145]

The importance that American politicians attributed to the Jewish arena is likewise manifested in the events leading up to the declaration conveyed by President Roosevelt via Senator Wagner to the November 1944 Zionist convention in Atlantic City. In his declaration Roosevelt reiterated the resolution adopted at the Democratic Party Convention in July 1944, which stated that "We favor opening Palestine to unlimited Jewish immigration and settlement and a policy that will lead to the founding of a free Jewish and democratic state there." Roosevelt further promised to make an effort to realize this policy at the earliest time, adding that should he be re-elected, he would assist in promoting the realization of the party's resolutions.[146] Roosevelt's declaration was made public three days after Thomas Dewey, the Republican presidential candidate, had announced his support for the establishment of a Jewish community in Palestine. Silver maintained that the decision to publicize the declaration had been made during a meeting between Wise and President Roosevelt at which they addressed the Democrats' preparations for the upcoming elections and discussed fundraising for the Democratic election campaign.[147] Silver revealed that the details of the meeting and the expected content of the president's declaration had reached him through leaks from the White House. He was unhappy with the content of the declaration, especially that it suggested that the Palestine question would be addressed only upon conclusion of the war. Furthermore, Silver was concerned that Roosevelt had publicized the declaration as a presidential candidate rather than as president, thus reducing his commitment to work toward its practical implementa-

---

145 We may surmise that Wagner tried to take the middle road; taking care not to do himself electoral damage in New York on the one hand, while on the other hand maintaining a friendly and close relationship with Wise, who opposed the idea of submitting the resolutions. In his letter Silver referred to this aspect, asserting that Jewish advisors were associated with the senator's mode of operation. See Silver's letter, June 9, 1944, Silver Archive, 2/188.
146 Emanuel Neumann, *In the Arena of the Zionist Struggle: A Memoir* [in Hebrew] (Jerusalem, 1977), 217.
147 Silver's diary, October 12, 1944, Silver Archive, 2/468.

tion. Silver added that the only way to influence the content of the declaration was to ensure that the Republican candidate make a more significant pro-Zionist declaration. Silver accordingly contacted the Dewey camp and subsequently met the candidate himself. Upon conclusion of these contacts, Silver lost no time in informing the press of Dewey's imminent pro-Zionist declaration. This move forced the president to alter his declaration by underscoring the need for immediate action toward implementing Zionist aspirations.[148] Silver explained that Roosevelt had a dual objective in making the declaration: to gain Jewish support for himself, and to assist Wagner, who was waging a fierce campaign for reelection in New York, where the was particularly important to him. Silver's version is supported by Wise, who in a letter to Supreme Court Justice Felix Frankfurter relates that he had advised Roosevelt to make the statement regarding the administration's policy toward Palestine through Wagner, who required all possible support to gain reelection. By delegating Wagner to deliver his declaration to the delegates at the Zionist convention in Atlantic City, Roosevelt could assist in building up Wagner's image as someone close to the president who had actively promoted this pro-Zionist declaration, thereby gaining him a good many Jewish votes.[149]

These statements by Silver and Wise indicate that Wise and Roosevelt initiated a pro-Zionist declaration in order to gain the Jewish vote even though this was likely to create foreign relations difficulties for the administration. The links between American party politics and Jewish politics operated in both directions. In waging their campaign on behalf of Palestine, American Jewish leaders sought to exploit the election year; at the same time, the country's elected representatives could not ignore the political importance of the Palestine issue. The competition between the two parties was likewise manifested in the struggle among Jewish leaders, who sought to exploit their influence on the Jewish vote in the direction

---

148 Ibid. Regarding Roosevelt's remark that he had made the statement as a presidential candidate, see the transcript of Silver's lecture on the activity of the Emergency Council, 1944, Silver Archive, 5/653. On the publicizing of the contacts between Silver and Dewey in the Jewish press, see, for example, the headline revealing the Republican candidate's declaration following his meeting with Silver, "Dewey Issues Statement After Conference With Rabbi Silver," *The Jewish Post*, October 20, 1944.
149 Silver Diary, October 12, 1944, Silver Archive, 2/468. Wise's letter to Frankfurter, October 16, 1944, CZA, A-243/137. Frankfurter and Wise consistently supported Wagner. In 1932 Frankfurter had supported Wagner's candidacy for the Senate even though he was running against a Jewish opponent. See Frankfurter's letter to Wise, October 18, 1932, CZA, A-243/139. In 1937 Wise again took steps to ensure that Wagner would be elected to the Senate in the next elections. He even tried to gain Republican support for Wagner's candidacy. See Wise's letter to Frankfurter, October 18, 1937, CZA, A-243/139.

of the party they supported on the one hand, and to compel the national party leaders to support the Zionist interest in a more forthright manner on the other.

During the course of the intra-Jewish debate on the resolutions submitted to Congress, Neumann and Silver maintained that they had always intended to win the administration's approval before submitting the resolutions, and that Silver had made every effort to obtain a "green light" from the administration for this move.[150] This explanation contradicts the passage in his draft autobiography in which Silver states that his objective was not to gain the administration's blessing, but to reap the utmost political benefit from the Democratic administration's attempts to foil the submission of the resolutions. He stresses here that making the submission conditional upon the administration's endorsement negated the fundamental intention underlying the move, and that he and Neumann had never expected to receive such authorization. Their objective had been to activate members of Congress of both parties, who, in response to the demand of the Jewish and general American electorate, were to urge the administration to press Britain to change its Palestine policy. Silver and Neumann had offered the argument concerning the "green light" that they expected from the administration only after the event and for internal Zionist purposes, since the majority of the Jewish public would have rejected a move intended to create a rift with President Roosevelt. Silver and Neumann, in fact, had not merely foreseen the administration's opposition, but because it served their interest, had formed part of their political scheme around it. Naturally, they would not have rejected the administration's endorsement of the resolutions, but were simply convinced that this could not be attained, given the political reality in 1944.

In his notes on the second round of submission of the resolutions, Silver clarifies why he believed that it would be impossible to obtain the administration's blessing for the move. Senator Taft, who had advanced the pro-Zionist resolution in the Senate Foreign Relations Committee, informed Silver about his conversations with senior Defense Department officials who had told him that there were no military reasons for opposing the resolutions. They added that the issue had been discussed by the war cabinet, with most of those present expressing the belief that the passing of the resolutions was a purely political matter and that the security bodies thus had no reason to oppose a debate on them.[151] Evidence of a similar position is provided by a letter from Defense Secretary Henry Stimson to Senator Taft in response to the latter's request to continue the submission process. Stimson wrote that upon consideration of the issue he had withdrawn his opposition to the submission of the resolutions because the objections that

---
150 A declaration by Silver, 1945 (no location or precise date given), CZA, A-375/67.
151 Silver Diary, October 9, 1944, Silver Archive, 2/468.

had been valid in the past were no longer so, adding that continued opposition to the resolutions stemmed from political rather than military considerations.[152] On the strength of these revelations Silver concluded that it was not feasible to overcome the administration's opposition to the resolutions, since the opposition rested upon a world view that rejected the goals of the Zionist movement.

In concluding the chapter in his autobiography on the resolutions controversy, Silver rejects the prevailing perception that the status of an American Zionist leader was determined by his good relations with the White House. According to that view, to the extent that such a leader was accepted in the White House, his stature should grow, and vice versa. Silver was in effect attacking Stephen Wise, who enjoyed a close relationship with Roosevelt. Wise was subsequently to remark that when Truman was elected president in 1948, his stature within the World Zionist movement was weakened because he was now less welcome in the White House. On the other hand, when the Republican Dwight Eisenhower was elected president in 1952, Wise was once again considered to wield political power. Silver rejects this conception, maintaining that personal factors did not shape U.S. foreign policy. He argues further that his own political achievements on behalf of the Zionist movement and the State of Israel had been far greater during the presidency of Truman even though he had then been persona non grata in the White House, and that his good relations with Eisenhower's foreign secretary John Foster Dulles had exerted less influence on America's foreign policy than had his activity in Truman's time.[153]

Silver's views on relations with the White House were exceptional among the Zionist leadership. During a discussion of the resolutions episode held by the Jewish Agency Executive, Ben Gurion stressed the considerable importance of the personal links between an American Zionist leader and the president.[154] Israel Goldstein, Chairman of the Zionist Organization of America, believed that maintaining a cordial relationship with the White House was vital to American Zionists and to the Zionist movement altogether. He pointed to the harm that had resulted from the fraught relationship between Silver and the White House, and commended the close and friendly relationship that Wise maintained with the

---

152 Ibid., October 13, 1944.
153 See Silver's Autobiography, 1963, Silver Archive, 7/3. Silver's ability to influence the US administration's policy despite being unwelcome in the White House is clearly manifested in his effort to persuade Truman and his administration to support the UN partition plan, and thereafter to recognize the State of Israel. See Ian J. Bickerton, "President Truman's Recognition of Israel," *American Jewish Historical Quarterly* 58 (1968): 173–240; William F. Levantrosser, ed., *Harry S. Truman. The Man from Independence* (New York, 1986), 37–65. On the antagonism between Truman and Silver, see David McCullough, *Truman* (New York, 1992), 598–589.
154 Ben Gurion at the Jewish Agency Executive, February 4, 1945, CZA S-100.

State Department and with President Roosevelt. Chaim Weizmann, president of the Zionist movement, was likewise critical of the pattern of relations between Silver and the White House that had come to light during the resolutions matter, wondering "why it had been necessary to try the violent?"[155] Silver on the other hand, as mentioned, asserted that the president and the State Department made their decisions in light of political considerations, and were not swayed by personal relationships. He believed that Roosevelt was more likely to act in support of the Zionist movement owing to fear of electoral damage than because of his personal relationship with Wise. On the strength of their analysis of the course of the relationship between the Zionist movement and Roosevelt's administration, Neumann and Silver maintained that American Zionism had failed to reach significant political achievements during his presidency despite the close links between Wise and Roosevelt. The pro-Zionist resolutions marked a change of the Zionist approach and strategy in the United States and were intended to bring about a change in this situation.

Silver and Neumann were well aware of the gulf between their positive assessment of the process whereby the resolutions had been submitted and the sense of failure felt by the American Jewish public; and they were likewise cognizant of the negative effect of this gap on Silver's political stature and the concomitant reinforcement of Wise's position. For this reason, Neumann was more concerned about the probable effects of Roosevelt's pro-Zionist declaration at the gathering of American Zionists in Atlantic City than about the resolutions' expected failure to pass. The president's declaration allowed the administration to maintain its ambivalent policy on the Palestine question while preventing the Zionist institutions in the United States from attacking this policy. Likewise, the president's declaration had drawn the sting of the Zionists' threat to harm the Democratic Party in the electoral sphere, and had undermined the position of Silver, whose opposition to the administration's policy could now be attributed to party political considerations and shown to harm Jewish interests. By contrast, Roosevelt's declaration would portray Wise as having taken the better course of action and as someone whose personal ties with the president had benefited the Zionist movement. In an attempt to preempt such interpretation, Silver and Neumann argued that Roosevelt merely appeared to be supporting the political aspirations of the Zionist movement, and that his declaration at Atlantic City did not reflect his true policy, but had been made for electoral purposes. This assessment was subsequently confirmed when, contrary to Wise's expectations, Roosevelt's actions at

---

155 Public pronouncement by Israel Goldstein, 1945 (no precise date given), CZA, A-375/67. Regarding Weizmann's view, see Weizmann's letter to Wise in Chaim Weizmann, *The Letters and Papers of Chaim Weizmann*, vol. 21 (Israel, 1975), 258–259.

the Yalta Conference and beyond proved detrimental to the interests of the Zionist movement. The Jewish public in the United States took note of the discrepancy between Wise's presentation of Roosevelt's policy and the president's actual tendencies. Roosevelt's anti-Zionist policy at Yalta did indeed strengthen the status of Silver and Neumann and contribute to Wise's retreat from the center of Zionist political activity in the United States.

Silver and Neumann achieved their goal with the submission of the resolutions to the House and the Senate. They were aware of the discrepancy between their sense of achievement and the feeling of failure generated among the American Jewish public and the Zionist establishment in Palestine. In order to alter this situation, they used the crisis created by the failure and Silver's removal from his post to strengthen his political standing and to transfer to him responsibility for all Zionist political activity in the United States. Silver argued that the mode of operation of the Emergency Council regarding the resolutions controversy had revealed that it could not continue to function with two chairmen at its head, namely himself and Wise. The resolutions episode was instrumental in bringing about changes in the structure of American Zionist leadership, facilitating Silver's appointment as sole chairman of the Emergency Council with far-reaching organizational and political authority in the American Jewish sphere.[156] The successful third attempt to submit the resolutions (which were passed by both houses of Congress), alongside Silver's appointment to head the Emergency Council enabled Silver and Neumann to portray the entire move in a positive light. The resolutions episode was conducted in the shadow of the rivalry between Silver and Wise, and Silver's triumph spelled failure for Wise.

The failure to pass the resolutions had given Silver'srivals in the Zionist movement a pretext to remove him from his position at the head of the Emergency Council.[157] The administration, which could have suffered damage from the resolutions affair coming so close to the election, likewise attempted to exploit the failure to influence the composition of the Zionist leadership in the United States. The administration's motives for opposing the resolutions and the reasons for its attempts to influence the composition of the Zionist leadership are revealed in the words of David Niles, political assistant to presidents Roosevelt and Truman and the person in charge of minorities in Roosevelt's administration. At a meeting of Niles with Leon Feuer, Silver's assistant in Cleveland and subsequently head of the Emergency Council office in Washington, and James Heller, Vice President of the Zionist Organization of America, Feuer began the discussion by asserting

---

156 Transcript of Silver's lecture on the Emergency Council's activity, 1944, Silver Archive, 5/653.
157 See the utterances of Dov Yosef and Moshe Shapira at the meeting of the Jewish Agency Executive in Jerusalem, February 4, 1945, CZA, S-100.

that the heads of the movement had sought clarifications from State Department representatives prior to submitting the resolutions, and had been told that there were no political reasons to object to their submission. Feuer pointed to the broad support for the resolutions in the Senate and the House of Representatives and underscored the public anger at the administration's opposition, which had blocked their adoption. Niles responded by explaining that the unexpected opposition to submission of the resolutions on the part of the military stemmed from the connection that had evolved between those who initiated the resolutions and Roosevelt's political opponents. According to him, the members of Congress who had proposed the resolutions did so in order to gain electoral benefit, by winning both the support of the Jewish vote and public sympathy, and to harm Roosevelt and his administration as well as the chances of the Democrats in the upcoming elections—particularly among Jewish voters.[158] From what Niles divulged at the meeting it appears that the administration had initially tried to prevent the submission of the resolutions because it feared that the broad public sympathy and the support of the majority of Congress for their adoption would make it increasingly difficult to oppose them as the process progressed. Furthermore, the move was being led by Congressmen who opposed Roosevelt and who had gained both the support of the Jewish vote and broad public sympathy, which was harmful to Roosevelt. The administration had therefore sought to block discussion of the resolutions from the outset in order to minimize political damage and to preempt the need to confront them in sessions of both houses, or even to be faced with their adoption despite its opposition.[159] Niles' revelations likewise throw light on the dilemma that confronted Democrats such as Wagner and Bloom. They both depended on Jewish votes for their reelection, and could therefore not oppose the resolutions; but on the other hand, as Democrats they recognized the damage that the process of the resolutions' adoption may do to Roosevelt and the Democratic administration. Therefore, they presented themselves in public as supporters of the resolutions, while covertly operating to delay the adoption process, thereby enabling the administration to remove the issue from the public agenda. Thus they prevented the loss of the Jewish votes without which they could not have gained reelection, while minimizing the harm done to Roosevelt and the Democratic Party. Silver's documents indeed reveal that Wagner and Bloom had

---

158 Minutes of the Meeting between Feuer and Heller and Niles, February 23, 1944, Silver Archive, 2/183.

159 Roosevelt gained over 90 percent of the Jewish vote in the 1940 and 1944 elections. The danger that Silver would alter Jewish voting patterns and bring about the loss of many votes previously promised to the Democratic Party was among the reasons that administration functionaries sought to oust him.

merely created the impression that they were actively promoting the resolutions so as to keep up appearances.

Niles' pronouncements demonstrate the blurring of the boundaries between the Jewish and the overall American political worlds, indicating that they had, in fact, become integrated. The process of submission of the resolutions constituted a field of rivalry between Roosevelt's supporters and his adversaries, and became part of the effort made by Congressmen, supporters and opponents of the administration alike, to gain an advantage prior to the elections. Silver, as noted, believed that the only path available to American Jews to influence that administration's policy on the Palestine question was to turn the Zionist question into an issue within the American political system. Silver had sought to create an electoral threat to the Democratic administration by means of the resolutions, thereby influencing its attitude toward demands pertaining to Palestine. Proposing and discussing the resolutions in Congress and its committees was intended to turn the Palestine matter into a factor that played a role in inter-party rivalry, thereby placing it at the center of the American political agenda. Once the resolutions had become a topic of political debate, the administration was obliged to reveal its clear opposition to their content, and this in effect had allowed Silver to achieve the goal toward which he had worked. Silver believed that the administration would not have supported the Zionist movement in any event and the resolutions were thus not designed to alter Roosevelt's policy, but rather to impel him to reveal it and to expose it to public criticism.

Contrary to the initial impression, the resolutions affair did not damage Silver politically, but in fact strengthened him. Unlike Wise, Silver's political stature and public power were not dependent on his close relations with the Democratic establishment. He did not maintain personal or political ties with Roosevelt and his associates and therefore, in contrast to Zionist leaders connected to the Democrats, who were confronted by a contradiction between their Zionist, Jewish, and party activism, he was undamaged by the rift that developed between him and the president. On the contrary, in the wake of the resolutions affair, Silver began to emerge as an independent and powerful political figure. He mobilized a large number of senators and representatives and succeeded in leading a political campaign in the face of Roosevelt's opposition. Silver thus strengthened his standing as a Zionist leader who was able to influence the American political system. Roosevelt's opponents, as well as administration functionaries, could not ignore him.

It was because of Silver's success and the damage that he had done to Roosevelt and his government that administration officials attempted to intervene in developments within the Zionist movement in the United States in order to reduce Silver's power in the movement, and even to bring about his removal. These attempts emerge from the minutes of a meeting between Nahum Goldmann and Samuel Rosenman, a judge and close advisor to President Roosevelt as well as his speech writer. Rosenman attacked Silver for neglecting to consult with him or with Frankfurter before submitting the resolutions and added that in light of this, neither he nor Frankfurter could be expected to assist the cause of American Zionists in Washington. He stressed the futility of proposing the resolutions, which could not have been adopted because of the administration's opposition, and which had changed nothing in Roosevelt's policy.

Rosenman told Goldmann that the president was planning to proclaim publically both his support for Jewish immigration to Palestine and his opposition to the 1939 White Paper, but that he would not say a word about Palestine's political future, which was a topic he intended to address only in the future. The president's declarations had been planned far in advance, and had nothing to do with Silver's endeavors. Rosenman divulged that in the wake of Silver's assumption of responsibility for American Zionists' political activity in place of Wise, the president had begun to exhibit an attitude of coldness to the point of hostility toward the Zionist movement. He expressed the opinion that with a Democratic administration in place, American Zionists had been crazy to exchange Wise, who was liked by and close to Roosevelt, for Silver, whom Roosevelt detested. A further element in the president's hostility toward the Zionist movement was provoked by the ties created between American Zionists and Roosevelt's opponents. Rosenman expressly pointed out that the president himself had noted the fact that all the pro-Zionist speeches delivered in Congress had been made by factions hostile to him. He added that Silver's policy and activity concerning the resolutions had led the president to change his attitude toward the Zionist movement. In the past, Roosevelt had viewed Zionist settlement in Palestine as a daring and noble enterprise, whereas he now considered it only a nuisance. In light of these circumstances, Rosenman told Goldmann that, in his opinion, Wise should direct the political activity of American Jews, and that he, not Silver, should be presented as the foremost Jewish leader in the Washington political arena. He therefore recommended that Wise be brought back to the center of Zionist activity. Goldmann agreed with Rosenman; he too sought the removal of Silver and preferred Wise to lead Zionist political activity. He nevertheless pointed to the difficulties involved in ousting Silver, who enjoyed wide popularity among the Jewish public as well as the support of a considerable number of Emergency Council members. An attempt to oust him would most assuredly culminate in a severe internal crisis among American Zionists. Thus, as an alternative to removing Silver, Goldmann proposed setting up a small leadership group that would direct the political activity of American Zionists. While Silver would not actually be deposed, the new structure would curtail his political power and enable others to restrict and supervise his actions.[160]

Given Rosenman's high standing in the White House, it can be assumed that, though perhaps not coordinated directly with Roosevelt, his words to Goldmann accurately reflected the president's position. Rosenman expressed the president's wish to reinstate Wise to a senior position in the American Zionist leadership and to depose Silver. Rosenman indicated that Silver's incumbency as chairman of the Emergency Council was primarily responsible for Roosevelt's negative attitude toward the Zionist movement. He maintained that Silver's modus operandi had caused serious damage to American Zionists and to American Jews in general. Not only had it precipitated a rift with the president, but it had also made it impossible for Rosenman himself to promote the idea of a Jewish state in White House circles. Rosenman's utterances contained a political threat designed to bring about a change in the composition of the leadership of American Zionists to bring it into line with the president's wishes. He pointed to the resolutions as the major factor that had led Roosevelt to want to see Silver ousted. Indeed, through its opposition to the resolutions the administration itself had created the necessary political circumstances for action against Silver. The White House's stance was a blend of opposition to the resolutions per se and the desire to see that Silver failed, and then to use his failure to damage his standing among American Zionists, to bring about his downfall, and to ensure the appointment of an American Zionist leadership more congenial with the president.

Roosevelt's influence on the composition of the American Zionist leadership was discussed in a letter from Wise to Frankfurter in which Wise describes his activity in Washington and tells of a meeting he held with Secretary of State Edward R. Stettinius at which Silver was also present, much to Wise's annoyance. Wise writes that he would like to see Silver removed. He admits that such a move was impractical given the prevailing circumstances, but expressed the hope that this would become feasible after the election. Following Roosevelt's reelection, Silver would have to realize that he had to stand down.[161] Like Rosenman, Wise assumed that the rift between Silver and Roosevelt meant that Silver could not function as chairman of the Emergency Council. This assumption conferred an obvious political advantage on Wise, who enjoyed a close relationship with Roosevelt. Yet beyond this, it meant that the president played an important role in determining the complexion and composition of American Zionist leadership. Roosevelt's knowledge of the Zionist power structure was likewise revealed

---

160 Top secret minutes of the meeting between Nahum Goldmann and Rosenman, April 27, 1944, CZA, Z-5/382.
161 Letter from Wise to Frankfurter, October 28, 1944, CZA, A-243/137.

in connection with the nomination of the Zionist representation to the United Nations conference, which convened in San Francisco in May 1945. In conversation with Wise, Roosevelt showed that he was well versed in the controversies that divided the Zionist leadership, and was particularly aware of the rivalry between Ben Gurion and Weizmann. Roosevelt preferred that Ben Gurion assume chairmanship of the Zionist delegation to the conference because he believed that a Jew from Palestine should head the delegation. It was only after considerable persuasion on the part of Wise that the he agreed that Ben Gurion and Weizmann should jointly head the delegation.[162]

Goldmann's subsequent activity regarding the resolutions episode shows that he acted in the spirit of Rosenman's guidelines and cooperated with the administration against Silver. Goldmann failed to pass on to Silver details of his meetings with administration officials, and tried to thwart attempts to revive discussion of the resolutions in both the House and the Senate. He reported to Wise that at the forthcoming meeting of the Emergency Council's planning committee, Silver would press for a decision enabling the resolutions to be proposed once again to Congress, despite the opposition of General George Marshall, Head of the Joint Chiefs of Staff. Since he could not be present at the meeting, Goldmann asked Wise to attend, even though it was to take place during his vacation. Goldmann referred to Silver and his supporters as "a gang," adding that every effort should be made to block the authorization of Silver's proposal by the Emergency Council's institutions.[163] Meanwhile, Goldmann approached Weizmann, appealing to him as well to take steps to foil Silver's initiatives. He requested that Weizmann approach Silver and demand that he desist from taking action designed to resubmit the resolutions so long as the administration withheld its express support for the move. He stressed that the Zionist movement could not afford a second rejection of the resolutions, and that a further setback was likely to cause serious damage in the United States.[164]

The meeting between Rosenman and Goldmann was not an isolated event. Administration officials continued to convey Roosevelt's anger at the submission of the resolutions. They made it clear that Silver's actions were harming the campaign for the founding of a Jewish state and intimated that if Silver were to be replaced, Roosevelt's attitude would change, thus helping the Zionist cause. Stettinius said as much to Wise and Goldmann at an informal meeting in his office that preceded a larger meeting with Zionist representatives. He told the two men that the president was angry with the Zionists for continuing their campaign

---

162 Minutes of a meeting between Wise and Roosevelt, March 16, 1945, CZA, Z-5/1161.
163 Letter from Goldmann to Wise, August 10, 1944, CZA, Z-6/2759.
164 Letter from Goldmann to Weizmann, August 10, 1944, CZA, Z-6/2759.

despite his explicit request to halt the process of submitting the resolutions. According to him, Roosevelt regarded the resolutions issue as an attempt to use the Senate to exert pressure on him, which made him feel as though American Zionists had lost faith in him. Given the circumstances that had evolved, Stettinius declared, he himself felt that he could not continue to promote the Zionist cause in the White House.[165] A fortnight later, Stettinius held a meeting with Goldmann and Dov Yosef, a member of the Zionist executive who later became a minister in Israeli government. Yosef noted that although he had planned to discuss matters concerning Palestine with the secretary of state, political developments in Washington obliged him to address the resolutions issue instead. Yosef and Goldmann explained that the Jewish Agency had full confidence in the president and his desire to act in the interests of the Zionist movement, that there had been no intention of acting in defiance of the president's request, and that instructions along these lines had been given to Zionist activists in the United States. Stettinius complained to Goldmann and Yosef that a group of American Zionists had caused serious damage to the Zionist cause in Washington. He described the egoism and stubbornness of the members of this group, which had induced the president, who had been a friend of the Zionists, to become impatient with the Zionist movement.[166]

Although he did not mention him by name, Stettinius was clearly referring to Silver. Speaking as a secretary of state who played a large part in shaping and prosecuting the administration's policy on the Palestine question, Stettinius's comments on Silver did not manifest personal hostility toward him, but rather conveyed the position of senior echelons in the administration. The conclusion to be drawn from the picture of the political situation portrayed by Stettinius was that the Zionist interest required the removal of Silver from the American Zionist leadership. Silver's continued incumbency as chairman of the Emergency Council, coupled with his choice of procedures, was likely to exacerbate the damage he had done by causing the president to change his attitude toward the Palestine question, and stoking the anger already felt in the corridors of the administration toward the Zionist movement. Like Niles and Rosenman, Stettinius mentioned the personal angle, emphasizing that Silver's activity made it impossible for him to continue to support the Zionist movement in Washington. A declaration of this sort by the secretary of state carried considerable significance and lent great weight to the demand to remove Silver from his post. It was

---

[165] Summary of the conversation between Stettinius, Wise and Goldmann, December 13, 1944, CZA, Z-6/2755.
[166] Minutes of a meeting between Dov Yosef, Nahum Goldmann and Stettinius, December 27, 1944, CZA, Z-5/394.

difficult to imagine how the chairman of the Emergency Council could continue to represent the Zionist cause while being politically ostracized in Washington.[167]

This caustic response on the part of the administration's officials in fact indicates that Silver's political assumptions were correct and demonstrates the effectiveness of the political steps he took. His success in winning the support of many senators and congressmen for the resolutions in addition to the public campaign he waged on this issue threatened to restrict the president's freedom of action with regard to the Palestine question. Roosevelt and his associates responded in two complementary ways: They blocked the adoption of the resolutions and took action to ensure that this set of circumstances would not happen again by attempting to bring about Silver's replacement. According to various elements in the administration, the dead end that Silver had engineered in his dealings with the administration regarding the resolutions episode and the rift that had emerged between the two parties indicated the need to replace Silver forthwith.[168]

An additional letter from Wise to Stettinius concerning the matter of the resolutions demonstrates why Roosevelt's staff wanted Silver replaced and preferred to see Wise leading American Zionists. Wise asked Stettinius to find out what Roosevelt thought about renewed efforts to promote the resolutions in the Congress. The secretary of state replied that the president had asked to leave matters of policy on Palestine to him and to freeze further Zionist activity regarding the issue. Wise made it clear that as far as he was concerned the president's request marked the end of the matter and that he had no intention of taking any further action on the resolutions.[169] Nevertheless, having accepted Roosevelt's demand

---

167 Ibid.

168 The reciprocal relations between the Zionist movement and the administration came to bear on an additional sphere. The importance of the Zionist issue conferred political power on the administration officials who engaged with it. Therefore, the senior officials approached by Zionist representatives gained political advantages. This was manifested in the attempt to persuade the Zionist representatives to refrain from approaching Under Secretary of State Sumner Welles, and to turn directly to Secretary of State Cordell Hull. It was impressed upon them that it would be preferable to use Hull rather than Welles as a channel to the president. See meeting between Nahum Goldmann and Dov Yosef with Treasury Secretary Morgenthau, January 6, 1944, CZA, Z-6/2755. Goldmann conveyed Morgenthau's suggestion to refrain from contacting Welles to Silver. He noted that Rosenman had informed him that Silver was planning to arrange a meeting of Zionist representatives with Welles, and asked him to cancel the meeting. See letter from Goldmann to Silver, January 7, 1944, CZA, Z-6/2306. On the relationship between Hull and Welles, see Benjamin Welles, *Sumner Welles: F. D. R's Global Strategist* (New York, 1997), 258–270.

169 Letter from Wise to Stettinius, December, 1944 (no precise date given), CZA, A-243/104. Wise mentions in his letter a forthcoming meeting between Senator Wagner, Silver, and Stettinius. According to Raphael, this meeting was held on December 4, 1944, indicating that the letter was written in early December, before the fourth of the month. See Raphael, *Silver*, 122–123.

not to initiate the immediate adoption of the resolutions, Wise requested Stettinius to enquire whether it would be possible to promote their adoption in the near future. Wise stressed that such a move was subject to Roosevelt's approval and would be implemented only on condition that the president's instructions were strictly adhered to. He added that he himself felt that there was no need for the resolutions, since he had every confidence in Roosevelt's support for the founding of a Jewish state, as manifested in his "historic" declaration to the Zionist Congress at Atlantic City. Wise explained, however, that the administration's withdrawal of its opposition to passage of the resolutions would be important in both Zionist and Jewish American contexts because their endorsement by the Senate and the House would be greatly welcomed by many American Jews. At the end of the letter Wise repeated that despite the internal Jewish significance attached to the adoption of the resolutions, if the president chose for whatever reasons to maintain his opposition to their adoption, he, Wise, would continue to act according to the president's guidelines, and he asked Stettinius to convey this position to Roosevelt.[170]

Wise's letter to Stettinius indicates that he was aware of the political repercussions of the administration's opposition to the resolutions and sought to moderate them. This opposition was likely to generate antagonism on the part of American Zionists and Jews sympathetic to Zionism toward Roosevelt and his administration, and to harm him and other Democratic candidates in the forthcoming election. As we shall see, Wise was likewise aware of the implications of such a development on his own political future in Zionist and American Jewish circles. The deteriorating relationship between Roosevelt and American Jews and the revelation that Roosevelt had not actively supported Zionism weakened Wise's standing, which largely depended on his closeness to the president. Thus, even though he believed that the resolutions could not benefit the Zionist movement in any way, Wise asked Stettinius to reconsider the State Department's opposition to them because of its ramifications on Jewish support for Roosevelt and on Wise's own standing among American Zionists.

Shortly after dispatching this letter to Stettinius, Wise wrote two additional letters, one to the secretary of state and one to President Roosevelt. Written on the same day—despite their differing content—these letters complemented each other and reinforced the themes raised in Wise's previous letter to Stettinius. In

---

170 Ibid. A further indication of Wise's unwillingness to support the resolutions may be found in a statement by Bloom, who claimed that Wise had refused his request to appear before the House Foreign Affairs Committee in order to support the pro-Zionist resolution during the course of one of the discussions on the issue. See the summary of the meeting with Bloom in Silver's diary, November 30, 1943, Silver Archive, 2/467.

his letter to Roosevelt, Wise underscored his reservations regarding the manner in which the Emergency Council had handled the resolutions episode, differentiating between the activity of Silver and the official policy of American Zionism's institutions. According to him, as he had conveyed to Stettinius, the Emergency Council had from the outset decided that American Zionists would not actively promote the resolutions without Roosevelt's support and authorization. Furthermore, the council believed that it would be unwise to take any further action, given Roosevelt's pro-Zionist declaration. Wise portrayed Silver as someone who consistently disregarded the decisions of the institutions of American Zionism, and termed his actions unfortunate. He explained that Silver's mode of activity had left him no choice but to submit his resignation from the post of chairman of the Emergency Council.[171]

In his letter to Stettinius, Wise suggested that the secretary of state make a public declaration clarifying the State Department's attitude toward the resolutions and setting out Stettinius's position regarding the Zionist aspects of U.S. foreign policy. He explained that such a declaration was vital in light of the action taken by the State Department's representative to block the resolutions in the Senate Foreign Relations Committee; the evidence given by Stettinius to this committee on December 11 in which he had presented the president's and the State Department's opposition to the pro-Zionist resolution, thereby preventing its adoption, and Stettinius's press releases criticizing the resolutions. Given the major role that Stettinius had played in opposing the resolutions, Wise asked him to state clearly in his letter that the State Department had merely sought to put the resolution adoption process on hold temporarily in both the Senate and the House of Representatives, and was adhering to administration policy on the Zionist movement as expressed by President Roosevelt in his pronouncement to the Zionist Conference in Atlantic City. Stettinius should, Wise believed, define Roosevelt's declaration as a commitment on the part of the American people, including the State Department. Wise's request that it be publicized in the form

---

171 Letter from Wise to Roosevelt, December 12, 1944, CZA, A-243/83. The differences between Silver and Wise may be further appreciated upon reading one of Silver's public pronouncements attacking Wise's comments in the letter to Stettinius. He accused Wise and his associates of hesitating to take any action that was in opposition to the will of the State Department and the president, portraying Wise as someone who considered American Zionism to be his private property, who ignored the fact that Washington had done nothing for the Jews, and who, despite this, continued to defend the administration. Silver stressed that the administration would authorize the resolutions only prior to a presidential election, driven by the electoral considerations of the White House. See Silver's public pronouncement, December 29, 1944, CZA, A-243/38.

of a letter sent to him by the secretary of state was no less important than the content of the declaration.[172]

Wise's letters to Stettinius and to Roosevelt indicate that he was aware that by dint of his absolute commitment to the president, his standing among the Jewish public had been affected by the administration's steps with regard to the resolutions. Wise reiterated his commitment to act according to Roosevelt's directions in the Jewish arena as well, out of a desire to minimize the electoral damage to Roosevelt and the various Democratic candidates. He furthermore sought to ensure that the president would have a free hand in conducting his policy on the Palestine question, thus displaying his confidence in the president's considerations. In contrast to his own loyalty to the president, Wise portrayed Silver as someone who had exhibited his distrust of Roosevelt and had conducted a political campaign that had unjustly harmed the president and sought to dictate to him how to conduct America's foreign policy. Wise took care to stress that Silver was an exception, who acted contrary to the instructions of the American Zionist institutions and the Jewish Agency, both of which continued to believe in the president and his policy. Wise's confidence in Roosevelt's support for the Zionist movement was demonstrated again some months later when he summarized the events concerning the resolutions controversy and Roosevelt's meeting with Ibn Saud. He persisted in describing Roosevelt as having remained a friend of the Zionists, just as he had been prior to the resolutions issue, and asserted that Roosevelt had acted in the interest of the Zionist movement in his contacts with both Churchill and Ibn Saud, and that his pro-Zionist pronouncements were genuine. Wise discounted the assertions made against Roosevelt and believed that Roosevelt had always maintained that Palestine should be a national Jewish home, citing Roosevelt's support for free Jewish immigration to Palestine.[173]

Wise's letter to Stettinius nevertheless indicates that he recognized the difficulties that would probably ensue from the administration's opposition to the resolutions, which created a contradiction between Roosevelt's pro-Zionist declaration to the Zionist Conference in Atlantic City and the activity against the resolutions being carried out by Stettinius and other administration officials. He warned that unless this contradiction was resolved, Roosevelt's credibility among Jewish voters would most likely be harmed, and that his declaration could be perceived as a manipulative move designed only to win the Jewish vote. Such a situation would work in Silver's favor, since he sought to unmask Roosevelt as having

---
172 Letter from Wise to Stettinius, December 12, 1944, CZA, A-243/104.
173 For letters in this spirit, see Wise's letter to Weizmann, March 21, 1945, CZA, Z-4/14471; Wise's letter to Benjamin Aktzin, attacking his assertions against Roosevelt, May 20, 1946, CZA, A-243/201.

acted contrary to the interests of the Zionist movement. Silver's and Neumann's papers indicate that they had indeed sought political gains in the American and Zionist spheres by exploiting the disparity between the president's declaration and the actions that he and his officials had taken to block the resolutions. From Wise's point of view this state of affairs would cause damage on two fronts: It would harm the electoral prospects of the Democratic Party and of Roosevelt, and it would undermine Wise's status within American Zionist circles. For this reason Wise asked Stettinius to publicize the president's declaration in a letter to him, presenting Wise as the foremost American Zionist leader, who by virtue of his political skill was able to influence the State Department's policy toward Palestine. Addressing the letter to Wise would add a further dimension to his image as someone who maintained close relations not only with President Roosevelt, but also with the administration in general. Wise asked Stettinius to publish the declaration in order to minimize the potential damage that the administration's opposition to the adoption of the resolutions would cause, and to narrow the gap between the State Department's actions and the president's declaration. With these objectives in mind, Wise underscored the commitment of the entire American people as well as that of the State Department to act in accordance with the Atlantic City declaration. He further requested Stettinius to present his opposition to the resolutions as a temporary step that did not indicate an anti-Zionist bias on the part of the State Department. He sought to portray Stettinius's opposition as a step dictated by international political events, implying that should these international circumstances change, the State Department would drop its opposition and the resolutions would be approved. Wise asked Stettinius not to publicize his declaration until after the resolution had been rejected by the Senate Foreign Relations Committee, so that its publication could not be interpreted as a move designed to thwart its adoption. Wise added explanations to the draft declaration suggesting that its publication would serve only internal Zionist purposes. In other words, Wise was seeking to influence events within the American Zionist movement by means of manipulating the actions of the Roosevelt administration. Like Silver, Wise was well aware that Zionist activity in the United States was bound up with American politics, and that the two systems maintained a reciprocal relationship. In the present case, the administration's efforts to prevent adoption of the resolutions affected the political standing and fate of both Wise and Silver and impacted the voting patterns of American Jewry. Thus did Wise, who supported Roosevelt, seek to limit the political damage that he himself and the Democratic Party were likely to suffer as a result of the administration's actions.

The resolutions issue provides further evidence to suggest that although they proceeded from different political points of departure, Wise and Silver shared the same understanding of the political rules of the game. Wise combined his activity in the World Jewish Congress and in the Zionist sphere with engagement in the Democratic establishment. Silver, by contrast, exerted influence on the American political system through his connections with elements that opposed the administration. Both men sought to influence the political agenda by means of the Jewish vote; they both knew that their standing as Zionist and Jewish leaders, as well as their ability to influence party politics and U.S. policy with regard to the future of Palestine, was a function of the interdependence of the Zionist and the wider American arenas. An American Zionist leader could only operate within the American political system by exploiting the opportunities that American democracy offered him, and by harnessing his influence on the Jewish vote to the Zionist cause. This could be achieved by exerting political pressure and making veiled threats, as Silver chose to do, or by participating in party politics, which was Wise's approach.

A letter that Wise wrote to David Niles upon his appointment as sole chairman of the Emergency Council following Silver's dismissal furnishes additional evidence of his attempts to influence the various forces operating within the American Zionist sphere through manipulation of the administration's activities. Wise described the rivalry between him and Silver, noting that Silver had instigated most of the anti-Roosevelt activity in the Senate. He termed the activity of Silver and his supporters as "dirty," and referred to Neumann as the leader of "a brigade of scavengers." Wise made it clear that he would not employ the methods used by Silver and that he felt that Roosevelt's Atlantic City declaration was altogether satisfactory, adding that he was certain that it would not be annulled or altered.

Having declared his loyalty, Wise asked Niles to use his influence with Roosevelt to persuade the president to welcome a delegation headed by Wise before his imminent trip to attend the Yalta Conference. Wise emphasized—by literally underscoring the sentence—that Roosevelt's meeting with the delegation was of paramount importance and that it was vital that the delegation be received at the White House despite the short notice and the president's tight schedule. He added that it was safe to assume that the Palestine issue would be discussed at the conference and it was thus important that the president be acquainted with the Zionist perspective before his departure. Wise then went on to link his efforts to block the resolutions to the meeting with Roosevelt. He noted that he and his colleagues, who had rejected the overtures made to them and had steadfastly supported Roosevelt's reelection, were not asking for preferential treatment on the strength of their courageous stand in support of the president and for having defended him in face of his enemies' malicious attacks. Nevertheless, he stressed, the meeting that he requested with the president was indeed a political move that would go far to strengthen him and his associates in the American Zionist movement. Roosevelt acceded to Wise's request, and before leaving for Yalta held two meetings with him at which the Palestine question was discussed.[174]

Wise thus pointed out that Silver's ousting and his own appointment to the post of chairman of the Emergency Council was not merely a change of personnel, but spelled the abandonment of the policy promoted by Silver and its replacement by a policy and mode of operation that would be far more acceptable to Roosevelt's administration. Yet although he adopted a different policy and different working methods, Wise sought to achieve political gains by means of participation in the American political arena, just as Silver had done. While Silver had acted against Roosevelt, Wise underscored the importance of his support for the president. He believed that by virtue of his actions in support of the president, he had gained the right to influence administration policy to a greater degree than had Silver. He believed further that the president should publicly recognize their cordial relationship in order to reinforce his own and his supporters' standing among American Jews. Like the declaration that he had requested from Stettinius, Wise's request to meet with the president prior to attending the Yalta Conference was meant to serve a complex objective. It constituted both an attempt to persuade the president to act in the interest of the Zionist movement and an effort to reinforce his own standing among American Jews. This meeting would once again enable Wise to appear to enjoy free access to the president, who wished to consult him before attending a political event of the utmost importance. Yet the pressure that Wise exerted to gain a meeting with Roosevelt prior to the Yalta Conference may likewise indicate that despite his pronouncements, he too was not convinced of the extent of the president's commitment to the Zionist cause and sought to ensure this support, both in substance and because of the meeting's implications for his public stature, particularly in the context of his rivalry with Silver. The close bond between Wise and Roosevelt was recognized by contemporaries and scholars alike; yet its depth, the extent of Wise's commitment to the president, and the fact that Wise was aware of the damage this did him in the Jewish sphere (which he tried to minimize) did not fully emerge at the time and were exposed only later in the press conference issue mentioned previously, in the context of the pro-Zionist resolutions submitted to Congress, and the political maneuvering associated with the resolutions within the American Zionist arena.

A meeting that Wise held with the Roosevelt following his return from the Yalta Conference and the meeting with Ibn Saud well illustrates the close link between Roosevelt's policy and Wise's stature in the American Zionist movement and among American Jews in general.[175] The outcome of the Yalta Conference was

---
174 Wise's letter to Niles, January 8, 1945, CZA, A-243/39.
175 Minutes of a meeting between Wise and Roosevelt, March 16, 1945, CZA, Z-5/1161.

met with disappointment by the American Jewish public, particularly in light of the rumors that had circulated beforehand suggesting that Roosevelt was about to win the agreement of the Allies to found a Jewish national home.[176] Silver, Neumann and their adherents were quick to seize on this apparent failure of Wise's strategy. They won over the requisite majority in the Emergency Council, Silver was duly invited to reassume the post of chairman, all the functionaries who supported him were reinstated, and he was given the authority to direct the Council's ongoing business. Wise informed the president of the tricky political circumstances in which he now found himself within the American Zionist movement following the failure at Yalta. He explained that in his capacity as the elected leader of American Zionists he was required to answer their questions and to present the prospects for positive political developments in the future, which he found difficult to do. Roosevelt responded by maintaining that Wise's standing had not been undermined, adding that Wise could declare on his behalf that he had refused to endanger the Jews of Palestine by supporting the immediate establishment of a Jewish state in Palestine. Roosevelt further stated that should the Zionist movement continue to trust him and allow him to proceed in handling the Palestine issue, he would fight with all his power on its behalf.[177] The degree

---

176 The Zionist issue was not officially raised at Yalta. Roosevelt briefly mentioned it after a dinner with Stalin, an event that received no mention in the official report on the conference. Roosevelt asked Stalin whether he was a Zionist. When Stalin expressed his reservations, Roosevelt informed him that he intended to meet with Ibn Saud after the conference. Later in the conversation, in response to Stalin's question about what Roosevelt intended to give Ibn Saud in return as concessions on his part on the Palestine issue, Roosevelt replied with a smile that all he was prepared to give to Ibn Saud were six million American Jews. See the testimony of a participant at the Yalta Conference, Charles E. Bohlen, *Witness to History, 1929–1969* (New York, 1973), 202–203. Rosenman writes about Roosevelt's meeting with Ibn Saud in his memoirs. He quotes Roosevelt's statements to Congress, and asserts that the president had never exhibited such an attitude following the meeting or on the trip back to the United States. He finds Roosevelt's pronouncement to be strange, suggesting that it may be linked to the acute deterioration in the president's health. See Samuel I. Rosenman, *Working with Roosevelt* (New York, 1972), 527–528. William Eddy offers a different interpretation. He served as the American envoy to Jedda. By virtue of his position and his command of Arabic, he served as translator at the meeting between Roosevelt and Ibn Saud, at which he was the only other person present. He recounts that toward the end of the meeting Roosevelt assured Ibn Saud that the United States would not adopt any policy hostile to the Arabs, and that US policy on Palestine would also be coordinated with the Arab states. He portrays Roosevelt's letter to Congress not as a political accident, but as a reflection of Roosevelt's Middle East policy and his attitude toward Ibn Saud. See William A. Eddy, *F. D. R. Meets Ibn Saud* (New York, 1954), 35–41. Other sources record that Roosevelt gave a favorable account of his meetings with Ibn Saud and King Faruk of Egypt. See James Bishop, *F. D. R's Last Year* (New York, 1974), 299–300.
177 Wise's meeting with Roosevelt, March 16, 1945, CZA Z-5/1161.

of Wise's distress arises from this meeting with Roosevelt. His ties to the president constituted a major component of his political power, yet had contributed to his political downfall when it transpired that the president was pursuing a policy detrimental to Zionism and that Wise was powerless to change it. The general sense of disappointment at the outcome of the Yalta Conference and Roosevelt's meeting with Ibn Saud did indeed lead to Wise's exclusion from the center of Zionist political activity in the United States, and contributed to Silver's success in regaining the role of chairman of the Emergency Council. This would support the conjecture that Wise became more active in the WJC as an alternative to his public activity on the American Zionist scene.[178]

The close link between Zionist and American party politics manifested itself once again when the pro-Zionist resolutions were presented for discussion for the third time in the Senate and the House in late 1945. They were adopted at the end of December and while they did not include specific mention of the founding of a Jewish state, they clearly expressed support for the objectives of the Zionist movement. In contrast to the previous attempts, this time Wise approved of the resolutions and supported their submission. He maintained that the resolutions should be submitted without delay owing to the danger of Anglo-American cooperation, which could harm Zionist interests in Palestine.[179] Further evidence of Wise's support for the resolutions is provided by his agreement to their speedy submission without obtaining the appropriate authorizations from the American Zionist institutions. Wise justified the urgency of submission and his active support of the move by citing the international political constellation and the willingness of Senator Wagner to take immediate steps to have the resolutions adopted.[180] The considerations that prompted Wise to support submission of the resolutions in 1945 were no different than those cited by his opponents in favor

---

178 See the report in the English language Jewish journal *New Palestine* on Silver's reinstatement to the Emergency Council and the shifting of Wise away from the center of Zionist activity. Headline in *New Palestine*, July 27, 1945.

179 Silver's pronouncement to the members of the Committee of Eight, October 26, 1945, Silver Archive, 1/169. The Committee of Eight comprised the members of the Jewish Agency in the United States and representatives of the large Zionist organizations in the country: the Zionist Organization of America, Hadassah, Po'alei Tsiyon, HaMizrahi, and Ha Po'el HaMizrahi. It was charged with coordinating Zionist diplomatic activity in the United States. The decision to set up the committee was made at the Zionist gathering held in London in August 1945, where it was agreed that the Committee of Eight would assume responsibility for conducting Zionist policy in the United States. Approaches to the US administration were to be made jointly with the Emergency Committee. Should disagreements emerge, the final decision was to be made by the Committee of Eight. See Statute of the Committee of Eight, 1945, Silver Archive, 1/239.

180 Silver's diary, October 26, 1945, Silver Archive, 2/468. Furthermore, Wise participated in the political negotiations that facilitated the submission of the resolutions. He was instrumental in

of the resolutions on the two previous occasions, when Wise had opposed the move. The danger posed by potential cooperation between Britain and the United States and the willingness of both the Senate and the House of Representatives to promote the resolutions had also prompted their submission in the past, raising the question of what had led Wise to change his policy. One cannot assert that Wise now, in 1945, supported submission of the resolutions because the administration no longer opposed the idea. The actions of both Neumann and Silver testify to the fact that pressure had also been brought to bear in 1945 in order to prevent the adoption of the resolutions by Congress—or at least to put the process on hold.[181] It would appear that the change in Wise's position was associated with the rotation of presidents and with the different types of relationship that he enjoyed with Roosevelt and Truman. Wise refused, for example, to sign an open letter of support for Truman during his contest for the Presidency with Dewey. He explained his position by criticizing Truman for having failed to act with sufficient vigor on behalf of the Zionist movement. While he had indeed assisted it, his support had been neither systematic nor wholehearted.[182] Wise had not made similar assertions about Roosevelt, even in the wake of the publication of the correspondence between them and Roosevelt's meeting with Ibn Saud. The difference in Wise's attitude toward the two presidents may be attributable to the fact that he was far less close to Truman than he had been to Roosevelt. Since he no longer felt totally committed to the Democratic administration, he now felt free to support the resolutions, and thereby perhaps also to reinforce his standing within the Zionist movement.

Wise's about-face on the resolutions issue might also be explained by means of an analysis of the Zionist camp in the United States. Silver and Neumann

---

persuading Senator Wagner to submit them without delay, before Truman's meeting with Atlee, the British Prime Minister. See Silver's letter to Wise, November 10, 1945, CZA, A-243/40.

181 Silver's letter to Frankfurter reveals the difficulties encountered on the way to passage of the resolutions. As on the previous occasions, Silver maintained, elements within the administration promised to refrain from opposing the resolutions but subsequently reneged on this. Silver noted that he had not previously realized what a treacherous place Washington was. See Silver's letter to Frankfurter, November 6, 1945, Silver Archive, 1/171. Reinharz notes that Truman's policy on Palestine was based on a compromise between political considerations such as Arab oil and the inter-bloc rivalry, which worked against American support for the founding of a Jewish state, and internal electoral constraints that prompted a converse policy. See Reinharz, *Great Powers*, 13–14.

182 Wise reported to Goldmann on a conversation he had held with David Niles, who continued to serve as Truman's advisor and asked Wise to sign an open letter of support for the president, which was to be publicized as part of the presidential contest between Truman and Dewey. See Wise's letter to Nahum Goldmann, October 7, 1948, Archive of the American Jewish Historical Society, P-134/211 2/11.

exploited the resolutions not only to exert pressure on the administration, but also to win the support of the American Jewish public for Silver and his mode of operation within American politics. Silver's actions with regard to the pro-Zionist resolutions served to place him at the center of the Jewish stage in the United States, to damage Wise's standing, and to create a more militant pattern of activity among both American Zionists and American Jews in general. Wise's initial opposition to the resolutions, therefore, stemmed from a blend of internal Zionist and general American considerations. Yet the process whereby the pro-Zionist resolutions were submitted, along with Silver's return to the center of Zionist activity in the United States and revelations of Roosevelt's attitude toward Zionism, all of which occurred upon the conclusion of World War II and the Holocaust, generated a new political and social situation within American Zionism and American Jewry. Given this development, there was no longer any point in continuing to oppose the resolutions—particularly since doing so would have harmed Wise's standing in the American Jewish community without bringing any political benefit.

The affair of the pro-Zionist resolutions is indicative of the fierce rivalry between Silver and Wise. The dissension between these two Zionist leaders was clearly manifested in issues of general concern to Americans that became entwined with Zionist activity in the United States in 1944, such as attitudes toward President Roosevelt and links to the opposing political establishments on the American scene. However, the ferocity of the rivalry between them must also be viewed against the backdrop of their contrasting outlooks regarding key issues that occupied the world Zionist movement, the settlements in Palestine, and American Zionism. Of particular note here is Silver's advocacy of intensifying the Zionist struggle against Britain both in Palestine and in the United States, which contrasts with Wise's opposition to Zionist action directed against Britain in the United States and his support of Weizmann's moderate policy in the mid-1940s. Weizmann's standing in the Zionist movement itself was a bone of contention between Wise and Silver that came to a head at the 1946 Zionist Congress, where Silver sided with the forces that led the anti-Weizmann campaign, contrary to Wise's position at that time. Weizmann's removal from the post of president of the Zionist movement enabled Silver to undermine Wise's position and to edge him out of his various official Zionist roles. One may assume that the political rivalry between the two men was exacerbated by personal animosity. Both of them were charismatic Zionist leaders and political figures, and both possessed impressive rhetorical skills and wielded considerable influence on their communities.[183]

---

183 A pro-Zionist policy in the United States necessarily involved waging an anti-British campaign in the American arena. On Silver's opposition to Britain and his presentation of the British

The Party Platforms

Alongside the attempt to pass the resolutions through Congress, Silver and his associates lobbied for the endorsement of pro-Zionist declarations and for their inclusion in the platforms of both the Democratic and Republican parties at their conventions, when they assembled in Chicago prior to the 1944 election, and. This activity in the party political sphere was intended to complement and reinforce the move to submit the resolutions to Congress. Discussion of the Zionist issue at the party conventions and its appearance in the platforms did indeed elicit wide media coverage, placing the Palestine question at the center of the U.S. public agenda, and turning it into a major topic in the election. This public debate was intended to deter decision makers from pursuing a policy incompatible with the pro-Zionist resolutions adopted by their respective parties and to which they had publicly committed themselves.

Silver prepared his campaign to promote the adoption of pro-Zionist resolutions at both conventions just as the debate on similar resolutions was put on hold in the Congress. The party conventions were scheduled for summer 1944; the Republicans were due to convene at the end of June and the Democrats in mid-July. As we shall see, one of the factors working in Silver's favor was that the Republican convention took place before the Democratic gathering. A further factor that facilitated the move was the appointment of Senator Robert Taft to the role of chairman of the Republican Party's Platform Committee. Taft had maintained close political ties with Silver, had been among those who initiated the pro-Zionist resolutions in the Senate, and sought to assist Silver within the Republican Party. Silver traveled to Chicago and took up residence close to the Republican headquarters a week ahead of the convention's opening. He was given official recognition by the party apparatus and was invited to conduct the traditional prayers at the opening ceremony. From his strategic location he tirelessly held meetings with Republican Party leaders, exhorting them not to delete a single element of the pro-Zionist section of the platform that Taft had submitted. Adoption of the section was a particularly tricky endeavor since the Republicans had traditionally refrained from addressing foreign policy in their platform,

---

issue as the major cause of his rift with Weizmann, see Silver's draft autobiography, 1963, Silver Archive, 7/3. On Wise's support of Britain and his opposition to Silver's anti-British policy, see Wise's letter to Frankfurter, May 21, 1942, CZA, A-234/138. In his reply to Wise Frankfurter expressed his complete agreement with Wise's view of Britain and with the need to refrain from Zionist action directed against Britain. See Frankfurter's letter to Wise, May 25, 1942, CZA, A-234/138. On Wise's support of Weizmann, see Wise's letter to Meir Weisgal (a journalist and Zionist activist, and Weizmann's permanent personal representative in the United States), CZA, A-243/43.

particularly in time of war. When, on the eve of the convention's opening, Silver learned that the Platform Committee was not prepared to endorse the Zionist paragraph, he suggested—or warned—that were his proposals to be rejected, the party leaders would be advised not to include any reference to Zionism whatsoever. Following a meeting between Silver and Republican presidential candidate Dewey, the section was accepted intact. It included the following statement:

> In order to give refuge to millions of distressed Jewish men, women and children driven from their homes by tyranny, we call for the opening of Palestine to their unrestricted immigration and land ownership, so that in accordance with the full intent and purpose of the Balfour Declaration of 1917 and the Resolution of a Republican Congress in 1922, Palestine may be constituted as a free and democratic Commonwealth. We condemn the failure of the president to insist that the mandatory of Palestine carry out the provision of the Balfour Declaration and of the mandate while he pretends to support them.[184]

The pro-Zionist resolution adopted by the Republican convention paved the way for similar success at the Democratic convention. The Democrat's resolution called for the opening of Palestine to unrestricted Jewish immigration and settlement, and for the adoption of a policy that would lead to the founding of a free and democratic Jewish Commonwealth.[185]

Silver believed that the resolutions adopted by the party conventions were of considerable public importance. Both parties expressed public support for the goals of the Zionist movement and undertook to implement them; Silver hoped that this would facilitate the adoption of similar resolutions by Congress.[186] Referring to the process whereby the pro-Zionist resolution had been adopted by the Republican convention, Silver recalled that he had broached the matter of including the section in the party's platform with Taft prior to the convention. He requested that the formulation of the resolution to be put to the Republican convention be similar to that which Taft had proposed to the Senate Foreign Relations Committee. Taft acquiesced to the idea and suggested that Silver meet with Dewey to ensure that the resolution would be passed. Taft promised to arrange

---

[184] Raphael, *Silver*, 112.
[185] The description of events at the Republican and Democratic conventions relies on Raphael, *Silver*, 109–115.
[186] Silver's letter to his son Daniel, July 21, 1944, Silver Archive, 3/311. The importance of the Democratic and Republican parties' resolutions is indicated by the reference to them in the resolutions of the Zionist Executive Committee, which convened in Zurich on September 1, 1947. The parties' resolutions were presented as being among the major political events that symbolized recognition of the Jewish people's right to a state. See The Zionist Executive Committee's Resolutions, in Meir Avizohar, ed., David Ben Gurion, *Stepping Toward a State (Memoirs from the Legacy: March–November 1947)* [in Hebrew] (Tel Aviv, 1993), 518–521.

the meeting, which indeed took place in early June. On Taft's suggestion, Zionist activity prior to and during the convention, which included submission of background material on the objectives of Zionism and the exchange of drafts of the section between Silver and Taft, was conducted mainly behind the scenes. Silver explained that this was done in order not to create the impression that a Jewish lobby was at work, which would probably have generated a reaction on the part of the opponents of Zionism. This tactic accorded with Silver's preference for obfuscating American Zionism's operation as that of a political pressure group that was driven purely by Zionist motives. Silver opposed attempts to modify the text of the Republican resolution, specifically to exclude the term "Jewish community," and demanded that the resolution clearly state that the immigrants to Palestine were Jews. He argued that only if the resolution were clear-cut and unequivocal, would the Republicans in both houses of Congress feel fully committed to voting for the pro-Zionist resolutions under debate there. He threatened to leave Chicago without conducting the prayers at the convention unless his demands were met. Silver recorded that he had reported the developments at the convention to Wise, who, in contrast to himself, had been prepared to accept the changes in the wording, asserting that the revised formulation was positive. Yet Silver decided not to compromise, and to insist on the original wording that he had proposed. He was convinced that, despite opposition within the Republican Party, its leadership understood the benefit to be gained from consideration of the wishes of America's Jewish citizens and would accede to his demands.

Silver's demands were accepted in the wake of intensive diplomatic negotiations in which Dewey himself and his political advisor John Foster Dulles took part. The Republican resolution included stern criticism of the president. Roosevelt was portrayed as someone who had reneged on his commitments to the World and American Zionist movements. Silver divulged that he had tried to exclude this attack on Roosevelt but had encountered a flat refusal on the part of Dulles, who asserted that this was a Republican and not a Zionist resolution. The Republican Party, he added, had every right to criticize all areas of the administration's activity, including its policy on Palestine.[187]

---

[187] Silver Diary, 1944, Silver Archive, 2/467. An example of the ongoing and close political ties between Silver and Dulles is provided by a letter in support of Dulles that Silver sent to a Zionist activist in Philadelphia. Silver explained that Dulles had supported the Zionist movement and Silver's activity in the United States for many years. He noted that Dulles had taken action on behalf of German Jews upon the Nazis' rise to power, had supported the pro-Zionist resolution at the Republican convention in 1944, and had assisted in gaining American backing for the UN partition resolution. See Silver's letter, September 25, 1948, Silver Archive, 1/930.

Examination of Silver's efforts to promote a pro-Zionist resolution at the Republican convention indicates that this was a meticulously planned political move designed to complement the campaign that Silver had waged in Congress. As he had done in Congress, Silver sought the assistance of political figures with whom he maintained a close relationship, such as Senator Taft and John Foster Dulles. Despite his efforts to conceal this fact and to operate behind the scenes, Silver's ability to influence the convention's decisions stemmed from the Republican leadership's desire to transfer as many Jewish votes as possible from Roosevelt and the Democrats to their party. This was why Silver's threat to refrain from conducting the prayers at the convention carried so much weight. Such a refusal would have demonstrated dissatisfaction with Republican policy and have detracted from the value of the pro-Zionist resolution, which was likely to have been portrayed as unsatisfactory in the view of American Zionists.

The Republicans' desire to reap electoral benefit from the Zionist section is manifested by Dulles's opposition to removing the references critical of Roosevelt. The Republicans sought to demonstrate in the clearest terms that Roosevelt had failed in the matter of Palestine, and to bring the differences between Roosevelt and the Republican candidate on this issue into sharp relief. While Silver agreed with the content of the wording concerning Roosevelt, he objected to its inclusion in the Zionist section in keeping with his overall policy of downplaying the parties' pursuit of the Jewish vote. The drawing of a clear line between the pro-Zionist resolution and the attack on Roosevelt was likely to have provided ammunition to Silver's opponents in the Zionist camp and in the general American domain, enabling them to claim that he was driven by opposition to Roosevelt and was exploiting his Zionist activity in order to harm the president. This would have hindered Silver in his attempt to win support among the Jewish public, which had traditionally supported Roosevelt. Portraying Silver as a tool in the hands of the president's opponents would have enabled administration officials to take action against him and to ignore all of his demands, particularly those regarding the Palestine policy. It would also have hindered Silver's efforts to persuade Democrats to support his Zionist endeavors in Congress and elsewhere, and turned support for Zionism into a partisan political matter. In effect, although Silver publicly declared that he was pursuing a bi-partisan policy, his central role in securing the Republican resolution and the fact that he had chosen to focus his efforts on the Republican rather than the Democratic convention indicate that his connections there were closer and therefore more influential.

The differences in outlook between Wise and Silver also become apparent in a telephone conversation between them during the course of the Republican convention. Observing events through the perspective of the Democratic Party's interests, Wise was prepared to accept a rather vague declaration that would have placed less of a commitment on the Republican Party to adopt a pro-Zionist policy. Indeed, the more pro-Zionist the Republican resolution, the more it would bring out the differences between Roosevelt's Zionist policy and the Republican's warm embrace, which would very likely result in Jewish voters transferring their allegiance from Roosevelt to Dewey. Wise realized that the Republican resolution required the Democratic Convention to adopt a similar one. A pro-Zionist resolution of this kind would make it difficult for Roosevelt to refrain from implementing it in future, and would thus restrict his freedom in conducting his Middle-East policy in the way he saw fit. Therefore, Wise from the outset sought to modify the Republican declaration in a more moderate direction in order to protect Roosevelt from such constraints.

Wise was well aware of the damage that the Republican resolution was likely to cause among the Jewish public. Writing to Roosevelt, he declared that as a Jewish and Zionist American he felt deeply ashamed of the manner in which the president had been portrayed in the Republican platform. He termed the Republican resolution unjustified, adding that he believed that the Jewish public understood this. Wise ended the letter by expressing his full confidence in Roosevelt's victory in the upcoming election, since the American electorate would not make the mistake of voting for Dewey despite the false propaganda that his camp was disseminating.[188] In his letter to Frankfurter, Wise once again called the Republican resolution a shameful and unwarranted attack on Roosevelt. He made it clear that he had had nothing to do with the anti-Roosevelt resolution, and that he had no connection whatsoever to the Zionist activity conducted at the Republican convention. Wise added that in his capacity as chairman of the Emergency Council he was considering whether to make a public declaration regarding his reservations toward the Republican resolution, and planned to ask the council to publish a similar declaration. He wrote that were the council to reject his request, he would consider resigning his post as chairman. Wise furthermore stated that the Republican resolution, which he termed an attack on Roosevelt inspired by Silver, had led him to alter his political plans. He had not planned to attend the Democratic Convention in Chicago, but he was now obliged to participate and to make sure that it would pass a pro-Zionist resolution—which he had previously deemed unnecessary—in order to mitigate the damage done by the Republican resolution.[189]

---

188 Wise's letter to Roosevelt, June 28, 1944, Archive of the American Jewish Historical Society, P-134/68.
189 Wise's letter to Frankfurter, June 28, 1944, CZA, A-243/137. Wise did not explain in the letter why he had not intended to attend the Democratic Convention. He merely noted that the reasons were known to Frankfurter. Silver would in the future be accused again of engaging in

Wise makes no mention in his letters to Roosevelt and Frankfurter regarding the Zionist aspects of the Republican Convention resolutions. What concerns him most of all are the implications of these resolutions on the political future of President Roosevelt and the Democratic Party. He considers the Zionist issue to be a means of attaining political achievements in the general American sphere rather than as an end in itself. He asserts that Silver was motivated by a similar, yet opposite, objective—namely, to damage the Democratic Party and to harm Roosevelt politically.

The correspondence between Wise and Silver—joint chairmen of the Emergency Council—pertaining to the Republican and Democratic parties' conventions allows us a glimpse into the differences between the official Zionist position, which ostensibly favored the adoption of pro-Zionist resolutions by both parties, and what actually occurred behind the scenes with regard to Zionist activity. In his report to Wise on events at the Republican Convention, Silver describes his cooperation with Senator Taft and the Republican presidential candidate Dewey, pointing out that their assistance had been instrumental in assuring the Zionist achievement. Silver distanced himself from the criticism leveled at Roosevelt that appeared in the Zionist section, insisting that this had been included despite his opposition at the demand of John Foster Dulles. He believed that the political significance of the Republican resolution for American Zionism lay in the possibility of extracting a similar resolution at the Democratic convention. He thought that, in the long run, theresolutions of both parties would facilitate final approval of the pro-Zionist resolutions at the forthcoming session of Congress.[190]

Wise replied by expressing his satisfaction at the Republican Convention resolution and, of course, agreed with Silver's assessment of the damage caused by the criticism of Roosevelt. Furthermore, Wise approvingly noted Dewey's cooperation, and undertook to bring about a similar resolution at the Democratic Convention with the help of Senator Wagner, who was due to be nominated as chairman of the Democratic Platform Committee.[191] Yet Wise responded very differently to Silver's report in a letter to David Niles, to which he attached a copy

---

political activity because of his support for the Republican Party. The leaders of the Zionist labor movement sent him an open letter in this vein. While complaining about Truman's policy on the Palestine question, they opposed Silver's activity, which they defined as being pro-Republican. In their view, support of the Republicans was harmful to Zionist interests and to the American people in general. See a report on the letter in the New York Post, October 16, 1946.

[190] Silver explained that he had sent the letter after repeatedly failing to contact Wise by telephone prior to the official release of the resolutions of the Republican Platform Committee. See Silver's letter to Wise, June 28, 1944, CZA, A-243/132.

[191] Wise's letter to Silver, June 29, 1944, Archive of the American Jewish Historical Society, P-134/119.

of Silver's letter. Wise maintained that Silver was not being truthful in denying any involvement on his part in the criticism leveled at Roosevelt in the Zionist section of the Republican platform. Referring to Silver's threat to withdraw from the Republican Convention, Wise asserted that here, too, Silver had not accurately described the political events. He surmised that the entire move had been coordinated in advance by Silver and the Republican Party leadership, and that the story of his threat was designed to cultivate his image as an uncompromising politician who campaigned for the objectives of the Zionist movement.[192] Wise informed Niles that he had assured Silver that he would endeavor to see that the Democratic Convention would adopt a pro-Zionist resolution at least as favorable as that passed by the Republicans. He repeatedly stressed that at the Democratic Convention he would act not of his own free will, but rather in order to balance the Republican resolution and to protect President Roosevelt.

Wise chose to publicize his reservations about the criticism leveled at Roosevelt in the Zionist section of the Republican platform in a lecture he delivered at an evening arranged by the New York branch of the American Zionist Organization in honor of Congressman Bloom. He asserted that the criticism was unjust and called on Bloom to prove to the Jewish public just how misguided it was.[193] Following this address, Silver sent Wise a second letter that further revealed and exacerbated the differences in outlook between the two Zionist leaders. Silver began by saying that he understood Wise's natural reaction in trying to protect the president from unwarranted criticism as he regarded it. Nevertheless, maintained Silver, it would have been preferable had an official spokesman of the Democratic Party come to the president's defense rather than Wise. He added that this was an altercation between the parties since it was the Republican Party and not the American Zionist movement that had brought the accusations against the president; thus it was appropriate that a representative of the Democratic Party rather than a Zionist leader should respond to them. Silver went on to admonish Wise's reaction to the Republican resolution, complaining that Wise had ignored the Zionist achievement at the core of the resolution and had not bothered to compliment Silver on this in any way. He underscored the success in winning the support of one of the two main parties for unhindered Jewish immigration, for the abolition of the land law, and for implementation of the principles of the Balfour Declaration and the Mandate document. This was the first time that the Zionist issue had appeared in a party platform, and American Jewish leaders should not ignore it; rather it was their duty to exploit it in order to achieve further Zionist gains in the political sphere. Silver pointedly stated that if Wise wanted the Dem-

---

[192] Wise's letter to Niles, June 29, 1944, CZA, A-243/83.
[193] The dinner was held on June 29, 1944.

ocratic Party to adopt a similar pro-Zionist resolution, then the Republican resolution was the most efficient means to achieve this. He foresaw difficulties in passing the pro-Zionist resolution at the Democratic Convention and informed Wise that according to information that he had received, the State Department would attempt to prevent this from happening, just as it had in the Congress. Silver maintained that precisely in light of the State Department's expected action, it behooved the Zionists to let the Democratic leadership know that the Republican resolution had been greeted with considerable joy and appreciation by the American Jewish public. He reiterated his contention that the heads of American Zionism should exploit the Zionist section in the Republican platform so as to turn it into a means of extracting a similar or even more favorable resolution at the Democratic Convention—and that it was not their business to come to Roosevelt's defense.[194]

The correspondence conducted between Silver, Wise and Niles following the endorsement of the Republican resolution and prior to the gathering of the Democratic convention indicates the rift and the conflict of outlook between Wise and Silver. Silver wanted to neutralize Wise's endeavors in his capacity as a Democrat activist and as Roosevelt's man by restricting his activity to the American Zionist-Jewish sphere alone. He maintained that Wise should have assessed the Republican resolution solely from the Zionist perspective, and left the defense of Roosevelt to the Democratic leadership. He further asserted that despite the ties between Wise and Roosevelt, it was the Zionist interest that should dictate Wise's political actions. Silver noted in a letter to Neumann that the critical response on the part of a section of the Emergency Council's members to the Zionist section in the Republican platform confirmed his view that these members regarded themselves as more committed to the Democratic Party than to the Zionist movement. He maintained that their opposition to the Republican resolution because of its criticism of Roosevelt demonstrated that in the case of a conflict of interest between their Zionist and Democratic loyalties, they would choose to support the Democratic Party and were prepared to sacrifice the Zionist interest in so doing.[195]

In his autobiography Silver portrays his efforts at the Republican and Democratic conventions as non-partisan, adding that his position differed from that taken by a large section of the members of the Emergency Council, who regarded themselves primarily as Democrats and fervently defended President Roosevelt,

---

194 Silver's letter to Wise, July 1, 1944, Archive of the American Jewish Historical Society, P-134/119. As he had maintained previously, and unlike Wise, Silver believed that Senator Wagner's nomination to the position of Chairman of the Democratic Platform Committee did not assure adoption of the pro-Zionist resolution.
195 Silver's letter to Neumann, July 17, 1944, Silver Archive, 2/165.

who in their eyes could do no wrong. He notes that these elements looked askance at his success in bringing about the inclusion of the pro-Zionist section in the Republican platform because of the damage it could do to the Democratic Party. Silver concludes that the dispute regarding the Democratic Party and President Roosevelt was among the main issues that engaged American Zionism, affected overall Zionist activity in the United States, and led to his resignation from the Emergency Council in 1945. He notes that he harbored no doubts about Wise's loyalty to the Jewish world and to Zionism and underscored his longstanding contribution to the movement. Wise was, however, a loyal and devoted member of the Democratic Party and on close personal terms with President Roosevelt, factors that influenced his political activity to no less and perhaps to a greater degree than the fact that he was an American Zionist leader.[196]

Wise took a very different view of these matters, as evidenced by his actions in the wake of the Republican Convention and his letter to Niles. As on the issue of the American Jewish response to the Holocaust, Wise saw no contradiction between his role as an American Zionist leader and being part of the Democratic establishment. He regarded the cooperation between Silver, Taft and Dewey at the Republican Convention as a conspiracy between Silver and Roosevelt's enemies designed to harm the president. He thus considered it his duty as a Democratic leader to defend the president. He failed to see any contradiction between Zionist and Democratic interests because he was convinced that Roosevelt was entirely sincere in his intention to work on behalf of the Zionist movement. Thus he believed that his endeavors as a Democratic leader to ensure the continuation of Roosevelt's incumbency served Zionist objectives better than did Silver's achievements at the Republican Convention.

Following Roosevelt's death, Wise wrote that the Palestine question had been among the major issues of concern to the president during all the years of his presidency and that Roosevelt had supported free Jewish immigration to Palestine and believed that it should become a national Jewish home. Wise maintained that the criticism leveled against Roosevelt's policy on the Zionist issue was part of a well-planned and mendacious propaganda campaign intended to besmirch and vilify the late president. He believed that Roosevelt had taken care not to exhibit hostility toward the Arab world, and that this was compatible with the policy espoused by American Zionists, who had never urged the president to take action against the Arabs.[197]

---

196 Silver's draft autobiography, 1963, Silver Archive, 7/3.
197 See Wise's letter to Benjamin Aktzin, May 20, 1946, CZA, A-243/41; Wise's letter to Sumner Welles, May 20, 1946, CZA A-243/201; and Wise's letter to Meiron Weil of New York, October 22, 1945, CZA, A-243/83.

The letters of Silver and Wise are once again indicative of the blending of spheres that typified the Zionist leadership's activity in the United States. While Wise's mode of operation manifests this blurring of boundaries between the Jewish-Zionist and the overall American arenas more clearly, this phenomenon is also discernible in Silver's comportment. Silver was fully aware that his political successes were possible only because of the attempts on the part of Republican leaders to alter the voting patterns among the American Jewish public by coaxing it away from the Democratic Party. It is safe to assume that Silver was unperturbed by such an eventuality. Although he did not openly support Dewey, he enjoyed a close relationship with Taft and John Foster Dulles, as well as with other figures in the Republican establishment.[198] Reducing Jewish support for Roosevelt and the Democrats suited Silver's political strategy. His opposition to Roosevelt's third and fourth terms in office, which he regarded as posing a danger to American democracy, and his desire to bring an end to the overwhelming Jewish vote for Roosevelt and the Democratic Party, were intended to turn the Jewish vote into a significant and powerful political tool.[199] As had been the case with his efforts in the resolutions issue in Congress, the fact that Silver was closer to the Republicans than to the incumbent Democrats made it easier for him to achieve political gains for the Zionist movement. Contrary to the sentiments expressed at the meeting of the Jewish Agency Executive in Jerusalem, given the political reality of 1944 it was actually Wise's links to the Democratic establishment that brought about his downfall within Zionist politics, whereas Silver's standing as a persona non grata in the White House somewhat paradoxically served to reinforce his stature as an American Jewish and Zionist leader.

Wise's commitment to the Democratic Party and his dispute with Silver on this account surfaced all the more clearly during the course of the Zionists' activity at the Democratic Party convention that convened in Chicago in 1944. Silver let it be known that the reports he had received from Chicago suggested that the actions of Wise and his supporters at the convention had been guided primarily by their allegiance to the Democratic Party rather than their duty as Jewish and Zionist leaders. The arguments in favor of a pro-Zionist resolution that Wise

---

[198] While at first glance it may appear that Silver did indeed support Dewey during the various election campaigns, internal Zionist memorandums and the correspondence between associates of Dewey and Silver reveal that this was not so. One example is provided by a letter from Dan Alfeng, one of Dewey's senior advisors, to Silver, in which he castigated Silver's deportment prior to the 1948 election, asserting that Silver's support of Dewey was merely a pretense. See Dan Alfeng's letter to Silver, 1947, CZA, A-123/327.

[199] See Silver's sermon "Thoughts on the 1944 Election Campaign and Election," November 5, 1944, Silver Archive, 6/711; Silver's sermon on the topic of Roosevelt's third term, March 31, 1940, Silver Archive, 6/608.

and his followers put forward in the Democratic Platform Committee had focused solely on the benefit that the Democratic Party would derive from it; they had foregone the opportunity of expounding on the Zionist cause. Wise attacked the Republican Party and commended the nobility that the Democratic Party had exhibited toward the Zionists. He further asserted that there was no substantive need to adopt the pro-Zionist section, which had been required only by the Republican resolution. Silver's assistant Harold Manson, who attended the convention, particularly emphasized the words of Israel Goldstein at the Democratic Platform Committee. Goldstein spoke as a member of the Democratic Party, not as a Zionist leader, in warning the committee of the effects of the Republican platform on American Jews. He stressed that during a tour of Cleveland he had gained the impression that the Republican resolution was likely to have far-reaching electoral repercussions, which would be manifested in a shift of allegiance on the part of Jewish voters from the Democrats to the Republicans. Silver went on to report that convention delegates had told him that Wise and his followers had disseminated a rumor among the delegates that Silver was planning to deliver a series of speeches in support of Dewey. They presented Silver as someone who was intent on destroying the Democratic Party and who meant to use the Zionist movement to achieve this aim.[200] Neumann similarly asserted that Wise was deeply involved in Democratic politics and was committed to President Roosevelt. He termed Wise an emissary of the White House who coordinated his positions with Roosevelt and worked for him among the American Jewish community.[201]

Owing to the opposition of some of its members, Wise encountered difficulty in his efforts to have the pro-Zionist section endorsed by the Democratic Platform Committee. Fear that the pro-Zionist resolution would not be included in the Democratic platform induced Wise to dispatch a hasty letter to President Roosevelt in the hope of persuading him to apply all his political weight toward ensuring its adoption. In his letter Wise spelled out the main reasons compelling the Democratic Party to exhibit public support for the Zionist movement, warning that failure to endorse such a resolution would cause irreparable damage to the party. Wise explained that he himself, along with other Zionist leaders, was eager to work actively toward a victory for the Democrats and Roosevelt in the forthcoming election campaign, adding that the absence of a pro-Zionist section in the Democratic platform would make it impossible for them to combat the president's opponents. Inclusion of a meaningful pro-Zionist section to the platform, on the other hand, would provide an appropriate response to the Republicans' pro-Zionist resolutions. Wise made it clear that the Jewish voting public, which

---

200 Silver Diary, July 17, 1944, Silver Archive, 2/764.
201 Interview conducted by Professor Yehuda Bauer with Neumann, July 21, 1967, CZA, A-123/413.

he described as supportive of the Democrats, expected the party to endorse a pro-Zionist resolution. Such a resolution would enable them to maintain their traditional support for the Democratic Party and to vote for Roosevelt. The absence of a pro-Zionist section, on the other hand, would induce these voters, despite having supported the Democrats in the past, to vote for the Republican candidate because of the pro-Zionist section in the Republican platform. Wise informed Roosevelt that his apprehension regarding a change in Jewish voting patterns rested upon data that had been collected by his followers throughout the country, which suggested that many Jews, from all social strata, were intending to transfer their allegiance to the Republicans based on the absence of a pro-Zionist section in the Democratic platform. Wise reiterated that the Democratic Party should include in its platform a section that was more supportive of Zionism than the one appearing in the Republican platform—or at least equally so—in order to preserve the allegiance of the Jewish voting public.[202]

It can be argued that Wise chose to promote the inclusion of the Zionist section by stressing that it served the interest of the Democratic Party by making it easier for him to persuade party institutions to support its endorsement. Yet Wise had made this same assertion in his letters to Felix Frankfurter, with whom he maintained an exceedingly cordial political and personal relationship. Wise had no need to present Frankfurter with a manipulative set of arguments in order to persuade him of the necessity of passing the pro-Zionist section. The fact that Wise, in his letters to Frankfurter, nevertheless expressed the same view that he had presented to Roosevelt and to Niles indicates that his mode of operation at the Democratic Convention was not dictated by tactical considerations, but demonstrated a political world view and his genuine convictions. In his letters to Frankfurter, Wise argued that it would have been preferable had the Zionist issue not figured at all in the two parties' platforms, but since the Republican Party had adopted a pro-Zionist section, he had been obliged to endeavor to bring about the endorsement of a parallel section at the Democratic Convention. He stressed that failure on the part of the Democrats to adopt a pro-Zionist section, or the passing of a lukewarm and insignificant resolution in support of the Zionist movement would have been tantamount to offering a political gift to the Republicans. Wise asserted that the Republican resolution was a calculated and well-planned plot designed exclusively to harm Roosevelt's prospects of reelection by altering Jewish voting patterns. He maintained that this scheme had been foiled by his own action at the Democratic Convention and the adoption of the pro-Zionist section in the party's platform. In a subsequent letter to Frankfurter, Wise left no room for doubt: He categorically stated that Silver had led the political activity

---

202 Wise's letter to President Roosevelt, July 19, 1944, CZA, A-243/38.

directed against Roosevelt, defining Silver's deeds at the Republican convention as monstrous and describing him as having connived with Senator Taft to wage war on Roosevelt.[203]

These sources reveal that Silver's assertions regarding the precedence that Wise accorded to the Democratic interest above the Zionist cause did indeed reflect Wise's political outlook. Unlike Silver, Wise saw nothing wrong with this order of priorities, believing that Roosevelt's continued incumbency in office and assured freedom of action on the Palestine question would serve American Jews in the best way possible.

Wise's order of political priorities surfaced yet again during the course of another occurrence in the 1944 election campaign. Because of his influence on the Jewish voting public, Wise was asked to express public support for Congressman Hamilton Fish. Fish had traditionally shown support for the Zionist movement and had been one of the initiators and submitters of the pro-Zionist resolution of 1922. Consequently, Fish's adherents believed that Wise would support him despite his Republican allegiance.[204] Wise, however, explained that despite the damage that may be incurred by the Zionist movement in the event of Fish's failure to be reelected, he was not prepared to sign the requested letter of support because of Fish's energetically conducted opposition to President Roosevelt and the Democratic Party. Thus the decisive reason for Wise' decision not to support Fish despite the latter's record of fierce and ongoing support for the Zionist movement was the damage that this could do to the Democratic Party—and therefore to Wise himself.[205]

Wise's support for Roosevelt during the 1944 election campaign was not an isolated occurrence, but was a part of the deep and continuous relationship between them, not merely pertaining to the Palestine context, but also with regard to toning down the American Jewish response in the wake of the Holocaust. Wise told Frankfurter that he had supported Roosevelt ever since the political infighting in the Democratic Party in 1924. In 1944 Wise reiterated the words of praise for Roosevelt that he had uttered in the past, portraying him as a defender of the American people and as someone who had been of historic service to the United States.[206] In a letter to David Niles, for example, Wise attacked those who opposed

---

203 Wise's letters to Frankfurter, March 22, 1945, CZA, A-243/137.
204 Letter to Wise, April 13, 1944, Archive of the American Jewish Historical Society, P-134/64. A draft letter of public support for Fish is attached to the letter. Concerning the Congress resolutions of 1922, see Carl J. Friedrich, *American Policy Toward Palestine* (Washington, 1944), 14–19.
205 Wise's letter, April 18, 1944, Archive of the American Jewish Historical Society, P-134/64.
206 Wise's letter to Frankfurter, January 28, 1936, CZA, A-243/139; a classified personal letter from Wise to Roosevelt, March 4, 1938, CZA, A-243/32.

Roosevelt's election to a third term, maintaining that the issue should not have been raised in the first place since the country needed another four years of Roosevelt's presidency. He described the efforts he had made to persuade Roosevelt's Democratic opponents to drop their resistance and announced that he intended to travel to Maine and Vermont to lead the campaign for Roosevelt's reelection to the presidency at the Democratic Convention. In a further letter to Niles, Wise argued that the Democrats should not have addressed the issue of a third term. The Democratic campaign should be conducted in light of Roosevelt's successes and should disregard the number of times he had been elected. Wise asked Niles to exert his influence on Democratic leaders so as to ensure that they did not raise this issue in their speeches, since even a pronouncement of support for a third term would likely be detrimental to the effort to secure Roosevelt's reelection in the forthcoming vote.[207]

Wise's writing on the resolutions submitted to Congress and on the Zionist lobbying at the Republican and Democratic conventions demonstrates that he attributed to Silver an approach similar to his own, albeit with the opposite intention. He believed that Silver's moves were designed to assist the Republican Party by harming Roosevelt, thus garnering votes for its own presidential candidate and representatives in Congress. He lent no credence to Silver's protestations of political neutrality. Moreover, he was contemptuous of Silver's and Neumann's claims that their endeavors in the American political arena were intended to achieve political gains for the Zionist movement and were not motivated by their opposition to Roosevelt. Wise warned that political use of the Jewish vote and the modes of operation that Silver had initiated were jeopardizing American Jewry's future.[208] It is difficult to assess the truth of Wise's accusations against Silver. On the strength of the material presented thus far, it would be fair to conclude that Silver's Zionist activity was a blend of his opposition to Roosevelt and his support of certain sections of the Republican Party leadership. It is safe to assume that his predisposition toward the Republicans facilitated his anti-Roosevelt activity and enabled him to exert a more significant influence on Republican Party institutions. Silver attached more weight to his status as a Zionist and Jewish leader than Wise did to his own. While Silver, too, combined the roles of Zionist leader and American politician, he gave clear priority to his work for Zionism.

Silver's freedom to give precedence to Zionist interests was a function of the reciprocal relationship he had with the American political system, within which he maintained particularly close ties to Republican Senator Robert Taft, a member of the opposition party who, having failed to win the Party's candidacy

---

207 Wise's letters to David Niles, January 9, 1939; December 22, 1939, CZA, A-243/33.
208 Wise's letter to Frankfurter, October 18, 1946, CZA, A-243/137.

for president, maintained a rivalry with the Republican presidential candidates throughout the 1940s.[209] The fact that Silver maintained a reciprocal political relationship with Taft enabled him to oppose both the Democratic and the Republican leadership without fear of reprisal on the part of his party contact. On the contrary, activity directed against both the Democratic administration and the Republican presidential candidates served Taft's political interests and suited his standing within the party. It is difficult to assess how Silver would have acted had he encountered a conflict between his Zionist effort and his general American endeavor, but his opposition to American policy in Europe upon the conclusion of World War II and his advocacy of a policy of compromise in U.S.–Soviet relations provides some idea. His utterances elicited an angry reaction within broad sections of the Jewish public, and were detrimental to his standing in the Zionist sphere and his ability to harness the Jewish vote. Silver nevertheless steadfastly adhered to his position and was prepared to bear the political consequences of championing an unpopular cause.[210] Wise's activity in the sphere of American politics, on the other hand, was conducted through his connections with the political force that dominated the American arena during the 1940s. He therefore found it difficult to promote Zionist interests in the face of the administration's opposition, and it is abundantly clear that he was, above all, an American politician. Wise believed that this did not compromise his loyalty to the Zionist cause. On the contrary, unlike Silver, he was convinced that this was the best way to serve the interests of the Zionist movement, of the Jewish state that was about to come into being, and of American Jewry.

The desire of the WJC leadership to restrain American Jewry's efforts to promote the founding of a Jewish state surfaced once more with regard to the publication of the report by the Anglo-American Committee of Inquiry at the end of April 1946. By virtue of his senior position in the Jewish Congress, Nahum Goldmann was appointed to represent the organization at the Committee of Inquiry's meetings in London.[211] The full political significance of his nomination to represent the Congress on the committee emerged only after the committee had completed its work. At that point, Goldmann exploited his standing in order to restrain the Jewish response in the United States to the committee's conclusions.

---

209 On Taft's ties to Silver see, for example, evidence of Silver's support for Taft during the Senate elections of 1944 in Ohio. Letter from Paul Walter, a former member of Taft's election staff, to Daniel, Silver's son, January 27, 1989, Silver Archive, 7/154. On Taft, see, for example, James T. Patterson, *Mr. Republican, A Biography of Robert A. Taft* (Boston, 1972).
210 See, for example, Silver's sermon in Cleveland, "Russia and the USA – Is there not a bridge between them?" October 19, 1947, Silver Archive, 6/767.
211 On this nomination, see Wise's telegram to Goldmann's wife, January 18, 1946, CZA, A-243/124.

Goldmann's status as representative of the Congress rather than of the Zionist movement gave him room to maneuver because he was not bound by the decisions of the Zionist institutions, particularly in view of the opposition on the part of Abba Hillel Silver, the foremost Zionist leader in the United States at the time, to the committee's conclusions.[212]

Moderation and Restraint: The Response by American Jews to the Holocaust and the Struggle for the Establishment of the State of Israel

On these three separate occasions—the maneuvering related to the Palestine context in 1944 and again in 1946, and the attempt to restrain Jewish reaction to the Holocaust between 1942 and 1944—the World Jewish Congress in the United States served as a singular political instrument whose existence alongside the Zionist movement enabled Goldmann and Wise to act independently of the authority of the institutions of the World Zionist Movement and its American branch. By restraining the activity of the Jews as a group pursuing an ethnic policy of its own, they acted in accordance with the political strategy they had employed within American politics.

Although Wise and Goldmann employed a similar mode of operation, both in toning down the Jewish campaign calling for the rescue of Jews being waged in America and in attempting to restrain the activity in America with regard to the founding of a Jewish state, there is a significant difference between the two instances. This difference is clearly manifested in Wise's address to the American Jewish Congress in August 1943. As noted above, Wise used the occasion to dampen the audience's urge to agitate for the rescue of European Jewry, but magnified and stressed the role of Palestine as a refuge for Jews and the vital need to establish a Jewish state after the war. He took issue with British policy on Palestine and was particularly critical of the 1939 White Paper, which severely limited the number of Jews allowed to migrate to Palestine and placed restrictions on Jewish purchase of land there. Wise expressed his surprise that this policy had not been modified despite the tragic situation of the Jews throughout the world. He asserted that the distressing condition of European Jewry made it imperative to allow Jews to migrate to the United States and Britain, and that opening up Palestine to Jewish immigration under the surveillance and control of the Jewish Agency was an essential move that should be undertaken during the war. Wise

---

212 Goldmann's letter to Wise, April 18, 1946, CZA, A-243/124. On Silver's objections to the committee's conclusions, see Silver's letter to Wise, April 12, 1946, CZA, A-423/132.

did not stop at calling for a campaign to bring about Jewish migration to Palestine; he sought to induce the audience to conduct an active struggle for Jewish independence under the slogan "For the sake of Zion I will not be silent." He noted that alongside the pressing campaign for the rescue of Europe's Jews, the overriding objectives of the American Jewish Congress in 1943 were to preserve Jewish rights in Europe after the war and to work toward the founding of a Jewish state in Palestine to be put in place following victory. Immediately following his words on Palestine, Wise noted also that the struggle for the rescue of Jews was an important goal of the Congress, but he refrained altogether from calling for an active campaign on this matter, thereby creating a significant difference between the two issues.

The struggle for Palestine also figured as the main topic in Nahum Goldmann's address to the same conference in 1943. He began by asserting that the Congress's primary objective was to create a united Jewish American front that would campaign for the establishment of a Jewish state. To his mind, this struggle transcended customary party divisions and unified all sections of American Jewry because of Palestine's tremendous importance to present and future Jewish life. Goldmann explained to his audience that this importance was not purely an ideological matter since in practical terms Palestine should serve as a refuge for the masses of Jews who would require somewhere to live after the war and would not want to remain in Europe.[213]

Goldmann described the success of Jewish settlement in the Land of Israel, maintaining that the achievements of the Jews of Palestine were conclusive proof of the validity of the claim for immediate Jewish control over Jewish immigration to Palestine, for unhindered purchase of land, and subsequently for the founding of a state. He extensively reviewed the various arguments offered by those who opposed the establishment of a Jewish state, from the Arab problem to the question of dual loyalty of the world's Jews. He rejected all of them as being irrelevant and urged his audience to place the struggle for a Jewish state at the top of the American public agenda.[214]

As had Wise, Goldmann had received first-hand reports of the dimensions of the extermination of Europe's Jews and foresaw that the vast majority of European Jewry would be murdered by the Nazis, yet chose to give top priority to the struggle for the Land of Israel at the central convention of American Jewry in the summer of 1943.

---

213 Goldmann's speech to the American Jewish Congress, New York, August 30, 1943, AJA, 361 A2/3.
214 Ibid.

The papers of Goldmann and Wise pertaining to the operation of the WJC during the thirties and forties with regard to the Holocaust and the struggle for the establishment of a Jewish state, as well as the Congress's practical activity in the United States during this period, shed light on the factors that shaped its mode of operation in the American sphere. These documents reveal that the founders of the WJC were aware of the fate of European Jewry, and that their attempts to restrain the political and public activity of American Jews stemmed from their belief that by so doing they could best serve the interests of world Jewry and of the Jewish-American community.

Stephen Wise, Nahum Goldmann, and their associates among the senior executives of the WJC did not operate in a vacuum as they addressed Jewish issues. Their public and political standing in the country must be taken into account when assessing their actions. From their papers we learn that they regarded themselves as an integral part of the Democratic establishment in general, and of Roosevelt's administration in particular. They saw no difference between themselves and Jews who occupied senior posts in the White House. They sought to conduct Jewish public activity in a manner that would not harm the Democratic administration, thus to their minds best serving their interests as Jews.[215] They were not misled by the president or by Jewish and non-Jewish administration officials. They did not persuade themselves that Roosevelt's government had done what was needed to rescue Jews from the Holocaust, or that President Harry Truman supported the founding of a Jewish state as part of the post-war arrangements. On the contrary, they applied their policy in the knowledge of the tragic situation of European Jews and despite the awareness that their efforts to influence the administration's policy on Jewish and Zionist matters were—as they themselves termed them—muted. Nevertheless, the continuation of Roosevelt in office and assuring a Democratic majority in Congress were, in their view, a supreme strategic objective of the American Jewish public—simply because they were American Jews.[216] They were convinced that curtailment of the Democratic administration's freedom of action, and worse still, the possibility that Roosevelt would be replaced, were far worse alternatives than the status quo.[217]

---

215 See the top secret minutes of a meeting between Nahum Goldmann and Samuel Rosenman, Roosevelt's close advisor and speech writer, April 27, 1944, CZA, Z-5/382. See also Wise's letter to Felix Frankfurter, October 28, 1944, CZA, A-243/137.
216 On coordination with the administration, and on their attempts to prevent electoral damage to Roosevelt owing to his policy on the Jewish and Palestine issues, see Wise's letter to Frankfurter, July 26, 1944, CZA, A-243/137; Goldmann's letter to Weizmann, August 10, 1944, CZA, Z-6/2759.
217 On the definition of Roosevelt as defender of the American people and as having done historic service to the United States, see Wise's personal and classified letter to Roosevelt, March 4, 1938, CZA, A-243/33. It should be noted that during Roosevelt's term as Governor of New York,

The evidence suggests that the policy of restraint practiced by Wise, Goldmann, and their associates in the WJC leadership does not indicate that they were impervious to the fate of the Jews during the Holocaust or that they feared for their personal standing in America. We should note that both Wise and the Congress as an organization had signed financial guarantees that provided economic assistance to Jewish refugees who came to the United States during the war. These guarantees were essential to gaining authorization from officials in the State Department to accept Jewish refugees into the United States.[218]

At the end of July 1943, Wise wrote to Goldmann about his effort to persuade the administration to take more strenuous action on behalf of European Jews. He told of a telegram he had sent to Henry Morgenthau, Roosevelt's Secretary of the Treasury, and of his telephone conversations with Democratic senators, singling out the Democratic Senator from New York, Bob Wagner. Toward the end of the letter Wise concluded that, "I think we have done what could be done."[219] On other occasions both Wise and Goldmann spoke of the limits to their public and political power in the United States during time of war, and ascribed the actual restrictions they faced in campaigning for rescue to their status as representatives of an ethnic minority in the American arena during a time of world war. Wise, Goldmann, and their colleagues in the Congress leadership felt that, according to their world view and given the prevailing circumstances in the United States during the 1940s, they had done all they could to rescue Jews during the Holocaust. The political partnership and close personal ties between Wise and Goldmann reinforce the impression that Wise's words were sincere, and that he firmly believed that no-one could have attained more in the struggle to rescue Jews during the Holocaust.[220]

Beginning in the latter half of the 1930s, the American Jewish public became far more ready to engage in Jewish and specifically Zionist activity, despite fearing rising anti-Semitism stemming from the economic crisis and the anti-Semitic propaganda emanating from Germany. Although American Jews were not quick to respond to Hitler's accession to power in 1933, early signs of a growing

---

tensions emerged between him and Wise following Wise's demand that he deals firmly with cases of corruption in the Democratic establishment. See Urofsky, *Wise*, 246–249.

218 On this issue, see Wise's letter to the State Department, March 31, 1941, AJA, 361 H295/2; and Tartakower's letter to a Jewish refugee in Porto, Portugal, about Wise's agreement to sign a financial guarantee for him, August 28, 1941, AJA, 361 H295/2.

219 Wise's letter to Goldmann, June 27, 1943, CZA 243/124.

220 It is indeed difficult to assess Goldmann's actions in the United States in the summer of 1943 dispassionately, when alongside his endeavors to promote the rescue of European Jews he took the time to submit an application to the State of New York to renew his fishing permit. Goldmann's letter to the Conservation Department, July 20, 1943, CZA, Z-6/18.

Zionist endeavor in the United States were now becoming discernible. There was sharp rise in the amount of money collected by the Jewish philanthropic foundations and the Zionist appeals in the early 1930s; membership of the women's Hadassah Organization increased considerably; a growing number of people were joining the Zionist movement; and even more were participating in Zionist events.[221] Fear of anti-Semitism in the United States grew alongside awareness of the deteriorating situation of Jews in Germany, of the burgeoning anti-Semitism in Central and Eastern Europe, and of the emerging rift between Britain and the Zionist movement. These factors enhanced the sense of Jewish solidarity and the willingness to engage in public and political activity as an ethnic group in the American arena.[222]

A guide to community action published by the Congress's women's league demonstrates the growing ethnic activity within the Jewish community in the wake of the Holocaust and World War II.[223] The document reports on the collection of thousands of tons of clothes for Jewish survivors, the struggle against racism in America, the encouragement of purchasing and reading the *Congress Weekly*, and dissemination of U.S. government bonds to fund the struggle against the Nazis. A large section of the guide is devoted to a gala dinner that was to be held in New York in honor of the Congress's women activists who had met their fundraising goals. The authors explain that the drama of the period necessitated setting a high standard, and that only women who had succeeded in raising fifty dollars or more would be permitted to attend the event. There would be none of the customary concessions and compromises. It appears that the contemporary public, too, felt that the previous standards of ethnic activity were irrelevant to the World War II period, and the new norms gave practical expression to the expansion of the Congress's activity in the United States.[224]

---

[221] For a similar assessment, see the memoirs of Eliyahu Elath (then Epstein), the Jewish Agency envoy to Washington and subsequently a senior functionary in Israel's foreign ministry, Eliyahu Eilat, *The Struggle for the State* [in Hebrew] (Tel Aviv, 1979), 98–99; David H. Shpiro, *From Philanthropy to Activism: The Political Transformation of American Zionism in the Holocaust Years 1933–1945* [in Hebrew] (New York, 1994), 1–22. The membership of Hadassah rose from 24,000 in 1933 to 66,000 in 1939. The Zionist Organization of America boasted 43,000 members in 1939, compared to just 9,000 in 1933. See Samuel Halperin, *The Political World of American Zionism* (Detroit, 1961), 20–28, 189–217, 327.
[222] For an example of such activity, see the movement for a boycott of German products in the United States: Yfaat Weiss, "The Transfer Agreement and the Boycott Movement: A Jewish Dilemma on the Eve of the Holocaust," *Yad Vashem Studies* 26 (1998): 129–171.
[223] A guide to action by the Congress's Women's League, February 1945 (no precise date given), AJA, 361 C68/5.
[224] Ibid.

These trends did not go unnoticed by the founders of the WJC, which had been established in 1936 as a democratic organization with a view to enhancing public activity undertaken by Jews as a distinct ethnic group to promote the well-being of Jews around the world. Its founders recognized the existence of a worldwide Jewry and the need to act on its behalf, but believed that Jewish political endeavor should not be left to those unacquainted with the intricacies of diplomatic and public activity—all the more so given the crisis of European Jewry and the Holocaust.

Two considerations drove the founders to seek to channel Jewish ethnic activity in the United States and the world at large in a manner that they deemed to be correct. The first was linked to their perception of the constraints upon ethnic politics in America. They believed that uncontrolled activity could do untold damage to the standing of the Jews in American society, and would thus also restrict their ability to act in the interests of European Jewry. This outlook is expressed in a lecture delivered by Wise in his New York synagogue in 1946[225]. He felt that there was no such thing as the Jewish vote in the political and social reality of American Zionism and of American Jewry. By this he meant that the Jewish public in America would not allow any political body to determine its voting patterns, and that Jewish voters cast their votes freely and were by no means a "flock of sheep that is led to the polling booth".[226] Wise stressed that American society comprised many ethnic and religious groups, and it was thus of great importance that ethnic groups not be identified with one particular party. For the sake of the unity of American society it was essential to ensure that the ethnic and religious groupings remained non-partisan, or at the least refrained from supporting only one party. Aware that he was associated with the Democratic establishment, Wise thus declared that he opposed the use of the Jewish vote in 1946 on principle, and not merely because this was directed against the Democratic Party. He added that he would oppose the use of the Jewish vote even if doing so were to assist the Democratic candidates. He furthermore emphasized that throughout his public career he had never used the Jewish vote to promote the interest of the Democratic Party. When he joined Roosevelt's campaign he had sought the support of all the country's citizens, irrespective of their religious affiliation, in the belief that Roosevelt's election would serve the interests of the entire country. Catholics, Jews, and Protestants should not vote according to their religious affiliation, but as Americans! Wise maintained that it was disingenuous to claim that the Jewish vote had been turned against the administration rather than in favor of the Republicans, since, given the two-party political system, opposition to one party

---

225 Wise's lecture at New York's free synagogue, November 1, 1946, CZA, A-243/42
226 Emphasis in the original.

inevitably led to support for the other. Zionist agitation against the Democratic administration had therefore meant voting for the Republicans and their candidates in the elections.[227]

Despite his declared opposition to the idea of consolidating the Jewish vote, Wise went on to appeal to the Jewish voting public to vote for Democratic candidates as Jews for singular Zionist and Jewish reasons. His use of a reasoning that spoke only to the Jewish voter demonstrates that, despite his proclamations to the contrary, Wise sought to galvanize a pro-Democratic Jewish vote. He accepted the claims that the Democratic administration had not acted with sufficient vigor on the Palestine question, but maintained that it was incorrect and unjust to assert that the Democratic administration was responsible for the failure of efforts to transfer one hundred thousand displaced persons from Europe to Palestine. The true culprit was neither the White House nor the State Department, but the British government, which, unlike the president or the State Department, held the keys to Palestine. Wise maintained that Truman's failure to transport the hundred thousand displaced persons to Palestine was attributable to a lack of political skill and did not indicate that he was insensitive to the fate of these people or that he opposed their immigration. And once again, attempting to blur his desire to galvanize the Jewish vote in favor of the Democrats, Wise declared that the Land of Israel was dear to the hearts of American Zionists, who would resist pressure to persuade them to vote merely along ethnic and religious lines. He was of the opinion that the use of racial and religious arguments was unwise, since it was, in the last resort, likely to harm the Zionist movement. He rejected the call to American Jews to vote solely on the strength of Zionist considerations without taking into account internal American problems and other aspects of United States foreign policy. He stressed that it would be a serious mistake to turn the American Zionist movement into a tool of American party politics.[228]

Wise's lecture is indicative of the tension that existed between his allegiance to the Democratic Party and the possibility of turning the Jewish vote against the Democratic establishment in the hope of winning political gains for the Zionist movement. A concerted effort to galvanize the Jewish voting public so as to exert pressure on the administration may benefit the Zionist movement and the campaign for the rescue of Jews, but was apt to damage the Democratic Party. Wise opposed such an effort in principle. He asserted that such a move would jeopardize the Jews' assimilation into American society and would facilitate racist and religious tendencies, which, in the general long-term view, could endanger the

---

227 Wise's lecture at New York's free synagogue, November 1, 1946, CZA, A-243/42. A transcript of the lecture was distributed to the Jewish and general American media.
228 Ibid.

American Jewish public.²²⁹ Wise's uncompromising opposition to the use of the Jewish vote in 1946 was thus a function of his apprehension that doing so would harm the Democratic Party, which was his political home. He tried to resolve the contradiction by resorting to the argument that underpinned his political artfulness, namely that a Democratic election victory would serve the future interests of the Zionist movement—whose political and social outlook was more compatible with that of the Democrats.

The second consideration underlying the WJC founders' approach was linked to their standing within the American political sphere and their political and public position. An overwhelming majority of American Jews was prepared to take action on behalf of European Jewry during World War II, to resolve the problem of the displaced persons, and eventually to establish a Jewish state. Within the reality of a bi-party political system, such action was inherently damaging to the Democratic administrations of Presidents Roosevelt and Truman, who were accused of having been callous to the fate of Europe's Jews prior to and following the war, and/or of being opposed to the establishment of a Jewish state. The practical consequence of this criticism of the Democratic regimes was to hand a political advantage to the Republican Party, something that ran contrary to the WJC founders' political and ideological outlook.²³⁰ The fact during the war years, Wise and Goldmann were prepared to step up action on behalf of the founding of a Jewish state to a greater extent than on intensifying the campaign for rescuing the Jews of Europe does not contradict their overall policy within the American arena, and in no way stemmed from a disregard for the fate of these Jews. Wise and Goldmann believed that although American Jewish activity in support of a Jewish state and thus challenging Roosevelt's regime was undesirable, it did not resemble activity promoting the rescue of Jews. The issue of Palestine was of importance to the Jewish public and engaged the decision makers in the administration, but did not possess the same public and political significance as the rescue issue. Naturally, the American war effort was high on the country's agenda and personally touched a significant proportion of American citizens. Wise and Goldmann thus assumed that forging a linkage between the United States' par-

---

229 Ibid.
230 It is beyond the scope of this book to survey the copious literature on the activity of ethnic groups in general and Jewish groups in particular within American politics. On the patterns of Jewish voting for Roosevelt and the Democratic Party, see Henry L. Feingold, "From Equality to Liberty: The Changing Political Culture of American Jews," in Robert M. Selter and Norman J. Cohen (eds.), *The Americanization of the Jews* (New York, 1995), 114–116. For a general discussion of voting patterns in general and ethnic voting patterns in particular, see Thomas Sowell, *The Economics and Politics of Race* (New York, 1973); Angus Campbell, *The American Voter* (New York, 1960).

ticipation in the war and the rescue of European Jewry would most likely serve the interests of the president's opponents and cause significant electoral damage to Democratic candidates and to the president during the various election campaigns of the 1940s. The Palestine issue, on the other hand, was not a burning national issue in America, did not personally impact every American citizen, and did not, therefore, encompass the same potential to harm the president, whose opponents could not exploit this issue to his detriment.

The complexity involved in conducting Jewish ethnic and public activity during World War II required Wise, Goldmann and their colleagues in the WJC leadership to construct an intricate public campaign that would enable more intensive action to be taken on behalf of founding a Jewish state than on the issue of rescue, while allowing them to control and to restrain activity on both matters. They believed that by so doing they would be serving two objectives at the same time. The first objective derived from their realization that the American Jewish public was eager to act in response to the events in Europe. Wise and Goldmann feared that stepping up public pressure on behalf of Europe's Jews was dangerous, and they thus channeled Jewish public action into the struggle for the establishment of a Jewish state. By so doing they lent their hand to intensifying ethnic Jewish activity that was harmful to Roosevelt's administration, yet did not impact his ability to fight the Nazis in Europe. The second objective is revealed in the papers of Wise and Goldmann, which show that they genuinely desired the founding of a Jewish state as part of the international arrangements to be put in place after World War II. They therefore conducted a complex and controlled ethnic effort within the American sphere that facilitated the struggle for the foundation of a Jewish state while attempting to limit as far as possible the damage it would inflict.[231]

In 1944, in the midst of the war and while the Germans were still murdering the Jews of Europe, Abba Hillel Silver, the American Jewish leader considered by contemporaries and scholars alike to have skillfully harnessed the shock and upheaval caused by the Holocaust to turn the American Jewish public into a political force that conducted a Herculean struggle for the founding of a Jewish state in Palestine, chose to lead a public campaign to promote the pro-Zionist resolutions in Congress, rather than resolutions calling for the rescue of European Jewry.[232]

---

[231] On the support offered by Wise and Goldmann toward the establishment of a Jewish state, see, for example, Wise's speech at the opening of the Congress convention at Atlantic City, November 26, AJA, 361 A67/8; and Goldmann's address on the same occasion.

[232] See Ben Gurion's comments on Silver's actions in the United States in 1944 and 1945, Ben Gurion at the Jewish Agency Executive meeting in Jerusalem, CZA, S-100. See also Raphael, *Silver*, 97–115.

Silver's choice demonstrates that despite his disagreement with Wise concerning the proper way of conducting ethnic politics in the United States, he in fact concurred with Wise's and Goldmann's assessment of the dire implications of placing the issue of the rescue of European Jews at the top of the public agenda. Therefore, rather than making an effort to submit resolutions to the Senate and the House of Representatives regarding the need to intensify the administration's actions on behalf of rescue, he chose to wage a public campaign calling for the establishment of a Jewish state.

As may be gleaned from his sermons in his Cleveland synagogue, Silver feared that World War II would be dubbed a "Jewish war," and was aware of the limitations and difficulty of waging a Jewish political campaign of an ethnic nature. He maintained that the public discourse on minorities in the United States contributed to the perpetuation of the problem rather than to its resolution. Engagement with this topic was recreating those negative social patterns of the old world that people had attempted to alter and improve upon during the building of American society. Europe had been plagued by the problem of minorities for centuries, whereas Americans had tried to resolve the issue by focusing on the rights of the individual rather than on those of the minorities. Silver claimed that America was occupied in protecting the rights of all human beings, irrespective of race, color, or creed. Americans should be measured by their personality and achievements and not by the ethnic or religious group to which they belonged. These issues were the private affair of each American citizen. This outlook had enabled the United States to absorb immigrants from hundreds of lands and to turn them into upstanding American citizens. These immigrants and their descendants were unconditionally loyal to America and many of them were to be found among the injured and the fallen whose names appeared each day in the press. Silver did not gloss over the problem of racism in American society, but stressed in particular the problems of the black minority and anti-Semitism. He attacked those who employed anti-Semitic arguments to oppose legislation on labor relations, national insurance, and the New Deal. American anti-Semites had disseminated propaganda that portrayed international Jewish banking as having pushed the United States into the war. The Jews were presented as bearing responsibility for the deep economic crisis, and of controlling the movie industry, broadcasting networks, and the Democratic Party.[233] Silver noted that the problem of racism had existed in the United States long before the rise of the Nazis to power. The problem of the blacks was created in the United States and had not been imported by foreign elements. Millions of American citizens were still suffering discrimina-

---

[233] On the prominence and stature of Jews in the American movie industry, see Neal Gabler, *An Empire of Their Own, How the Jews Invented Hollywood* (New York, 1988).

tion because of the color of their skin—and not only in the Southern states. Discrimination against the black population was demonstrated in all walks of life: in schools, churches, residential neighborhoods, hospitals, public transportation, and entertainment. Blacks were unable to find work according to their skills and the standard of living of most of them was low. Silver proposed undertaking extensive educational actions to combat racism, as well as passing decisive legislation outlawing racist activity in the United States.[234]

Silver returned to the issue of the Jewish vote in a further sermon he delivered in Cleveland in the midst of the contest for the Presidency between Roosevelt and Thomas Dewey in 1944. He stated that he had no wish to influence the way in which his congregation would vote or to induce members of the audience to support one or the other of the candidates, adding that he would not express public support for a particular candidate because of his position as head of the Emergency Council. He said that the Zionist movement as a whole had not taken sides since there was support for both parties among American Zionists. He noted that both the Democrats and the Republicans had included pro-Zionist sections in their platforms and that there were loyal supporters of the Zionist movement in both parties. Given its political situation, the Zionist movement needed to ensure support for both Republicans and Democrats and to cooperate with both of them. Silver maintained that it would be a political mistake to declare public support for either of the candidates, and emphasized that the leaders of both the parties and the presidential candidates themselves understood and accepted his position. Nevertheless, despite refraining from active involvement in the election, Silver continued, by virtue of his role as rabbi and as an American citizen, he wished to discuss certain issues that had arisen during the course of the 1944 campaign. He noted that topics linked to the questions of religion and race had been raised during this election, citing the example of the attacks on the Jewish labor leader Sidney Hilman, who figured prominently in Roosevelt's campaign. While a politician could, indeed, expect to be attacked by his opponents, Silver felt that the propaganda directed at Hilman was of a different order, and rejected in particular the emphasis placed on the fact that Hilman was an immigrant who had been born outside the United States. At a time when our sons were serving in the armed forces, he asserted, sustaining injuries and dying, the fact that they had been born beyond the borders of America was of no consequence whatsoever. Silver considered it to be an un-American act and a Nazi-like mode of operation to emphasize that a person was an immigrant, thus exploiting anti-Semitic sentiments and diverting attention from the cardinal issues. He warned that the use

---

234 Silver's sermon in his Cleveland synagogue on the topic of minority groups in American society, 1942 (no precise date given), Silver Archive, 5/600.

of Nazi methods in the United States was an ominous sign, and expressed his hope that American society had not been irreparably harmed and that the issue would disappear once the election campaign had come to an end. He concluded his sermon by reiterating that no Jewish issue was at stake in the election, and that American Jews would vote not as Jews, but as American citizens. The first objective of American Jews, as American citizens and as Jews, was to reject intolerant and un-American activity directed at them; for this reason they should vote as American citizens and for the best interests of the country.[235]

Silver's sermons indicate how careful he was in addressing the topic of the Jewish vote and the voting patterns of American Jews. His use of Hilman as an example is instructive. Like many among his audience, Silver himself was born beyond the borders of the United States, and believed that referring to Hilman as an immigrant rather than as an American citizen was likely to bring the social standing of many American Jews into question. Such fears may explain the disparity between the public pronouncements of Silver, Wise, and other American Jewish leaders, who tended to downplay the importance of the Jewish vote or even to deny its existence, and the discreet use they made of it.

One gains an appreciation of Silver's unease with regard to racist and sectarian tendencies within American society. He referred in particular to a series of anti-Semitic claims pertaining to the ability of American Jews to exert political influence on the administration. Given such sentiments, Silver, like Wise, feared that engagement in political activity on the part of the American Zionist movement, the operation of a Zionist lobby in Washington, and the exploitation of the Jewish vote could easily provide ammunition to anti-Semitic elements within the American political system and reinforce anti-Semitic tendencies in American society. Silver pointed out that the Jews were not the only ethnic minority to be subjected to sectarian and discriminatory treatment, and that such treatment was a structural problem in American society. It was difficult to combat so deep-rooted a phenomenon—a fact that increased concern that the Jews might be deprived of their status as equal citizens in American society and instead be regarded as an ethnic group whose loyalty to the United States was subject to

---

[235] Silver's sermon on the topic: "Thoughts on the Election Campaign and the Forthcoming Election", November 5, 1944, Silver Archive, 6/711. Additional topics raised by Silver in his lecture included the following: the advantages and drawbacks of the two-party system in the United States; the blurring of the differences between the two large parties; and the uniqueness of the continuing existence of American democracy. Despite Silver's denials of his involvement in the election campaign, the Jewish press published reports suggesting that the pro-Zionist declaration by the Republican presidential candidate Dewey had been made following his meeting with Silver. See "Dewey Issues Statement after Conference with Rabbi Silver," *The Jewish Post*, October 20, 1944.

question. Silver's analysis affords a further perspective on the motives that drove him, Wise, and Goldmann to try to downplay the campaign for the rescue of European Jews. Emphasizing such a campaign could, according to their assessment, have brought only modest achievements in terms of rescue, but could very well serve both as a tool with which to harm Roosevelt's presidency and to turn American Jews into a minority that was unable to use its position as the largest Jewish community in the world to promote the interests of Jews worldwide.

Within the political and social reality of the early 40s, the founders of the WJC in America did not think of themselves as different, in many respects, from the Jewish financial elites of German origin represented by the American Jewish Committee or from Jews who occupied senior positions in the Democratic administration. These elites shared the same interests, which were generally associated with their support for the Democratic Party and/or for desirable ways of integrating Jews into American society. The growth of distinct Jewish ethnic activity during the thirties was inimical to their outlook, and was likely to encourage Jews to stray from what they perceived to be the desirable way to implement this integration. It was for this reason that they founded the World Jewish Congress, which in effect worked in close cooperation with these established elites.[236]

The term "congress" was deliberately chosen for the organization in order to convey to the broad Jewish public the sense that this was a democratic body committed to enhancing the public and political presence of Jews as an ethnic minority operating for the good of world Jewry. In fact, however, from the late 1930s onward, the WJC conducted itself in a different, non-democratic, manner designed to enable its leaders to conduct independent political activity free of supervision, and to guide the ethnic activity of the American Jewish public in the correct direction as they perceived it. Yet this inclination in fact moved the WJC away from activity on behalf of world Jewry and reduced the influence of non-establishment bodies such as the Bergson group, which operated independently of the American Jewish community's organizational structure, refused to accept the authority of Zionist institutions in the United States, and engaged in a militant campaign against the apathy and ineffectiveness of the American administration with regard to the rescue of Jews during the Holocaust period.[237]

In a letter to Gruenbaum, who was introduced in Chapter 1, Nahum Goldmann described a series of Jewish public activities in the early 1940s that had allowed the broad Jewish public to "let off steam" by creating an impression of public

---

[236] For a different view on this issue, see Gulie Ne'eman Arad, *America, Its Jews, and the Rise of Nazism* (Bloomington, 2000).

[237] On Goldmann's efforts to suppress the Bergson group, see Goldmann's letter to Shertok, May 19, 1944, CZA, Z-6/27755.

action, but in effect obviated the danger of harming the Democratic Party and President Roosevelt's administration by closely adhering to the boundaries that the WJC itself had set by refraining from employing the Jewish vote in a manner that its activists believed could damage their standing within American society. The singular position of world Jewry from the early 1930s onward, and the stature of the American Jewish community at this time as the largest and most powerful in the world, induced the Jewish public in the United States to act within ethnic political boundaries and to make its voice heard on behalf of Europe's persecuted Jews. Yet this tendency highlighted the problems that could emerge from such patterns of ethnic political activism. Given these circumstances, the Jewish leadership felt obliged to set up new organizational structures with a view to ensuring that these patterns of Jewish activism would not exceed what they considered to be desirable for the Jews and compatible with their political and public status within American society as a whole.[238]

---

238 A similar debate concerning the circumstances in which the Rescue Committee was founded is ongoing. Opinion is divided on the question whether it was an important tool in organizing rescue operations in the *yishuv*, or merely a means of defusing the frustration felt by the Jewish public in Palestine. See Frilling, Ben Gurion, 184–204.

Figure 1: A poster advertising the Foster Parents Plan for European Jewish Children. AJA, 361 J11/5.

Figure 2: Photographs of children hidden with peasant families in the Foster Parents Plan for European Jewish Children. AJA, 361 J11/5.

Figure 3: World Jewish Congress Children Division, 1946. AJA, 361 J11/5.

Figure 4: Nahum Goldmann. AJA, 361 J13/24.

Figure 5: Stephen Wise. AJA, 361 J14/23.

Figure 6: Program cover of the War Emergency Conference, Atlantic City, N.J., 26-30 November 1944. AJA, 361 J17/1.

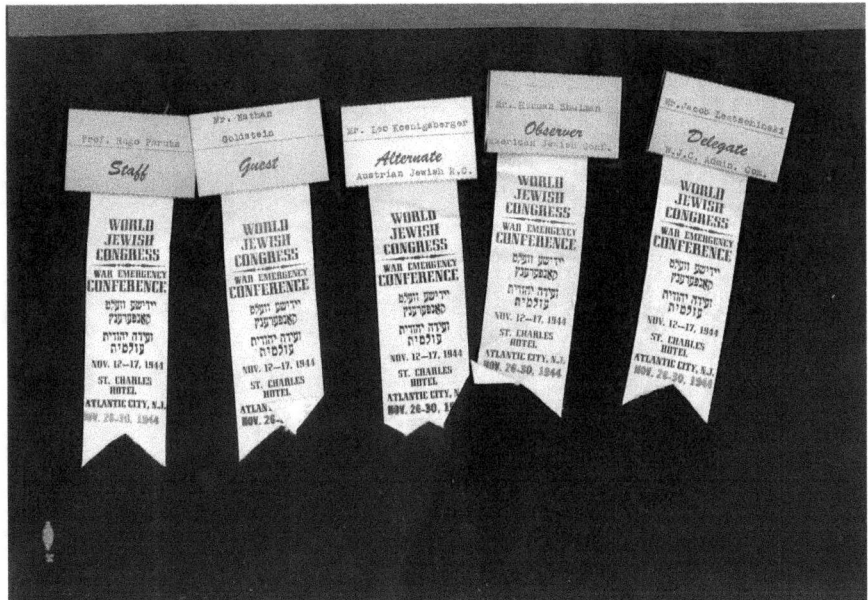

Figure 7: Participant tags of the War Emergency Conference, Atlantic City, N.J., 26-30 November, 1944. AJA, 361 J17/1.

Figure 8: Poster of the American Committee for the Rehabilitation of European Jewish Children. AJA, 361 J18/1.

Figure 9: War Emergency Conference at the St. Charles Hotel, Atlantic City, N.J., 26-30 November 1944.

Chapter 3
The World Jewish Congress's Rescue Effort

The "Soul Searching" Conference in Atlantic City

The wartime conference of the World Jewish Congress convened in Atlantic City in 1944. This was the first international Jewish gathering to take place since the outbreak of the war and was attended by delegates from 26 countries. They came from the United States, Palestine, South America, and the European countries that had been liberated from Nazi occupation. Even emissaries who had managed to escape from Jewish communities in areas that were still under Nazi control attended. Fifteen hundred people gathered for the opening evening to hear speeches delivered by Stephen Wise and Nahum Goldmann.[239] The WJC conference convened in the shadow of the reports on the horrendous dimensions of the loss even as the killing in Europe continued. This backdrop imparts particular importance to the minutes of the conference, brings the debates held there into relief, and illuminates the problems with which the WJC leadership contended during the Holocaust period. The records of the Atlantic City conference afford historians a singular opportunity to examine the outlooks of those in the United States involved in activity on behalf of the Jews of Europe as events were unfolding. Many of the debates held at the Atlantic City conference were devoted to critical assessment of the actions taken by American Jews, particularly by the WJC leadership, to rescue Jews during the Holocaust. Leon Kubowitzki, a native of Lithuania who migrated to the United States in 1940 and who directed the Congress's rescue effort in Europe, delivered one of the key speeches at the conference.[240] Kubowitzki estimated that five and a half million Jews had been murdered by the Nazis. American Jews and the WJC leadership had not even succeeded in slowing the pace of this mass murder and Kubowitzki termed the effort a total failure. Yet at the same time, and despite the dreadful sense of failure, Kubowitzki added a reservation to the effect that the WJC was under an obligation to itself and to future generations to explain the rescue enterprise from the

---

[239] See the press statement on the conference, November 1944 (no precise date given), AJA, 361 A68/4.
[240] Kubowitzki's speech at the Atlantic City conference, November 26, 1944, AJA, 361 A68/2. Kubowitzki immigrated to Israel in 1948 and occupied senior positions in Israel's Foreign Ministry. In 1959 he was appointed Chairman of Yad Vashem, continuing in this role until his death. To appreciate the significance of Kubowitzki's work at Yad Vashem one should note that the WJC was closely involved in establishing the body. See, for example, Minutes of Meeting on the topic of Yad Vashem, October 28, 1948, AJA, 361 D104/2.

point of view of the organization's leaders. He noted that history would judge the WJC leadership according to two major issues: whether it could have rescued more Jews, and to what extent had the leadership contributed to the rescue of those Jews who had managed to escape or to survive the Nazi inferno. Kubowitzki foresaw that even were one to conclude that it had been impossible to rescue more Jews, it would be unbearably difficult first to come to terms with the huge disparity between the number of those murdered and the number of survivors, and second to accept that the Congress leadership had been unable to persuade the Allies to take meaningful steps to assist the Jews.[241]

The policy of restraining the public campaign for rescue that the WJC leadership conducted in the United States during the war years added to the immense difficulty of coming to terms with the Jewish tragedy in Europe. This policy created the impression that the action taken to assist European Jews had been muted. Many of the speakers in Atlantic City were indeed scathingly critical of the actions of WJC leaders during the Holocaust. One representative of Polish Jewry stated that:

> Of course, the World Jewish Congress is a wonderful organization, but we have sinned, we have committed a mortal sin, we are mortally guilty. I have not heard one resolution yet that has any teeth in it. We ought to stand at the mourning biers and beg forgiveness from our dead. Every one of us here is partially to blame for these slaughters. None of the punishments of war crimes that we talk about will be of any avail if we do not take upon ourselves some of the guilt.[242]

Despite the sense of opprobrium manifest at the conference, the policy of restraining public activity on behalf of rescue in the United States was the conspicuous element of intensive efforts to come to the aid of Europe's Jews prior to the outbreak of World War II, during the war years, and following its conclusion, when assistance was given to the displaced persons. Other minutes of the Atlantic City conference, as well as other archival sources pertaining to WJC activity during the Holocaust period, demonstrate that alongside the policy of restraint, the WJC conducted extensive discreet diplomatic activity on behalf of European Jews and set up clandestine and underground machinery to engage in rescue. This sphere

---

241 Kubowitzki's speech, November 26, 1944. About Kubowitzki's proposal to bomb Auschwitz see, Breitman and Lichtman, *FDR*, 281–282. For a general discussion about this issue see, Breitman and Lichtman, *FDR*, 281–288.
242 Minutes of the Congress conference in Atlantic City, November 26–30, 1944, AJA, 361 A67/3. Other delegates at the conference asserted that responsibility for the terrible loss rested on the WJC in general and on its leaders in particular. See the address of another Polish delegate, AJA, 361 A67/5.

of activity complemented rather than vied with the policy of restraint and was, in effect, a part of it. The WJC leaders believed that clandestine, underground diplomatic activity was preferable not merely because it accorded with the policy of restraint, but because it was the only way to rescue Jews. This approach is detailed in a memorandum pertaining to the rescue of Jews composed by the Congress's Rescue department in March 1944, which states: "The rescue of Jews from the clutches of the Nazis now falls for the most on commando and guerila warfare. For example, there is no legal way, with the exception of exchange to get a Jew out of Nazi occupied Europe."[243]

Nahum Goldmann responded to the criticism in similar fashion—particularly to that leveled by the Polish delegates regarding the policy of restraint that he and Wise had led in the United States—and their failure to rescue a greater number of Jews from the Nazi horror. While he understood the indignation and anger expressed by these delegates, he pointed out the differences between the patterns of political action adopted by the Congress leadership—and by him and Wise in particular—and those employed by rank and file members of the Congress. He noted that "certainly it is easier for them to let their feelings come forward here since they are not in a political activity. It is easier for them to indulge themselves by releasing their emotions than for Dr. Wise, the Presidium or me."[244]

Goldmann continued to display his understanding of the anger and frustration expressed by many speakers at the conference, but stressed that one could not conduct political activity that was driven by such feelings. He referred to the Riegner telegram episode as a test case that clarified his position. We may deduce from Goldmann's address that many of the conference delegates were critical of Wise's acquiescence to the demand of Undersecretary of State Sumner Welles that he delay public revelation of the information contained in the telegram in 1942 until the competent officials in the State Department and in the American embassies and consulates in Europe had verified the dramatic news. Goldmann explained that Wise's initial inclination upon receiving the telegram had been to publicize the information forthwith. He had, however, been obliged to delay public revelation of the material because publicizing the telegram without the authorization of the State Department would have had dire ramifications for the WJC's ability to take action to rescue Jews. He explained that during wartime, the WJC leadership in the United States could maintain contact with its European

---

[243] Memorandum of the World Jewish Congress submitted to the War Refugee Board, March 3, 1944, AJA, 361 A68/2. About the failure of the political efforts to bomb Auschwitz. See, Friling, *Ben Gurion*, 767–768.
[244] Goldmann's statements in the minutes of the debates at the Atlantic City conference, November 26–30, 1944 (no precise date given), AJA, 361 A67/3.

bureaus only through the State Department's communications network. Unauthorized publication of the Riegner telegram, which had been sent through the American consulate in Bern, would have meant that it would be the last telegram sent in this manner, and would in fact have put an end to the WJC's entire European operation.[245]

Four days before the Riegner telegram was dispatched to Wise, a letter from the U.S. Consulate in Geneva arrived at Riegner's Geneva office,[246] informing him that the American embassy in Bern had not been given permission from the State Department in Washington to transfer the reports on German plans to exterminate the Jews of Europe to Stephen Wise in New York. The reason given for the refusal was that the information contained in the telegram was unreliable and had not been confirmed by other sources. This communication from the embassy in Bern adds a further dimension to the information previously available regarding the attempts on the part of the State Department to prevent dispatch of the report in the first place and subsequently to delay its dissemination.[247]

Wise took steps to disseminate the information covertly despite the State Department's opposition. Acting on Wise's behalf, WJC representatives in Europe approached Czechoslovakian President Edvard Benes and informed him of the appalling news that had arrived from Switzerland.[248] Following this meeting, a representative of Czechoslovakian Foreign Minister Jan Masaryk wrote to Wise likewise requesting him to delay publication of the information and not to distribute it freely. The leaders of the Czechoslovakian government-in-exile also believed it was highly likely that the information was erroneous. The letter raised speculation that the report might be an effort by the Nazi propaganda machine to generate an anti-German chain reaction among Jews and non-Jews in Europe that would enable the Germans to intensify their actions against local populations. Benes was quoted in the letter as having questioned the credibility of the information on the grounds that were the Germans indeed implementing an overall move to exterminate European Jewry, this information would have already reached him from other sources. Despite these doubts, he promised to make every effort to check the veracity of the information contained in the Riegner telegram.[249]

---

245 Ibid.
246 Letter from the American Consul in Geneva, Paul C. Squire, to Riegner, August 24, 1942, AJA, 361 A8/11.
247 . On the US State Department and the Riegner telegram, see Wyman, *The Abandonment of the Jews*, 42–45.
248 For information about the approach, see the letter of reply written by the envoy of Czech Foreign Minister Jan Masaryk to Wise, October 5, 1942, AJA, 361 A27/2.
249 Ibid.

The U.S. State Department's refusal to pass the information on to Wise four days before it actually reached New York and the Czechoslovak president's request to delay publication of the telegram indicate the magnitude of the political pressure exerted on Wise to concede to these demands. As becomes evident in the series of considerations that Goldmann laid out in Atlantic City, Wise felt that he had no choice but to comply with the State Department's decision Yet the letter Wise received from the Czechoslovak Foreign Ministry reveals that the head of the WJC in fact chose to operate clandestinely, in disregard of the State Department's orders, and to disseminate the information in the Reigner telegram. WJC representatives approached the president of Czechoslovakia, thereby contravening State Department instructions not to distribute the information. The Czechoslovak leaders' refusal to cooperate with Wise and their demand, which echoed that of the State Department, to put publication of the Riegner telegram on hold added to the already considerable difficulty that Wise, as president of the WJC, confronted in his attempts to distribute the dramatic news of the extermination of Europe's Jews.

Perusal of the papers of the WJC reveals an additional occasion on which the organization's leaders chose to prevent dissemination of the information that had reached them regarding events in Europe on grounds that they defined as political. Toward the end of 1943, the Congress's bureau in Lisbon, Portugal, received a report of the atrocities committed by Poles on Jews in Polish territory.[250] During consultations between the WJC offices in Portugal and New York, it was decided to delete the references to atrocities in the information disseminated to rank-and-file WJC activists around the world. The correspondence between Lisbon and New York indicates that the WJC leadership was fearful of damaging the cooperation between their organization and the Polish government-in-exile. The heads of the WJC made a point of informing the Polish government of the material in their possession and requested it to take action to modify the Polish population's treatment of the Jews via the underground forces operating in occupied Poland. They were of the opinion that such action would be more effective than publicizing the report, which would be of no benefit and could only embarrass the exiled Polish government, damage the ongoing relations with it, and compromise the strengthening of these ties in the future.[251]

The case of the suppression of information about the atrocities committed by Poles against Jews highlights the dilemmas that emerged from the Atlantic City debate and further underlines the reasons for the trenchant criticism that

---

[250] See the classified summary of the contacts between New York and Lisbon in Kubowitzki's report, January 4, 1944, AJA, 361 H296/2.
[251] Ibid.

WJC delegates leveled at their leadership. The heads of the WJC had decided to delay publication of the Reigner telegram, refrained from criticizing the Roosevelt regime's handling of the rescue effort at the press conference in April 1943, and suppressed altogether the reports of atrocities committed by Poles against Jews in Polish territory. The documents available to scholars show that the heads of the organization firmly believed in good faith that their mode of operation in all three cases was the only correct one. They felt that it was their duty as Jewish leaders at a time of crisis to take responsibility and refrain from making the information public. In all these cases, they believed, the benefit to be derived by revealing the information was negligible in comparison to the extensive and significant damage that could have been done to the Congress's clandestine rescue endeavor. On the other hand, as the Atlantic City debates clearly reveal, the rank-and-file Congress members and even delegates to the organization's conference believed that the leaders had no right to filter as they saw fit the information that reached them by virtue of their position. It may be assumed that the emphasis placed on democratic modes of operation upon the founding of the Congress served to exacerbate the anger felt by the organization's members toward its leaders for having concealed such supremely important information from them. Judging by the utterances of Kubowitzki and Goldmann at the Atlantic City conference, WJC leaders were clearly aware of the anger felt by the delegates in general and American Jews in particular, and surmised that future generations would likewise find them badly wanting. This assessment reinforces the impression that the Congress leaders were convinced that they had acted properly and were prepared to pay the public and personal price that this entailed.

In order to impress upon his audience the extent of the WJC's dependence on the various arms of the United States administration, particularly of the State Department, during the war, Goldmann told them how exceedingly difficult it was to transfer money from the United States to the organization's offices in neutral countries and from there to occupied Europe with a view to financing the effort to rescue Jews. During wartime it was impossible to transfer money through regular banking channels. Moreover, the transfer of a significant amount of money from America to occupied European countries was labeled by U.S. law as a monetary transfer to enemy lands and required the authorization of the president, the Treasury, and the State Department. Goldmann explained further that even if the president were to authorize the transfer, the Treasury and the State Department could delay the process on various grounds, and that the cooperation of its officials was vital to the success of so complex a transaction. He stressed that the WJC was obliged to operate within U.S. law and it was thus unrealistic to expect it to undertake illegal activity in the United States. Goldmann added that there was an enormous difference between conducting illegal activity in the United States and doing so in Europe during World War II. As will be made clear later in this chapter, the Congress successfully undertook underground activity in occupied European countries and in neutral states, but did this with the support and backing of the institutions of the State Department and of the Allied Forces. Activity of this sort could not be carried out in the United States itself.[252]

Congress documents reveal that Goldmann's explanation of the matter of money transfers to Europe was based on fact, and that the ability to transfer money to Europe was a necessary condition for conducting the rescue effort. After holding meetings with the Polish government-in-exile and members of the Polish underground, Congress leaders concluded that it was highly unlikely that money transferred to Poland would reach its destination and be used to rescue Jews; they therefore decided to focus the rescue endeavor on Western and Central European countries occupied by the Germans.[253] Millions of Swiss francs were dispatched to the WJC bureau in Switzerland; from there the money was transferred to various countries—chief among them France, Belgium and Holland—to be used to rescue and hide Jews. Hundreds of thousands of U.S. dollars were likewise sent to the Congress's Lisbon office to fund the smuggling of Jewish children to Spain and Portugal, and tens of thousands of dollars were transferred to the Slovakian underground to fund child-smuggling operations. Considerable sums were transferred to Italy, where they were used to enable the escape and concealment of children in that country, and thousands of dollars were paid in bribes in Romania.[254]

The record of a meeting held in summer 1943 between Tartakower and Captain Foulis of the Office of Economic Warfare gives us an inkling of the daunting bureaucratic hurdles confronted by WJC representatives as they strove to transfer

---

[252] Goldmann's statements in the minutes of the debates at the Atlantic City conference, November 26–30, 1944 (no precise date given), AJA, 361 A67/3.
[253] For an example of such a conclusion, see the records of a meeting between the heads of the WJC and Jan Karski, an emissary of the Polish underground, September 10, 1943, AJA, 361 H287/3.
[254] See the following documents: for information on the transfer of millions of Swiss francs by the WJC to Switzerland for the rescue effort, see the secret telegram from Riegner to Wise sent through the United States consulate in Bern, May 10, 1944, AJA, 361 H294/5. For a comprehensive report on the transfer of money, transfer of for rescue purposes in Europe, see Report of the Rescue Committee of the WJC submitted to the Atlantic City conference, November 26–30, 1944, AJA 361 A68/2. On the extent of the transfer of money, transfer of to Europe by the WJC, see the report by Arie Tartakower on his two month long visit to Britain, January 6, 1944, AJA 361 A1/4. On the transfer of money from the United States to Lisbon in order to undertake rescue operations there, see telegram from the WJC's Lisbon office to the organization's New York Executive, April 10, 1944, AJA 361 H294/5. A memorandum to the WJC's executive committee was brought by a refugee arriving from Lisbon, April 19, 1944, AJA 361 H294/5.

funds to Europe.²⁵⁵ Tartakower was attempting to send between $200,000 and $300,000 to Switzerland. The money was to be transferred to the International Red Cross to be used to send food parcels to Poland. Tartakower stressed that it was essential to transfer the money to the Red Cross in Switzerland since that organization lacked the funds required to finance the sending of the parcels, and without the money from the United States it would be impossible to dispatch the food to Poland. That same day, after meeting with Foulis, Tartakower held a long series of meetings with American Red Cross functionaries and with senior officials at the Civilian Internees Department of the United States Department of Defense. While the meetings were conducted in good spirits, Tartakower was told that final authorization of the transfer was required from the State Department and the Department of Defense. The complexity of the challenge facing Tartakower is revealed in his report of the discussion he held with senior officials concerning the legal status of the prospective Jewish recipients of the packages. Tartakower's interlocutors maintained that if the recipients of the packages were Polish citizens it would not be possible to employ the machinery of the International Red Cross to support them. They explained that according to the Geneva Convention, the Red Cross could not assist citizens arrested by their own country. To Tartakower's astonishment, they claimed that the Jews held by the Germans in camps in Poland were Polish citizens who had in fact been apprehended by the Polish government, and that it was thus impossible to send them food parcels through the International Red Cross. Tartakower explained that, first of all, not all the prisoners were Polish nationals, and that the Jewish detainees who were Polish citizens had been arrested by the German government and were thus entitled to the support of the International Red Cross. The officials, convinced by this argument, were happy to assist in the matter, promising to submit memoranda in support of the application to the State Department, and adding that the money would be transferred to Switzerland through the American Red Cross as soon as authorization from the State Department was received.²⁵⁶

Tartakower's report on his Washington meetings in the summer of 1943 demonstrates the difficult task that faced Congress functionaries as they attempted to dispatch food and money to the Jews of Europe. Tartakower emphasizes that the officials with whom he met genuinely sought to cooperate with the WJC. Still, they did not grasp the full significance of the implementation of the final solution with which the Germans were proceeding with increased vigor in the summer of 1943, even though reports of this development had reached the United States in the summer of 1942. This state of affairs made it difficult for the

---

255 Tartakower's report on his meetings in Washington, August 2, 1943, AJA, 361 B1/6.
256 Ibid.

WJC functionaries to break through the bureaucratic constraints that arose from the circumstances of a world war.

The World Jewish Congress could not conduct rescue operations in Europe without the monies sent from the United States, and the money could only be transferred subsequent to the prolonged process of receiving authorizations from various arms of the administration. To the administration, this was a matter of transferring American money to enemy countries during a time of war, which entailed maintenance of contacts with various elements in these enemy countries and in countries under German occupation—a process that was, of course, totally forbidden.[257]

The WJC papers pertaining to the transfer of funds from the United States to Europe continue to reveal the complexity of the rescue work engaged in by a public organization of a primarily philanthropic nature in the midst of a world war. A report by the WJC on its rescue efforts mentions a request submitted by the Geneva office headed by Riegner for tens of thousands of dollars in order to fund rescue activity in Romania and France during April 1943. Upon receipt of the request, the New York office sent urgent applications to the Department of the Treasury and to the State Department, which initially refused to authorize the request. Following intervention by the president, authorizations were received from both the State Department and the Treasury. Having obtained the necessary authorizations from all the U.S. authorities, the WJC leadership then had to deal with opposition on the part of Great Britain, which was concerned lest the money dispatched to Europe fall into the hands of the Germans or their allies, thereby weakening the economic blockade of Germany.[258] The final authorization arrived only on December 18, 1943. It read as follows:

> In order to arrange for the Evacuation to places of safety of persons in France and Rumania whose lives are in imminent danger and, pending possible evacuation, to sustain and safeguard the lives of such persons, your representative in Switzerland (including such agents as he may appoint) is hereby licensed notwithstanding the provisions of General Ruling No. 11 to communicate with persons in France and Rumania in any manner he deems necessary or expedient and to take all other appropriate action, including the payment to persons in France of French francs and the payment to persons in Rumania of Rumanian lei for goods and services.[259]

---

[257] On the prohibition published in general ruling no. 11, see a summary of the rescue activities of the World Jewish Congress 1940–1944, submitted by Leon Kubowitzki to the WJC conference at Atlantic City, November 26–30, 1944, AJA, 361 A68/2.
[258] Ibid.
[259] Ibid.

Thus did one of the significant bureaucratic processes conducted discreetly behind the scenes, but which was vital to the rescue of European Jews culminate in dry, legalistic language—carefully failing to mention that the objective of the money transfer was to rescue Jews. The document was important in that it did not limit the money transfer to a single event, nor did it specify that it should be conducted by a specific individual. Rather, it granted sweeping authorization for the transfer of money by WJC functionaries throughout the war years. This was the first document of its kind to be issued by the United States Department of the Treasury to a private organization, and paved the way for the WJC and other Jewish organizations to transfer funds in the remaining years of the war.

Philanthropy and Politics: The World Jewish Congress and the Jews of Europe 1936–1942

The debates at the 1944 WJC conference in Atlantic City focused primarily on criticism of the ineffectiveness of the WJC's leadership and institutions since 1942, when its leaders first heard of the Holocaust of European Jewry. Most scholarly debate on Stephen Wise, Nahum Goldmann and their colleagues likewise focuses on those years and levels similar criticism at them. The particular attention paid to the debate over the WJC's actions during the Holocaust years is understandable. However, a better understanding of the Congress's patterns of activity from 1942 onward—when they were aware of the Holocaust of European Jewry—may be gained by perusing WJC papers regarding the second half of the 1930s. These documents reveal that despite the significant differences between the two periods and the fact (elaborated below) that the WJC fairly rapidly adopted new modes of operation in early 1943, the same modes of political and organizational deportment had characterized the organization from its inception in 1936, through the outbreak of World War II, up to the endeavor to rescue the Jews of Europe once information on the Holocaust had reached the United States.

The organization's leaders began a political campaign on behalf of Europe's Jews immediately after convening its inaugural conference in August 1936. The main political effort focused on the American sphere with a view to persuading the administration, particularly the State Department, to convey to the Polish and Romanian governments that the United States viewed the attacks on the Jewish minority in those countries with disfavor and that it requested these governments to protect the rights of the Jews in accordance with the commitments they had made when signing the peace treaty at the end of the World War I.[260] The heads

---

[260] Classified letter from Goldmann to Wise, December 17, 1936, AJA, 361 A1/1.

of the WJC sought to exploit Wise's personal and political ties with Jewish figures such as Frankfurter and Brandeis in order to activate them within the corridors of the administration for the benefit of Poland's and Romania's Jews. During the course of clandestine meetings held by Congress representatives with senior administration figures in Romania and Poland, the latter conveyed to the emissaries that American pressure on the two countries was a powerful political tool that had the potential to bring about significant improvement in the condition of the Jews there.[261]

The WJC leadership was also active in the institutions of the League of Nations, where the organization's functionaries emphasized the League's obligation to protect the rights of minorities in general and those of European Jews in particular. They maintained that since the issue of minority rights was high on the League's agenda, it was obligated to promote the rights of Jews not only among its members, but also in non-member countries. This position enabled Congress leaders to demand that the League protect the rights of Germany's Jews, even though Germany had left the League.[262]

Despite the League of Nation's significant inherent structural problems, which came to the fore in the latter half of the 1930s, the WJC's leaders went out of their way to operate in this arena. The grave state of Europe's Jews left them no choice in the matter; they sought every available channel through which to ameliorate their situation. They thus made energetic efforts at the League's September 1938 assembly in Geneva. They held meetings with the British deputy foreign minister, senior members of the Romanian regime, and League of Nations functionaries responsible for addressing the refugee issue, among others.[263]

In 1937 WJC representatives in Europe held an internal meeting in Vienna.[264] The participants felt that the situation of Polish Jews was the worst in Europe and termed it tragic. At the conclusion of the meeting they decided not to publicize a resolution regarding the Jews of Poland, fearing that such a pronouncement would spark a sharp reaction on the part of the Polish regime and would endanger Congress emissaries operating in the country. However, a decision was made

---

261 Ibid.
262 Memorandum of the Executive Committee of the World Jewish Congress to the League of Nations committee dealing with the organization's charter, December 16, 1936, AJA, 361 A1/2. In order to impress upon the League's institutions the seriousness of the plight of the Jews in Germany and in Eastern Europe, WJC leaders made a point of passing on to them information on the deteriorating economic condition of Europe's Jews. See the memorandum of the WJC's Economic Committee submitted to the League of Nations, March 14, 1937, AJA, 361 A9/3.
263 Report on the activities of the Executive Committee of the WJC September – October 1938, October 15, 1938, AJA 361 A1/1.
264 For a report on the meeting, see Goldmann's letter to Wise, May 25, 1937, AJA 361 A27/1.

to step up clandestine efforts on behalf of Polish Jewry.[265] Consequently, WJC spokesmen in Europe held meetings with the foreign ministers of Poland, Italy, Romania, and Czechoslovakia.[266] Of particular interest are the secret meetings that Nahum Goldmann held with the French Prime Minister Leon Blum during the second half of 1937. Goldmann's objective was to have the French exert pressure on the Polish government to improve its treatment of the Jews. Congress leaders felt that French intervention was essential because the ongoing political instability in Poland was likely to exacerbate the regime's anti-Semitic policy as it sought to curry favor with the gentile Polish public. The WJC leadership especially sought French and British intervention to remove Foreign Minister Jozef Beck from his key position in the Polish leadership. Beck was a member of the troika that governed Poland following the death of Jozef Pilsudski in May 1935. Beck led a pro-German policy in Poland and opposed the minorities contract, and the WJC's leadership thus believed that his removal from power or restriction of his authority would be a significant step toward improving the lot of Poland's Jews.[267] Later in 1937, representatives of the Congress executive committee met with the French foreign minister's Chief of Bureau Rochat prior to Foreign Minister Yvon Delbos's forthcoming visit to Poland and Romania in December of that year.[268] They maintained that the Jewish question in Poland had become a yardstick and a symbol of the struggle between the fascist and democratic forces in the country, and that the French government was therefore obliged not merely to support Polish Jews on moral grounds, but also to assist the democratic forces there. As to Romania, the Congress representatives asserted that Romania's Jews were preparing to submit an affidavit to the League of Nations requesting League protection because of their intolerable situation. They foresaw that such a step would lead to a rift between the regime in Romania and the League of Nations and would reinforce fascist tendencies in the country. Thus, in this instance too, it was in the French government's supreme interest to moderate the Romanian

---

265 WJC leaders received reliable information on what was happening in Poland. Nahum Goldmann visited the country in 1936 and met with Jews and with key members of the Polish regime. On the visit, see Kubowitzki, *World Jewish History*, 94–95. At the same time, the Congress leaders received information in the form of letters sent not only by the organization's operatives but also by other constituents in the Jewish and Zionist world who recognized the importance of the WJC's work in Poland. See a classified letter from Baruch Zuckerman, a leader of the labor movement in the United States who was staying in Poland, to Wise, February 13, 1937, AJA, 361 A9/1.
266 On these meetings, see a classified report on the political activity of the WJC leadership in Europe, 1937 (no precise date given), AJA, 361 A5/1.
267 On the political activity in Europe, see Goldmann's letter to Wise, May 25, 1937, AJA 361 A27/1.
268 See the classified report of the meeting submitted to the Congress executive, November 29, 1937, AJA, 361 A6/9.

government's anti-Jewish policy in order to prevent a widening of the rift between Romania and the democratic forces.[269]

At their meeting with the minister's chief of bureau, WJC emissaries stressed the political advantages that would accrue to France if it supported the Jews of Poland and Romania. In attempting to persuade the French government to take action on behalf of the Jews of Poland and Romania, they did not raise moral aspects or invoke the fundamental right of Jews to equal civil rights. They probably felt that such arguments would not spur the French to take action of this kind, and were thus obliged to create a political world picture in which action to assist Jews would serve French interests. This approach provides an additional perspective on the dire straits in which European Jewry found itself, and the stern and complex challenge entailed in the conduct of political lobbying on their behalf.

In addition to their contacts with France, senior functionaries in the WJC cultivated ties with opposition elements in Poland who they felt could counteract the country's anti-Semitic policy. They believed it was essential to take action on behalf of Polish Jews within Europe as a whole as well as in Poland itself, an approach that set the WJC apart from other philanthropic bodies, and particularly from the American Jewish Joint Distribution Committee (JDC). Congress leaders believed that political activity would in the last resort be far more effective in ameliorating the condition of Poland's Jews than the vast sums that the JDC was funneling to them.

The meeting with the bureau chief of the French foreign minister was not the only occasion on which WJC functionaries in Europe, especially Goldmann, tried to turn the question of East European Jews into an international political issue that transcended traditional philanthropic assistance to Jews in need. Goldmann's meeting with the Polish ambassador to Washington in mid-January 1939 is a case in point.[270] Goldmann began by telling the ambassador of the close ties between Polish and American Jews, stressing that the condition of the Jews in Poland was causing deep concern among the American Jewish public, which could take action toward harming Poland's economic and political interests in the United States. He stated that the WJC and other Jewish organizations were prepared to cooperate with the Polish government only on condition that it ceased the systematic discrimination against Polish Jews and desisted from pressuring them to migrate against their will. Goldmann preempted the ambassador by saying that any claim that the Polish constitution contained nothing that discriminated against the Jews was of no significance since no one took this consti-

---

269 Ibid.
270 Top secret minutes of Goldmann's meeting with the Polish ambassador to the United States, no location given, January 19, 1939, AJA, 361 A1/1.

tution seriously. He added that he expected to hear clear-cut declarations and to observe practical measures on the part of the Polish leadership. Goldman categorically rejected the ambassador's proposal that he travel to Poland to meet with Beck, Poland's foreign minister, and requested that the ambassador make it clear to the foreign ministry in Warsaw that he, Goldmann, as the representative of the WJC, expected Beck to announce a change in Poland's policy toward the Jews in one of his forthcoming speeches. Should the Polish government fail to make such a declaration, American Jewry would go to war against Poland.[271] The ambassador responded by asserting that both the Polish government and Beck opposed the process of anti-Jewish legislation in the *Sjem*, the Polish parliament, fearing that the increasingly anti-Jewish policy in Poland would harm the country significantly in the international arena. He emphasized that the process of anti-Jewish legislation was led by minority groups with vested economic interests, and that the Polish government found it difficult to confront them. The government of Poland was well aware that any solution to the problem of Poland's Jews necessitated close collaboration with American Jewry, which would not agree to cooperate if the Polish government continued to conduct an anti-Jewish policy.[272]

In his conclusion Goldmann stressed that should Beck clearly declare in his forthcoming speech that Poland was committed to preserving its Jewish citizens' equal rights. Such a declaration would make a deep impression on world Jewry. This stipulation may be understood as a pre-condition set by the WJC for entering into discussion with the Polish government on the issue of the country's Jews, and for refraining from taking action against the government of Poland.[273]

This meeting demonstrates that in representing the WJC, Goldmann did not approach the envoy of the Polish government as a representative of a persecuted minority seeking the ambassador's favor, but rather as the spokesman of a formidable organization that wielded economic and political power. He refused the ambassador's invitation to visit Poland and laid down an ultimatum that obligated the Polish government to alter its policy toward its Jewish citizens as a pre-condition for curbing American Jewry's political and economic campaign against Poland.

These meetings—one with the French foreign minister's chief of bureau and the other with the Polish ambassador—are but two examples of a broad political and ideological process that demonstrates the desire of the WJC's founders to deviate from the patterns of conventional philanthropic activity traditionally adopted by American Jewish organizations in the latter half of the 1930s, and

---

271 Ibid.
272 Ibid.
273 Ibid.

to work on behalf of world Jewry by political means that involved blending the Jewish issue into Europe's international political and economic texture and promoting the Jewish cause in ways that transcended mere provision of economic assistance.

Congress emissaries in Europe conducted a wide range of additional activities along these lines during the second half of the 1930s, especially in 1938 and 1939 in the wake of the considerable deterioration in the condition of Europe's Jews. In accordance with one of the lessons learned from the Evian Conference, Goldmann and Wise sought to set up a united front of Jewish organizations engaged in assisting European Jews with a view to exerting more effective pressure on international bodies that addressed the refugee issue.[274] In addition, WJC spokesmen held clandestine meetings with Czechoslovak envoys, among them Jan Masaryk, son of the recently deceased Czechoslovak President Thomas Masaryk, and the Czechoslovak ambassador to Switzerland. These contacts were kept secret in order to prevent the Germans from using them to prove the existence, as it were, of a close relationship between Czechoslovakia and world Jewry. During the course of the meetings, and in light of the possibility that Germany would take control of the Sudetenland, the WJC officials requested their interlocutors to allow the orderly migration of the Jews of Sudetenland and to urge the government of Czechoslovakia to assure that Czechoslovak Jews would continue to live in that country as a national minority (this term was expressly used).[275] WJC envoys likewise met with the Romanian foreign minister in an attempt to halt anti-Jewish legislation proposed by the country's parliament. They succeeded in bringing about the appointment of an ad hoc committee of the League of Nations comprising British, French and Iranian delegates, which was charged with ensuring that the foreign minister's promises regarding the cessation of anti-Jewish legislation were indeed kept.[276]

The political campaign waged by the WJC on behalf of the Jews of Eastern and Central Europe coincided with an attempt at conducting a radical political and organizational shakeup within the internal Jewish sphere worldwide. The organization's leaders believed that the dramatic reality of the late 1930s necessitated a far-reaching change with regard to two major issues. The first of these was

---

[274] Goldmann's letter to Wise following the Evian Conference, Geneva, July 16, 1938, AJA, 361 A27/1.
[275] Secret minutes of the meeting between Goldmann and the Czechoslovak ambassador to Switzerland, Geneva, September 16, 1938, AJA, 361 A1/2. The Munich agreement was signed on September 29, 1938, forcing the Czechoslovak government to hand over the Sudetenland to Germany within 12 days.
[276] Report of the WJC executive on activity in Europe between September 15, 1938 and October 15, 1938, AJA, 361 A1/1.

Jewish migration. In closed meetings and documents circulated to a restricted circle, Congress leaders expressed their opinion that the campaign for the individual and communal rights of Jews in the countries of Eastern and Central Europe was, in the long run, destined to fail, and that only a well-planned and organized program of migration could solve the Jewish problem there.[277] They argued that ever since 1933 Jewish organizations, headed by the Joint Distribution Committee, had sought to resolve the problem of Jewish refugees from Germany. They had engaged in philanthropic activity intended to alleviate the distress first of German Jews and later of Austria's Jews as well. While this was a vital enterprise, it merely addressed the immediate needs of Jews in Germany and Austria; it did not address the fundamental issues concerning Jewish existence in Eastern and Central Europe. The WJC was, in effect, making a distinction between refugees and migrants as part of a broader political perception that differentiated between its efforts to assist the Jews of Germany and Austria and its struggle on behalf of the rest of Eastern and Central European Jewry. Its leaders believed that it was impossible to ameliorate the situation of German and Austrian Jews, and that the WJC should focus on the long-term organized migration of these Jews, while endeavoring to preserve their rights until they emigrated. Thus the only way to attempt to modify the German regime's anti-Jewish policy and to facilitate the migration of German Jews in as orderly a manner as possible was to exert public pressure through the media, mass meetings, and the movement to boycott German products throughout the world and particularly in the United States.

> By contrast to the situation in Germany and Austria, the Congress leadership believed that it was feasible to set up a long-term, structured migration process in the remaining countries of Central and Eastern Europe by means of quiet diplomacy. Alongside preparations for migration, political and organizational arrangements were to be established in these countries that would enable individual and communal Jewish life as long as the Jews remained there. In the case of these other East and Central European countries, therefore, WJC leaders sought to both minimize and play down the public dimension of their efforts to improve the lot of the Jews there, assuming that public activity to this end would harm these efforts.[278]

---

277 See a document titled "The Problem of Migration and the World Jewish Congress," distributed on February 28, 1939, among the papers of the organization's executive committee, Paris, January 14–16, 1939, AJA, 361 A5/1.

278 The WJC indeed supported the movement to boycott German products and opposed the transfer agreement. On the organization's resistance to any agreement involving the migration of Germany's Jews in return for the promotion of German exports, see the letter from the WJC's Paris office to New York, August 26, 1938, AJA, 361 A8/3. For a description of the muted form of public action taken with regard to Eastern and Central European Jews by contrast to the movement to boycott German products, see Kubowitzki, *World Jewish History*, 92–110. It should be noted that

Congress documents present Poland, Romania, Hungary and Czechoslovakia as the four countries whose political situation necessitated Jewish migration, and which could not, so the organization's leaders believed, sustain a significant Jewish community in the future. Efforts at promoting Jewish migration from these countries must be conducted alongside an ongoing endeavor to protect Jewish rights. Moreover, since the regimes in these countries were keen to see the Jews leave, the WJC was able to make its support for this move conditional on the various governments' willingness to assure their Jews' rights as citizens until such time as a destination for migration was found, even if this were to take several years. Congress leaders were aware that conducting Jewish migration in the second half of the 1930s presented a stern challenge because Palestine was closed to immigration and severe restrictions on immigration were also applied worldwide, certainly in the United States. They nevertheless believed that well-organized international action could resolve the problems because of the pressing nature of Jewish distress and the desire of Eastern and Central European countries to encourage the Jews to leave. They noted that despite the current closing of its borders, Palestine was the preferred and natural destination for Jewish migration in the late 1930s. The migration enterprise would be funded by an international loan scheme subsidized by the various states, according to which the Jewish migrants would undertake to repay only the interest at a future date.[279]

The heads of the WJC had come to the conclusion that the dire condition of Jews in the late 1930s, and the question of migration in particular, required the various Jewish organizations to reshape their modes of operation with a view to undertaking well-organized and coordinated steps to assist the Jews of Europe. The WJC leadership cited the case of the Evian Conference in support of their advocacy of a united Jewish endeavor that would bridge existing organizational boundaries. In their opinion, the conference had failed not only because of the ineffectiveness of the participating nations, but also because the many Jewish organizations that attended had failed to form a united front and thus in effect had enabled the delegates of the participating nations to avoid making practical and significant decisions.[280]

Wise treaded very carefully also on the matter of the boycott of German products. See Urofsky, *Wise*, 297–298.

[279] See a document titled "The Problem of Migration and the World Jewish Congress," distributed on February 28, 1939, among the papers of the organization's executive committee, Paris, January 14–16, 1939, AJA, 361 A5/1. On the international plan and the loan scheme, see the top secret document on the WJC's activity on the League of Nations Committee, January 24, 1939, AJA, 361 A1/1.

[280] "The Problem of Migration," February 28, 1939, see note 279. For an assessment of the damage caused by the appearance of many Jewish organizations at the Evian Conference, see Gold-

In September 1938, in the wake of the Munich agreement that forced Czechoslovakia to hand the Sudetenland over to Germany, Stephen Wise as president of the World Jewish Congress sent a Jewish New Year letter to the Jews of Czechoslovakia, which included the following passage:

> In this fateful hour we urge you not to despair and not to let your courage sink. The history of the Jewish people is full of trials inflicted upon our forefathers. They lasted through, as you will do. In the long run justice is stronger than injustice, and liberty stronger than oppression. He who does not renounce his faith in the victory of justice, will triumph over the worshippers of violence and tyranny ... We are at the threshold of a new year. However dark its prospects, we yet wish and trust that it may be for you, dear brothers, and all the peoples of Czechoslovakia, a year of life and peace. More than ever we are with you and send you our brotherly greeting.[281]

This letter indicates—as does the Congress activity in Europe in the latter half of the 1930s—the organization's deep commitment to act in the interests of the Jews of Eastern and Central Europe. Wise's use of the term "brothers" in his letter is likewise indicative of the Congress leadership's solemn commitment to come to the assistance of its brothers in their time of need.

Wise's letter demonstrates that while Congress leaders recognized the severity of the crisis of Central and Eastern European Jewry, they had yet to grasp the full immensity of the transformation. Wise could thus address the Jews of Czechoslovakia and offer encouragement on the strength of past Jewish experience of confronting crises, which he considered to have been essentially similar to what was occurring in 1938. This disparity between the Congress leadership's perception of the Jewish aspects of European reality and what would actually occur following the outbreak of war—and especially upon the commencement of mass murder of European Jews—created a false impression among contemporaries and scholars alike of the essential nature of the Congress's work in Europe in the late 1930s. The efforts undertaken by the Congress prior to the outbreak of World War II and before first reports about the final solution appeared, in retrospect, to have been muted and irrelevant, and to have made little impact on the terrible situation of the Jews of Eastern and Central Europe. This perception was widespread in spite of the fact that the actions taken were significant, and that in many cases Congress functionaries sought to break out of the conventional mold of Jewish

---

mann's letter to Wise, July 16, 1938, AJA, 361 A27/1. Congress functionaries in Europe continued to work toward consolidation of the various organizations' activities there following the outbreak of war. See minutes of a meeting of Congress activists in Europe held in Geneva, classified top secret, December 6, 1939, AJA, 361 A1/7.

281 Wise's letter to the Jews of Czechoslovakia, September 1938 (no precise date given), AJA, 361 A1/1.

philanthropic endeavor that pertained in Europe prior to the founding of the WJC in 1936.

The conclusion that the critical assessment of the WJC's modus operandi in Europe on the eve of World War II does not accord with the reality of the period is reinforced by the extensive scholarly debate over the great difficulty experienced by both the general Jewish leadership and the Zionist leadership, in absorbing and digesting the information about the final solution. In other words, if the Jewish and Zionist leadership throughout the world and in Palestine found it so difficult to process the reports on the final solution after 1942, it would be unrealistic to expect the WJC leadership to have totally transformed their modes of operation in Europe prior to the outbreak of war. From today's perspective, the changes introduced by the Congress leadership in the late 1930s appear highly significant. Moreover, it will become apparent in due course that once the Congress leadership was exposed to the information about the extermination of European Jewry in late 1942 and grasped what was occurring in Europe, they responded relatively quickly by modifying the organization's patterns of action and adapting them to the dramatic developments.

The methods employed by the WJC to assist the Jews of Europe remained essentially unchanged during the initial months of the war. Its emissaries in Europe held meetings with representatives of the governments-in-exile and international organizations with a view to transferring food to European Jews, while its functionaries in Washington endeavored to obtain visas enabling Jews to enter the United States and mobilized volunteers among the organization's members and the American Jewish community at large to serve as sponsors who would provide material support to immigrants. Finding a sponsor was crucial to completion of the immigration process, since without it the prospective immigrant was unable to enter the country. Congress leaders themselves volunteered to serve as sponsors on numerous occasions and went out of their way to dispel anxiety on the part of potential sponsors with regard to exposing their financial data to the government, explaining that this was not a long-term sweeping financial commitment to support the immigrant. In addition, meetings were held at this time with ambassadors and consuls of South American nations in order to obtain passports for Jews in occupied Europe.[282] By contrast, the entry of the United States into

---

[282] See, for example, the secret minutes of a meeting of Congress operatives in Europe, December 6, 1939 (no location given). Among other issues, participants at this meeting discussed cooperation with the Red Cross and other non-Jewish organizations, the establishment of a Jewish delegation alongside the Polish government in exile, and the vital need to transfer provisions to the Jews of Poland, AJA, 361 A7/1. See also the minutes of a meeting of WJC functionaries based in Europe, held in Geneva, December 9, 1939. Participants were informed of the ties with the Polish

the war, and news of the Germans' murderous deeds in Europe and plans for the final solution led the WJC to introduce dramatic changes to its mode of operation in Europe. The immensity of the changes in awareness and organization that occurred within the Congress can be appreciated in light of the fact that a large part of the information pertaining to the acts of mass murder in Europe and the Nazis' plans for the overall extermination of Europe's Jews was collected and dispatched to the United States by WJC operatives in Europe. This meant that the organization's leaders were exposed to the full impact of this dramatic information.

Upon receiving news of the final solution, the heads of the WJC stepped up their political endeavors, which deviated from the contours of the public activity traditionally conducted by Jewish aid organizations, as they developed the pattern they had employed before learning of the Holocaust of European Jewry. In conducting the operation to rescue Jews in Europe, Congress institutions were obliged to adopt an underground pattern of activity and to forge a web of contacts with underground elements in Europe. This was a complex and challenging task. The WJC was a voluntary philanthropic body unaccustomed to such activity, which was foreign to its organizational culture. Prior to the 1940s its leaders had always sought to operate in the public eye and to draw as much public attention as they could to the plight of the Jews. This approach was clearly inappropriate for clandestine activity in Europe. The Congress had no prior organizational infrastructure of an underground nature, compounding the challenge that faced its leaders as they prepared to conduct activity aimed at rescuing the Jews of Europe.

The Untold Story: The Operation to Rescue Children in Portugal

The centerpiece of the Congress's rescue activity was its clandestine operation to rescue children. The saga of the organization's efforts to rescue children is fascinating, but has yet to receive the public and scholarly exposure it deserves. Yet the telling of this story is significant not merely because of the importance of its exposure, but also because it epitomizes the complexity of the debate over

---

government in exile and disputes with the Joint organization, AJA, 361 A7/2; the correspondence between Wise and Undersecretary of State Sumner Welles regarding visas, November 11 and 19, 1941, AJA, 361 D16/6. For more on activity in Washington, see Activity report June 22, 1942, AJA, 361 D16/7. WJC envoys continued to operate in Washington during 1943. See the following report, October 25, 1943, AJA, 361 D10/9. Regarding sponsors, see, for example, the following letters, October 3, 1941; October 31, 1941; December 5, 1941; December 10, 1941; and December 11, 1941, AJA, 361 D10/9.

WJC activity during World War II. The apparatus for rescuing children was set up through a concerted economic, political and organizational effort conducted by the WJC's leadership and its rank and file members. Despite this extraordinary endeavor, however, only a few thousand children were eventually rescued. While the value of rescuing each individual child cannot be underestimated, the question remains whether the Congress's ability to undertake only the rescue of these children does not highlight failure on the part of the organization's leadership to rescue a greater number of Jews from the Nazi inferno.

The clandestine activity in Lisbon was conducted by Yitzhak Weissmann, an emissary of the WJC. Weissmann was born in Istanbul in 1892 to a family of Russian origin. His extensive business ventures took him to Berlin, whence he escaped with his wife to Lisbon in 1940. The Congress leadership recognized Portugal's singular status as a safe haven for Jewish refugees and therefore sought to appoint an official envoy in Lisbon. Although Portugal had no common border with France and refugees could be transferred to the country only through Spain, Congress leaders believed that the Portuguese regime, unlike its Spanish counterpart, would allow a clandestine rescue operation to function within its territory.[283]

Weissmann had been chosen by Gerhart Riegner, director of the Congress's Geneva office, who had been charged with the task of locating a suitable candidate to run the WJC's Lisbon branch. It is safe to assume that Riegner took into account the fact that the function of a WJC emissary in Lisbon during wartime would involve clandestine activity. Weissmann's varied business interests in Cairo, Istanbul, Vienna and Berlin, and his command of several languages suited him to the role. He operated as the WJC's official envoy in Lisbon from 1941 onward. This status enabled him to build an extensive network of connections with the Portuguese authorities, delegations of Allied countries in Lisbon, and the British and American intelligence services.

Even while overcoming a string of obstacles, Weissmann was able to reach an agreement with the government of Portugal that would facilitate the temporary sojourn of Jewish refugees in that country. The Portuguese authorities, under the despotic and nationalist regime of Antonio Salazar, conducted a policy of neutrality during World War II, but maintained close economic ties with the Nazi regime and sought to prevent Jewish refugees from entering the country.[284]

---

[283] Portugal was considered the only neutral state in which a significant rescue effort could be conducted. See Weissmann's letter to the Congress's New York headquarters, August 20, 1943, AJA, 361 H295/7.

[284] Avraham Milgram, "Portugal, its Consuls, and the Jewish Refugees" [in Hebrew], *Yad Vashem Collected Studies* 27 (1988): 95–122. On the ties between Nazi Germany and Portugal, see An-

A practical illustration of the difficulties confronting Weissman was his arrest, together with his wife, by the Portuguese secret police and their release after several days following intervention by the British ambassador. Internal Jewish opposition to the clandestine modes of operation adopted in Lisbon posed an additional hurdle to be overcome by the WJC in Portugal. Of particular significance was the opposition on the part of the American Jewish Joint Distribution Committee and Professor Moshe Amzelak, head of the small Jewish community in Portugal. The JDC refused to transfer money intended for rescue efforts in Portugal and its local representatives refrained from engaging in political activity on behalf of the WJC's rescue enterprise. Given the economic power and its seniority among American Jewish philanthropic organizations, JDC opposition posed a serious challenge and greatly hindered the work of WJC emissaries in Portugal. Amzelak's opposition was likewise of considerable political significance because he had been a classmate of the Portuguese ruler and was personal friend.[285] The full significance of the JDC's refusal to support WJC efforts in the first half of the 1940s can be seen in the rejection by the Hadassah organization of the WJC's request that it participate in funding Congress activity in Europe. Hadassah's decision was based on the conviction that the JDC was focusing its activity on Europe and that the Congress should thus apply there for support. Hadassah, on the other hand, had made prior financial commitments to the Zionist movement's rescue endeavor conducted from the United States, and was therefore unable to accede to the WJC's request. In its response Hadassah stressed that its rejection of the request for funding did not stem from reservations regarding WJC activity, but was due to its inability to provide the necessary financial resources.[286]

The JDC's objections to Congress activity in Portugal were not merely a matter of a bureaucratic power struggle over the two organizations' control of the care of Jewish refugees in Portugal and Spain. The correspondence between Weissman and the JDC's operatives in Portugal, as well as the impressions gained by Jewish refugees who lived in the country during those years, indicates that unlike the WJC, the JDC chose to adhere to its philanthropic patterns of operation and was totally opposed to the clandestine modes of activity that Weissman had devel-

---

tonio Louça and Ansgar Schäfer, "The Lisbon Connection Regarding the Sales of Gold Plundered by the Nazis" [in Hebrew], ibid., 81–94.

285 On the importance and power of the Joint Distribution Committee in Spain and Portugal and the difficulties presented by its aloofness toward Congress efforts in these areas, see Haim Avni, *Spain, the Jews, and Franco* (Philadelphia, 1982), 188–196. On Amzelak's ties to Portugal's ruler and his refusal to cooperate with the Congress's operation in Portugal, see Weissmann's letter to the members of the WJC's Executive Committee, February 19, 1945, AJA, 361 H295/3.

286 Letter from Mrs. Robert Szold, President of Hadassah's American Affairs Committee, on behalf of Hadassah's President to Taratakower, June 12, 1941, AJA, 361 H287/8.

oped there. Amzelak's opposition stemmed from similar grounds.[287] The JDC and the institutions of the Portuguese Jewish community believed that not only were they unable to undertake underground activity in their capacity as philanthropic bodies, but that if this illegal activity were to be discovered, they would no longer be able to conduct the philanthropic work that in their view took pride of place.[288]

In late December 1944, an editorial in *Congress Weekly*, the WJC mouthpiece, elaborated on the differences in the modes of operation adopted by the JDC and the Congress during the Holocaust period.[289] The article began by applauding the JDC for raising tens of millions of dollars toward assisting the Jews of Europe. The article makes clear that this massive fundraising was crucial because of the dual challenge that confronted American Jewry in 1944, namely to continue the effort to rescue European Jews and to care for those who had been and would be rescued from the Nazi hell. Alongside its appreciation of the JDC's fundraising ability, the article harshly criticizes the organization's modes of operation in Europe during the Holocaust. It suggests that fundraising for purposes of rescue and rehabilitation was a necessary, but not a sufficient condition for undertaking action on behalf of European Jews and constituted only the initial stage of a comprehensive political endeavor. The article's author stressed that such activity demanded ongoing ties with governments and international organizations as well as new initiatives and ideas, which often achieved far more than spending millions of dollars. Adding the political dimension to the sphere of activity of Jewish aid and welfare organizations had always been the correct way to proceed and had become absolutely vital in light of the dramatic events of the Holocaust and the immense tasks facing American Jewish organizations engaged in the campaign for European Jews. The Jewish American effort on behalf of European Jewry could succeed only through shaping a coordinated strategy that blended philanthropy with politics. The article's author believed that the WJC's willing-

---

287 See the following correspondence between Weissman and the JDC's representatives in Portugal and Spain: Weissmann's letter to the JDC delegation in Lisbon, May 19, 1944; the JDC representative's letter of reply refusing Weissman's request for support, May 21, 1944; a further letter of reply from Weissmann in which he notes the JDC institutions' refusal to participate in the underground rescue endeavor from the outset, May 22, 1944, AJA, 361 H296/3; a further telegram sent by Weissmann to Wise informing him that up to that date the JDC had refused to join the underground effort in Portugal and France, May 24, 1944, AJA, 361 H296/3. See also a report by a Jewish refugee on the JDC in Portugal and Spain, August 23, 1943, AJA, 361 H296/1; a further testimony regarding the JDC's avoidance of involvement in illegal activity, June 12, 1944, AJA, 361 H296/4.
288 On the JDC leadership's view that Weissmann's efforts in Portugal were not contributing to the rescue of Jews in general and children in particular from France, see a letter from the JDC's Vice President Joseph C. Hyman to Wise, July 7, 1944, AJA, 361 H296/4.
289 Opinion piece by M. Boraisha in the *Congress Weekly*, December 29, 1944, AJA, 361 A68/3.

ness to undertake intensive political action during World War II set it aside from other Jewish welfare organizations such as the JDC and enabled it to work in an optimal manner for the good of European Jews. Despite the differences in the nature of operations among the American Jewish bodies that acted on behalf of Europe's Jews, the article viewed cooperation among the various groups as being of vital importance given the grave circumstances of European Jews. The historical responsibility borne by American Jews required them to transcend their differences and work in unison. Jews worldwide, especially American Jews, had the right to demand that the JDC cooperate with other Jewish organizations, such as the Congress, to undertake activity on behalf of the Jews of Europe.[290]

The resistance on the part of the JDC and the Portuguese Jewish community to the WJC operation in the country provides evidence of the organizational development and change in awareness that the Congress underwent during the war, and its willingness to conduct a different order of political activity to that in which it had engaged before learning of the Holocaust. The WJC adopted underground methods in Europe after its leaders concluded that, despite the danger it posed to the organization and to them personally, this was the only way to rescue Jews during the Holocaust. Over time, following the success and expansion of its operations in Portugal and Spain, the organization's efforts there could no longer be ignored. As a result, an agreement between representatives of the WJC, the JDC, and the Jewish Agency was reached at the American embassy in Lisbon in summer 1944. The agreement delineated the areas of activity of the three bodies in Spain and Portugal and set up an apparatus for the transfer of information among them. A coordinating committee that was to convene at short intervals in order to ensure the rapid and free flow of information among the organizations was formed for this purpose. A similar joint committee was to care for children who had been rescued and had arrived in Portugal. The agreement between representatives of the Jewish Agency, the JDC and the WJC was signed long after the Congress office in Lisbon had begun to operate. This affords an additional perspective on the overwhelming difficulties attending the founding and operation of a clandestine rescue enterprise by a philanthropic and voluntary organization nature that lacked the legal authority and practical capacity to compel other organizations to toe its line.[291]

A letter penned by JDC Vice President Joseph Hyman to Stephen Wise as the agreement was about to be signed shows that the heads of the JDC genuinely feared that the mode of operation developed by Weissmann in Portugal would delay—or even prevent—the rescue of Jewish children and others from France and

---

290 Ibid.
291 For a copy of the agreement, see July 13, 1944, AJA, 361 H296/4.

Belgium. Yet when Weissmann's endeavor in Portugal proved effective, JDC leadership agreed to formalize the relationship between the two organizations and to contribute funding to the rescue operation in Portugal in the belief that a unified effort would facilitate the rescue of a greater number of individuals.[292] The American Embassy's involvement in achieving the agreement provides further indication that the Jewish rescue operation in Portugal had developed to the extent that it called for the participation of representatives of the U.S. administration in its regulation.[293]

Weissmann began his work in Portugal by taking steps to formalize the legal status of the Jewish refugees there. He approached the Portuguese police official responsible for refugees and together they came to an arrangement whereby he, as the Congress emissary, undertook to keep a record of Jewish refugees and to supervise them. According to this arrangement, beginning in December 1942, the Jewish refugees would be assembled in the town of Ericeira and those in detention would be released. WJC documents reveal that in the wake of the German takeover of Southern France during November 1942, the flow of refugees reaching Portugal increased considerably. This in turn led Portuguese authorities to take a more heavy-handed approach to the Jewish refugees, who already lived under the threat of imminent imprisonment. When Weissmann broached the matter with them, the authorities claimed that their firm handling of the refugees was not motivated by anti-Semitism, but by the assessment of the Portuguese security service that there were many Communists among the refugees, who were likely to disrupt public order in the country and endanger the regime. Weissmann met with the heads of Portugal's security apparatus and proposed that the Jewish refugees be concentrated in one location and that a system of identification and registration of the refugees be set up. The Portuguese authorities demanded that under the process of refugee legalization, lists of all the refugees be submitted to

---

292 Letter from the JDC's Vice President Joseph Hyman to Wise, July 7, 1944, AJA, 361 H296/4 and JDC archives New York Section 1933/44 File 897. Hyman's perspective wasn't unique among JDC leaders and activists in Portugal. See, Cables exchanges between the JDC offices in Portugal and New York, July 6.1944, the JDC archives, New York, Section 1933/44, File 897. Memorandum from JDC office in Lisbon to the JDC office in New York, August 22. 1944, the JDC archives, New York, Section 1933/44 File 897. The American Ambassador in Lisbon wrote to Washington about the struggle between the JDC and the WJC in Lisbon. The Ambassador's letter, May 10, 1944. WRB (War Refugee Board) Documents in Dr. Chaim Pazner Papers at Yad Vashem archives, Section P.12 File 105.

293 The Jewish Agency was represented by Eliyahu Dovkin, head of the Agency's Aliya Department. The JDC delegate was Robert Pilpel. Yitskak Weissmann represented the WJC. James H. Mann and Robert C. Dexter, members of the American Rescue Committee, participated as observers. See The Agreement, July 13, 1944 (note 53).

the authorities, that the refugees register with the consulates or delegations of their country of origin, and that proof be furnished that each refugee had applied for migration to a consulate that represented a viable migration destination for them.

Weissmann was officially appointed director of the registration process and the person responsible to the Portuguese authorities for its implementation. Alongside his activity in Portugal, international pressure was brought to bear on the Spanish regime to regulate the status of the Jewish refugees there. To this end Weissmann held intensive negotiations with Nicolas Franco, Spain's ambassador to Portugal, and brother of the Spanish dictator. According to the information he received from the ambassador, Weissmann surmised that the precedent created in Portugal had induced the Spanish to cease returning Jewish refugees to the French border and to grant them the status of temporary refugees in Spain. It is instructive to observe the differences between the JDC pattern of action in Spain and the WJC operation in Portugal. In Spain the JDC conducted strictly philanthropic activity among the refugees, providing the funding to meet their ongoing needs. By contrast, Weissmann, as the Congress emissary in Portugal, did not confine himself to caring for the refugees' welfare and initiated contact with the heads of the country's security structure as part of a political organizational effort that far exceeded the scope of traditional philanthropic work. Thus Weissmann's orientation toward undertaking political activity and setting up a clandestine organizational infrastructure was to gather momentum during 1943 and 1944, and would eventually lead to the establishment of the Congress's full-blown rescue operation in Portugal.[294]

Once the status of the Jewish refugees in Portugal had been regulated, Weissmann set about creating close ties with the intelligence attachés at the British and American embassies and with intelligence personnel at the delegations of the

---

[294] On the process of regulating the status of the Jewish refugees in Portugal, see a summary of WJC activity on this issue, no date given, AJA, 361 H294/5; Weissmann's report on Congress activity in Lisbon, September 15, 1944, AJA, 361 H296/4. On the outlook of Portuguese officials regarding the Jewish refugees' Communist tendencies and Weissmann's proposal for a solution of the problem, see Weissmann's memoirs, Yitzhak Weissmann, *Facing the Colossi of Evil* [in Hebrew] (Tel Aviv, 1968), 56–70. On the status of the Jewish refugees in Spain, the ongoing international diplomatic effort on their behalf, and the JDC's activity in Spain, see Avni, *Spain*, 94–127. The Spanish ambassador to Portugal visited Weissmann in early 1943 and provided him with information on Spain's policy on the Jewish refugees. See Weissman, *Colossi of Evil*, 71. The two men met again during April 1944 at the Spanish embassy, where they continued to discuss the condition of the Jewish refugees in Spain as well as that of Jews of Spanish nationality located in countries under German occupation. See the secret minutes of this meeting, April 8, 1944, AJA, 361 H296/3. For criticism of the nature of the Joint's activity in Spain, see Weissmann's report to Goldmann and Tartakower, July 28, 1943, AJA, 361 H285/6.

Polish and French governments-in-exile in Lisbon, with a view to establishing an organizational infrastructure for future rescue operations. One of the major concerns that occupied Weissmann, Congress emissaries in Europe, and the heads of the organization in the United States, was the establishment of a clandestine communications network. In the midst of a world war it proved difficult to communicate via letters and telegrams. Transfer of information between the various European countries and between Europe and the United States was exceedingly slow and sometimes altogether impossible. As a philanthropic rather than a government body, the communications structure of the WJC was totally exposed to the intelligence agencies of various nations. Given these circumstances it was not possible to conduct a clandestine rescue operation, which required the ability to transfer information rapidly and securely. Therefore Weissmann immediately proceeded to set up a clandestine system for the transfer of information and mail among the Congress's offices in Europe and between Europe and America. He approached the delegations of the French, Polish and Czechoslovak governments-in-exile and secured their agreement to transfer WJC mail via their diplomatic post bags, thus ensuring the orderly transfer of mail and telegrams. But Weissmann suspected that even the diplomatic postal channels were exposed to hostile intelligence activity and took steps to set up the organization's own independent communications procedure. He secured the services of an Argentinean diplomat who transferred the Congress's documents as diplomatic post, and an additional courier who clandestinely—and illegally—dispatched the organization's documents, as well as equipment vital to the rescue effort such as walkie-talkies. The clandestine system that Weissmann established was so efficient that the envoys of governments-in-exile in Lisbon sometimes preferred to send classified information through him rather than through regular diplomatic channels. They believed that information transferred in this way was more likely to reach its destination secure from exposure to hostile elements.[295]

Weissmann forged especially close cooperation with the French government-in-exile as well as with the French resistance. These ties between Weissmann and elements within the French underground are exemplified by the case of Pierre Mendes France, the future French prime minister. Mendes France later related that he had escaped from prison in France and had made his way to Geneva where he approached Riegner, head of the local WJC office. After growing a beard, he was equipped with forged documents identifying him as a Jew named Yehuda Lemberger; he then reentered France under this assumed identity. At the end of a long journey during which he was supported by the WJC, Mendes France arrived in Lisbon in early 1942. There he met Weissmann, who hosted him in the

---

[295] Weissman, *Colossi of Evil*, 45–48.

city until he departed for London in February of that year. Mendes France subsequently recalled that his visit with Weissmann left a deep impression on him and was a decisive factor in his decision to become involved in the rescue of Jews in Europe, particularly in France. From London he conveyed instructions to the French resistance regarding the concealment of French children and their transfer via escape routes to Spain and Portugal. He would later assist in funding WJC escape operation in Portugal.[296]

There is no mention in the scholarly literature of the episode of cooperation between the WJC and Mendes France. His escape from France and arrival in Geneva are documented, but any reference to WJC involvement in the process of his flight in Switzerland and his activities in Portugal has been totally excluded from the narrative. It is possible that following the war, circles close to Mendes France thought that mentioning the fact that his escape had been assisted by a Jewish organization was likely to harm him politically, particularly since he was a Jew, and to detract from the narrative of the French national struggle against the Vichy regime and Nazi Germany.[297]

Having settled the status of the Jewish refugees in Spain and Portugal, Weissmann and the apparatus that he had set up began to engage in obtaining information from occupied European countries on Nazi actions against the Jews, and in dispatching food and medication packages to the Jews of Europe. WJC documents from the period between the outbreak of the war and the receipt of detailed information on the final solution at the end of summer 1942 demonstrate that this was the major issue that occupied the leadership. At the time, the heads of the WJC believed that the orderly dispatch of food to Europe could significantly ameliorate the condition of the Jews there and induce the Nazi leaders to improve their treatment of the Jews. Opposition on the part of the United States and Britain to the transfer of food to Europe based on the fear that it would not reach its destination and would contribute to the German war effort prevented even an initial attempt to set up a comprehensive operation of food transfer to Europe, but failed to stop Congress leadership from persisting in its effort to transfer food to the Jews in smaller volumes and by indirect means. Even after receiving the information pertaining to the final solution, the WJC continued trying to transfer food to the

---

[296] See the letter written by Weissmann on this topic, July 17, 1944, AJA, 361 H296/4.
[297] See the testimony of Mendes France and a photograph of him with Weissmann taken during his visit to Israel in 1965, in Weissmann, *Colossi of Evil*, 143–147. For an example of the non-mention of the cooperation between the WJC and Mendes France, see Jean Lacouture, *Pierre Mendes France* (New York, 1984), 134–135.

Jews in the ghettos and the camps, believing that this was one of the few means of helping the Jews of Europe.[298]

During the war, the WJC sought to locate addresses of Jews in the areas under Nazi occupation in order to send food parcels to them. The organization's New York office engaged in extensive correspondence with its emissaries in Europe for the purpose of sending packages to needy Jews. The process of locating potential recipients was a lengthy one and there was considerable uncertainty as to whether they would, in fact, receive the packages. The Lisbon office, for example, wrote to New York to inform the office there that it had managed to locate an Ida Rotschild in Westerbork Camp in Holland, who would receive a weekly food package. Her case appears to be the exception that proves the rule; most attempts at locating recipients failed.[299]

The attempts to find addresses in Europe were part of a sustained effort by the WJC to locate the whereabouts and gather information on the fate of as many European Jews as possible in countries overrun by the Nazis and in those parts of the continent under German rule. To this end, in the fall of 1942 the Congress established a dedicated department in New York charged with gathering as much information as possible about the fate of Jews who had been forced for whatever reason to leave their places of residence in the various countries.[300] The department's files contained the names of over 82,000 Jewish refugees who could be located and on whom information could be found. In addition to the names of the refugees, the records included their last known addresses and their previous addresses, their ages, and any available details about their parents. Congress documents show, for example, that on October 15, 1944 the files contained names and additional information on over 45,000 refugees in the USSR, 1,000 in Teheran, and over 3,000 in Palestine. They not only contained information on Jews who had survived the horrors of the war, but also on those who had been deported to ghettos, to the death camps, and to various concentration camps. The fact that many of the refugees were living in the Soviet Union presented a particularly complex challenge to the WJC location machinery because of the county's vast area and the difficulty of communicating with the USSR during time of war.

---

[298] For information on WJC attempts to set up an official channel for the transfer of food to European Jews, see the organization's report submitted to the Committee for War Refugees, March 3, 1944, AJA, 361 A68/2.

[299] See, for example, a letter from Lisbon to the Congress's New York office regarding the location of Jews in German-occupied Europe, April 14, 1944 (13 names), AJA, 361 H296/3.

[300] See the report on the department's activity compiled by Haim Finkelstein, chairman of the department, November 26, 1944, AJA, 361 A68/1.

Letters sent from the United States to the USSR generally took a year or more to reach their destinations, and many telegrams went unanswered.[301]

The files themselves were important, but they also enabled families in the free world, particularly in America, to locate their relatives and attempt to find out what had happened to them. In order to make the information kept in the WJC offices available to the general public, the lists of refugees were typed onto stencils and sent to the organization's offices in the United States and around the world for duplication. The Congress likewise published full page announcements in the Yiddish press in the United States, Canada, South America, and Britain listing the names of refugees. Similar information was passed to over 120 non-Jewish papers in the United States and was broadcast over the radio there and in other countries. Many of those searching for their relatives chose to visit the department's office in New York in person. The department's staff recounted heart-wrenching scenes of relatives who had learned of their dear ones' deaths, as well as of moments of joy experienced by those who found names of their relatives and friends on the lists of refugees. The department's team estimated that some twenty percent of the refugees who sought assistance from the Congress's search staff were able to find relatives or friends. This was considered to be a particularly high rate of success, although only a relatively small proportion of applicants actually located members of their families—evidence of the total chaos in which the Jews of the world found themselves during the period of the Holocaust.[302]

Within the dramatic reality of the beginning of World War II, the WJC stood out as a body possessing a well-developed organizational capacity through which it might succeed in the complex task of dispatching food packages to the Jews of Europe. Thus it served as a clearinghouse for organizations and individuals seeking to establish contact with European Jews living under the Nazi occupation, as is indicated by the correspondence between the WJC and functionaries of the *Ha-Shomer Ha-Tsa'ir* (The Youth Guard). The latter submitted to the WJC a list of addresses of members of their movement in Poland so as to enable them to receive food parcels from the organization. Dozens of the movement's activists appeared on the list, including Mordechi Anielevich, who later became the commander of the Warsaw Ghetto uprising. Congress officials conducted a similar correspondence with functionaries of *Ha-Po'el Ha-Dati* (The Religious Workers Union in Palestine), who requested WJC assistance in funding the shipping of packages to Europe.[303]

---

301 Ibid.
302 Ibid.
303 See the letters on this topic between Tartakower and Ha-Shomer Ha-Tsa'ir functionaries, March 13, 1941; September 11, 1941; September 17, 1941, AJA, 361 H287/8; Tartakower's letter to

The organizational infrastructure erected by the WJC in Portugal played a key role in the process of dispatching packages. While Nazi Germany did not officially permit the transfer of food and medication to European Jews, Congress leaders believed that this could, in fact, be done. The main obstacle to dispatching parcels to Jews in occupied Europe was the refusal by the International Red Cross to recognize the Jews as prisoners entitled to its support. Weissmann and the Congress heads in Europe nevertheless succeeded in convincing the Portuguese Red Cross to recognize the Jews as civilian prisoners who were entitled to its services, thereby paving the way for the sending of food packages by the organization. The willingness of the Portuguese Red Cross to take part in the package dispatch operation was particularly important given the trenchant criticism generally leveled by WJC leadership at the International Red Cross because of their refusal to participate in the effort to rescue European Jewry. A passage written by Arieh Tartakower, chairman of the Congress's Welfare and Relief Committee, provides an example of this recalcitrance by the Red Cross during World War II:

> Since German policy was changing ever more from a policy of persecuting Jews to a policy of extermination and this had to be addressed by the rescue operation, inefficiency soon became apparent, and even an unwillingness to undertake genuine steps on the part of this institution. When it [the Red Cross], as a humanitarian institution, was required to protest against German policy toward the Jews as being contrary to the principles of justice and even to the 1929 convention regarding protection of prisoners of war as well as civilian detainees, it refused to do so, claiming that its role was to protect rather than to protest, and that such a protest was liable to jeopardize its activity on behalf of prisoners of war. And its refusal to pass on food parcels to the Jews in the ghettos and prisoner camps was far more glaring.[304]

The arrangement for sending packages from Portugal comprised one component of the WJC's extensive enterprise that oversaw the dispatch of tens of thousands of packages containing food and medical supplies to Europe. The leadership was

---

the League for the Ha-Po'el Ha-Dati in Palestine on the same issue, March 29, 1941, ibid. On the requests to send parcels submitted by the General Zionists and Ha-Mizrahi, see the letter from Ya'akov Greenberg to Tartakower, ibid. For a further request by the Jewish Cooperative movement in Poland, see the letter dated October 20, 1941, ibid.

304 Parcels were limited by weight to five kilograms. Weissman's letter to Tartakower, March 7, 1943, AJA, 361 H295/6. The quote is from Tartakower, draft of unpublished memoirs (undated), CZA, C-6/352. On a measure of cooperation between the Red Cross and the WJC in the context of the effort to rescue the Jews of Hungary, see Arie Ben Tov, *The Red Cross Arrived Too Late* [in Hebrew] (Jerusalem and Tel Aviv, 1993), 45–59. On the overall relationship between the Congress and the International Red Cross at the time of the Holocaust, see Monty Penkower, "The World Jewish Congress Confronts the International Red Cross During the Holocaust," *Jewish Social Studies* 41 (1979): 229–256.

aware of the fact that a large percentage of these packages did not reach their destinations. Still, believing that each package that reached its recipient might save a Jewish life, they continued the operation in the hope that at least some would fall into Jewish hands. An interim audit conducted by the Congress in November 1944 found that only 925 of 12,955 food parcels had reached their destination; of those, 855 had not been signed for by the recipient. This raised doubts as to the identity of the recipient.[305]

The matter of the parcels indicates the dual nature of the WJC effort to rescue European Jews. On the one hand it sought to set in motion a clandestine and underground operation (described at length later in this chapter), which was totally foreign to the essential activity of a philanthropic organization; and on the other hand it continued to operate in accordance with its previous philanthropic modes. While activities such as the dispatch of food parcels were frustrating and bore little fruit, given the harsh reality of the Holocaust, Congress leaders felt that they could not give up the effort despite the meager achievements.

Toward the end of 1943 the French resistance informed the WJC of an extensive German operation to apprehend Jewish children hiding in private homes and in Catholic institutions in areas of France under German control. WJC functionaries in Europe estimated that four to five thousand Jews were in imminent danger. Further reports told of the intensified German effort to locate and capture Jews—children in particular—in Holland and Belgium.[306] A report by Weissmann to the Congress's New York office provides an indication of the circuitous route whereby this information reached Lisbon. Weissmann told of a Dutch Jew who had escaped from Mauthausen concentration camp in Austria and had managed to reach Portugal via France. He was conscripted by the Dutch government-in-exile and shared whatever information he had with Weissmann. The survivor reported that 25,000 adults and 5,000 children were in hiding in Belgium and another 5,000 adults and 3,000 children were living underground in Holland. The report suggests that most of the people in hiding were Jews, although this had not been conclusively confirmed. The same source estimated that funding to the tune of 400,000 Belgian francs per month (roughly US$ 3,500 per family) was needed

---

305 See the report on the department's activity compiled by Haim Finkelstein, chairman of the department, November 26, 1944, AJA, 361 A68/1.

306 Lecture by Yitzhak Weissmann, the Congress emissary in Lisbon, January 19, 1945, AJA, 361 D71/2. For information on Jewish children in church institutions in Belgium, see a secret report from Belgium, September 18, 1943, AJA, 361 H295/6. For information on the hunt for Jewish children in France and a request to put out a radio broadcast from Algeria and London calling on the local population not to hand over Jews, see Weissmann's telegram to the WJC's New York office, December 20, 1943, AJA, 361 H296/1. For additional information on the numbers of Jews in hiding in France and Belgium, see an internal WJC document, February 4, 1944, AJA, 361 H296/2.

to enable the Jews in Holland to continue living underground. The money sent to Holland and Belgium would cover the needs of the Jews in hiding, which ranged from payment of bribes to the purchase of food.[307]

Upon receiving this information, Congress officials began by approaching the French government-in-exile to request that its representatives make a public announcement asking the French population not to cooperate with the Germans in their effort to find children, and to instruct the French resistance to take active steps to see that children were not handed over to the Germans. The French broadcasting centers in London and Algeria did indeed put out broadcasts to this effect directed at the French population at large and at the resistance in particular. Parallel meetings were held with senior Dutch and Belgian officials who promised to allocate special underground forces to the task of rescuing children in their respective countries, and to try to transfer the children to France as an interim staging post on their way to Spain and Portugal.[308]

The messages arriving from occupied Europe left Weissmann in no doubt as to the urgency of investing most of his effort in rescuing Jewish children from France and transferring them to Spain and Portugal. He and the Congress leaders concluded that the activity undertaken through the governments-in-exile and the various undergrounds was insufficient and they therefore took steps to set up an independent underground operation to rescue Jewish children in France. To this end Weissmann, who came from Lisbon, and Nahum Goldmann and Tartakower, who set out from the United States, met in London, where they held intensive meetings with envoys of the French, Dutch and Polish governments-in-exile. These meetings yielded promises of assistance and support for the establishment of the WJC's rescue machinery. Of particular importance was the decision of the Dutch government to send a contact person experienced in underground activity to Lisbon to assist Weissmann in creating the rescue machinery, and if necessary to enter areas of occupied France in order to provide practical assistance to its operation. With the support of the governments-in-exile and their embassies in Lisbon, Weissmann, Tartakower, and Goldmann also created an independent task force charged with rescuing Jewish children. Members of the group moved clandestinely between France and Spain as they implemented the rescue effort. Most were French-speaking Jews, some with experience in underground activity.[309] Their number was augmented by the addition of professional

---

[307] See the summary classified as secret of Weissmann's reports to New York, January 4, 1944, AJA, 361 H296/2.
[308] Printout of Weissmann's speech, January 10, 1945 (no location given), AJA, 361 H295/3.
[309] About the Jewish underground see, *La résistance juive: Un combat pour la survie* (Jerusalem, Yad Vashem, 2012), 196–264 (French; hereafter: Lazare, *La résistance*).

smugglers who could cope with the tremendous obstacles presented by crossing from France to Spain over the Pyrenees Mountains. Seeking to present Congress functionaries in New York with the profile of a typical member of one of these groups, Weissmann described a 24-year-old Jewish man of Polish origin who had lived most of his life in France. In the wake of the occupation he had joined the French resistance and gained extensive experience in operating communications equipment for the underground. He had come to London on a mission for the resistance and Weissmann had recruited him there.[310] In addition, Weissmann recruited peasant families on both sides of the border, who were paid to serve as a base for the departure of groups of children and smugglers.[311]

To establish and run an underground operation in a Europe under Nazi rule would have been a difficult task under any circumstances, but the challenge facing Weissmann was particularly daunting—and not simply because of the tremendous obstacles to be overcome in smuggling groups of children through tens of kilometers of border areas under close military supervision. Contemporary witnesses emphasized that Weissmann's mission was made significantly harder not only by the technical difficulties involved in undertaking clandestine activity, but also by the requirement that a philanthropic organization adopt underground modes of operation that were totally foreign to it and conduct missions far beyond the conventional sphere of such organizations.[312] A number of questions arose as preparations were being made for rescuing the children. To whom did they legally belong? Could any particular government claim that the children should be under its aegis? And did the WJC have the means to determine the children's original citizenship and establish their legal status? Those in charge of the rescue operation were severely critical of the various governments-in-exile, which for the most part ignored the children altogether once they had been rescued, making no attempt to establish whether these were children of their own citizens even when such an examination was feasible. This disregard and lack of concern was particularly galling in view of these governments' assiduousness in attending to their non-Jewish citizens and the dedicated financial resources at their disposal for the care of their citizens who were refugees or displaced persons. The WJC and other Jewish and Zionist organizations in effect took governmental functions upon themselves because of the ineptitude of the various countries.[313]

---

310 Weissmann's report in the WJC's weekly journal in the United States, *Congress Weekly*, December 29, 1944, AJA, 361 A68/3.
311 Ibid.
312 See the letter from Shmuel Roth, a refugee in Portugal, to Leon Kubowitzki, June 12, 1944, AJA, 361 H296/4; and Tartakower's draft memoirs, undated, CZA, C-6/352.
313 Weissmann's letter to Tartakower, February 2, 1944, AJA, 361 H296/2.

The fact that the Congress was merely a philanthropic organization had far-reaching consequences for its ability to function in Europe. Unlike the various governments-in-exile, the WJC was unable to make radio broadcasts to Europe or to operate a diplomatic postal service; its emissaries did not enjoy diplomatic immunity or preferential allocation of means of transportation during wartime; and the organization received no funding from the Allies. The Jewish philanthropic organizations took care of their brethren in a manner similar to that of the governments-in-exile, yet were not granted the economic and organizational infrastructure vital to their ability to operate in Europe.[314]

The operation to smuggle the children out of France began in Toulouse, where local women collected them and transferred them to a location close to the border. Because most of the children carried forged identity documents or had none at all, each woman was put in charge of only two children; any more than that could have aroused suspicion. The children were concealed in the homes of local families living near the border; there they waited to be led over the mountains to Spain. Passing through the border region was particularly tricky because an area some 20–25 kilometers wide leading up to the border had been declared a "military zone" within which movement was severely restricted.

Malka Azaria, a resident of Savyon, a suburb Tel Aviv, told of her escape from France by means of the machinery that Weissmann put in place in Portugal. Malka was born in Antwerp, Belgium, to orthodox parents of Polish origin. The family had passed from one concentration camp to another over the four years since Belgium was overrun by the Germans in May 1940. During this period Malka lost contact with her family, apart from her eldest brother, six years her senior. At the age of eleven, after a prolonged period of suffering, Malka reached a Catholic monastery, where she was found by emissaries of the WJC. She continued the tale of her escape over the Pyrenees to the Spanish border: She was part of a small group of children accompanied by professional smugglers. They wore improvised shoes and inadequate clothing unsuited to the cold air in the mountains. After an arduous journey they succeeded in passing the last Spanish border post and arrived at an isolated mountain village. Here they were cared for by a peasant family, sent on to Barcelona for a short while and then to Paco d'Arcos, a holiday resort on the sea near Lisbon. All their physical needs were attended to in the children's home there and Malka emphasized that the staff made them feel at home. In November 1944 all the children in the group set sail for Palestine, apart from a single girl who traveled to Philadelphia in the United States.[315]

---

314 Weissmann's letter to Tartakower and Goldmann, February 8, 1944, AJA, 361 H296/2.
315 The testimony of Malka Azaria delivered to Gershon Elimor (Wilkowski), in Weissmann, *Colossi of Evil*, appendix, 158–61. For two more testimonies, that tells the same story. See, Yad

In March 1944 the first two groups, each comprising six children, were led out of France. The youngest was a girl of five and the oldest a boy of 14. Weissmann reported to the Congress's New York office on the poor medical and emotional condition of the rescued children. Most suffered from various diseases, were underweight because of the prolonged lack of food, and were coping with emotional and psychological difficulties stemming from losing contact with their families and living in constant fear. These children's stories included the disappearance of parents whose fate remained unknown, loss of contact with siblings, and vague memories of relatives who lived mainly in the United States and Palestine.[316]

The arduous task of rescuing the children did not end with crossing the border. Since they had entered Spain without the permission of the government, they had to be concealed there as well. Weissmann requested the assistance of the American and British ambassadors in Lisbon in approaching the Spanish government to obtain authorization for the children to pass through the country. The request was made and authorization was duly granted. With the assistance of the higher echelons of the Catholic Church in Portugal, Weissmann likewise approached the Portuguese government to agree to accept groups of 300 children at a time. The agreement stipulated that after one group had left Portugal the next group could enter, and that this cycle could continue indefinitely.[317]

After the first two groups of children had successfully made their way to Lisbon, the rescue operation became ongoing, with some ten children crossing the border each week.[318] On average, with fluctuations owing to the weather, some sixty children per month crossed the border between France and Spain, making a total of over 700 children, joined by some 200 parents. While the Congress's operation in Spain and Portugal was intended to rescue children, its services were also extended to adults who were deemed at high risk and to parents of rescued children. In addition to the children smuggled into Spain and Portugal, 1350 youngsters under the age of 20 were ferried from France to Switzerland between October 1943 and September 1944. In addition, the WJC's Swiss office transferred considerable sums of money to France, which was used to conceal approximately 4000 children in France itself. The endeavor to smuggle, rescue

---

Vashem Archives, Record Group 03, file 7623. Record Group 093, file 19210.
316 For biographical details of the children, see a letter from Lisbon to New York, September 7, 1944, AJA, 361 H296/4.
317 Telegram from Weissmann to Wise, April 7, 1944, AJA, 361 H296/3. For a report on the condition of the children, see Weissmann's telegram to New York, May 9, 1944, AJA, 361 H294/5.
318 See, for example, a report from Lisbon regarding the ongoing arrival of groups of children. Weissmann's secret telegram from Lisbon, April 10, 1944, AJA, 361 H294/5; similar information is contained in a telegram from Weissmann to Wise, April 22, 1944, AJA, 361 H293/3.

and conceal children entailed extensive document forging activity. The WJC offices in Lisbon and Geneva supervised the forging of some 8000 documents, primarily ID cards and birth certificates. This rescue and forging activity was funded by a variety of sources and by indirect means, making it difficult to arrive at an overall figure. The Congress's Geneva office estimated the total cost to be in excess of 18 million French francs.[319]

As previously mentioned, the establishment and conduct of the rescue operation in Portugal and Spain presented a severe financial challenge to those engaged in it. Congress institutions estimated that the cost of rescuing each child was US$350. The organization's New York office ran extensive machinery to raise funds among WJC members in the United States, other Jewish public bodies, and individual Jewish donors. In addition, Congress fundraisers successfully approached non-Jewish organizations such as the American Quakers and the Unitarian Church in order to ensure that the rescue effort would not be impeded by financial constraints.[320] During 1944 considerable amounts of money were likewise received from the War Refugee Board (WRB), an agency of the administration set up in January 1944 on the instructions of President Roosevelt to rescue and assist victims of World War II.[321]

In the context of a world war, the raising of funds in the United States was merely the first stage of a complex process of transferring money to Portugal. WJC files for the year 1944 are filled with correspondence and telegrams between Lisbon and New York, by means of which functionaries in Europe and the United States sought to perform the transfer of funds, to trace the circuitous route taken by the money, to find out why it had not arrived, and even to try to obtain the most favorable exchange rates possible at the time.[322]

---

[319] The figure for the total number of children is based on the following sources: telegram from Riegner to Wise sent through the American consulate in Bern, May 10, 1944, AJA, 361 H294/5; summary of the WJC's rescue operation, November 11, 1944, AJA, 361 A68/2, 43. For a very positive assessment of the WJC activity in Portugal see: Secret letter of the American ambassador in Lisbon to State department, September 2. 1944, May 13, 1944. Letter to the Secretary of State, May 5, 1944. Yad Vashem archives, Section P.12 File 105. In parallel, the Jewish underground (with OSE) conducted a rescue operation of children to Spain. 88 children were rescued. See, Lazare, La résistance [in French], 230–231.
[320] For details on this topic, see Weissmann's letter to Lady Reading, widow of Rufus Isaacs, 1st Marquess of Reading, March 31, 1944, AJA, 361 H296/2.
[321] On WRB involvement in the rescue operation, see, for example, a secret telegram from the WJC Lisbon office to New York, April 19, 1944, AJA, 361 H294/5; telegram from Weissmann to Wise, April 22, 1944, AJA, 361 H296/3; report by Weissmann, September 15, 1944, AJA, 361 H296/4.
[322] Weissmann's letter to Kubowitzki, May 24, 1944, thanking him for the transfer of $10,000, AJA, 361 H296/3; telegram from Kubowitzki and Tartakower to Weissmann expressing their concern that he had not confirmed receipt of $23,000 transferred to Lisbon from New York and stat-

In order to care for the children, a home was established near the coast, some ten kilometers from Lisbon. Weissmann's wife Lily, who managed its operation, related that the staff at the temporary shelter tried to evoke the supportive atmosphere of a warm family in an attempt to assist the children's recovery from the trials of their escape from France and the loss of contact with their parents, siblings, and other family members. As part of the rehabilitation process the children also received schooling at the home. A Jewish refugee by the name of Shlomo Lifshitz was recruited to teach them. Lifshitz was a graduate of the Jewish gymnasium in Warsaw and taught the children a wide variety of subjects. On the assumption that most of the children would eventually reach Palestine, particular attention was paid to studying the Hebrew language. The topic of Hebrew instruction reveals the great difficulty that Weissmann and the Congress staff in Portugal faced during the war years in locating a destination to which the children could migrate. Apart from the conviction that finding a permanent solution would be in the best interest of each of the rescued children, Portuguese authorities permitted only 300 children to stay in the country at a time. It was therefore imperative to arrange for the children's migration while the war continued. Weissmann and the WJC leadership believed that the preferred destination for the children was the Jewish community in Palestine. Here, they explained, the *Aliyat Ha-Noar* (youth immigration) organization, founded in Berlin in 1932 to facilitate the immigration of youngsters and children to Palestine and to take care of their education there, provided a broad institutional infrastructure that had proved its effectiveness in absorbing children directly upon their arrival.[323] Aliyat Ha-Noar indeed played a major role in receiving the children to Palestine and its head, Henrietta Szold, informed Weissmann in late 1944 of the arrival of tens of children from Portugal in Haifa aboard the ship S.S. Guine. In telling the story of one child whose parents had been located in the country, she termed the ship's arrival a "unique event."[324] However, the choice of Palestine as the preferred destination for the children did not stem from purely bureaucratic considerations. Weissmann and his associates believed that ideological objectives should also play a part in caring for the children. Were they to send the children to other destinations, they would be unable to ensure adoption by Jewish families, which was likely to lead them to abandon

---

ing that they were willing to send additional amounts if needed, June 30, 1944, AJA, 361 H296/3. For a recommendation to transfer the money, transfer of directly to Portugal rather than to Spain owing to the better exchange rate, see Weissmann's telegram to New York, March 7, 1944, AJA, 361 H296/2. On the estimate that the cost of rescuing a child was $350, see memorandum to the WJC's executive committee, April 19, 1944, AJA, 361 H294/5. On fundraising for the rescue of children, see a letter on this subject, July 10, 1944, AJA, 361 D71/2.

323 Weissman's letter to Wise, April 22, 1944, AJA, 361 H296/3.
324 Henrietta Szold's letter to Weissmann, December 1, 1944, AJA, 361 H295/3.

their Judaism. By contrast, their absorption into Palestine would guarantee that the children would remain part of the Jewish people.[325] The clear preference on the part of the WJC for sending the rescued children to Palestine contrasts with the JDC's opposition to the choice of Palestine as the preferred destination for migration. The disagreement on this matter was a major factor in the JDC's refusal to participate in funding the children's upkeep in Portugal or their voyage to Palestine.[326] As mentioned, the JDC began to cooperate with the Congress's rescue operation at a very late stage after the two organizations and the Jewish Agency signed an agreement at the American embassy in Lisbon. The JDC's refusal considerably hindered WJC efforts because the necessity of arranging the children's migration during wartime required an exceptional financial endeavor. Seafaring vessels were hard to come by, and when a suitable ship could be found, the cost of transport was prohibitive. Thus, in addition to the usual effort to raise contributions toward the rescue of children from France, Weissmann sought creative solutions that might produce new channels of funding. He succeeded, for example, in persuading the heads of the Polish government-in-exile to treat Polish-speaking children who arrived to Portugal as the descendants of Polish citizens, even in cases where the requisite documents to support this contention were not available. The Polish government then undertook to provide the funding to arrange for the migration of these children.[327] Despite these obstacles, Weissmann succeeded in sending hundreds of children to Palestine and dozens to the United States in 1944 and 1945. In some cases children were equipped with basic items such clothes and bed-linen in order to facilitate their absorption in Palestine. Although Palestine remained the destination of choice, children who had relatives in America were sent there. The WJC made a point of publishing the names of the rescued children, along with as many identifying details as possible, to enable families in America to identify their relatives and to allow the Congress's New York office to attempt to locate families. If contact was established between a rescued child and relatives in the United States, the WJC took steps to reunite them, including handling all the bureaucratic and financial obstacles to migration during wartime.[328]

---

325 Weissman's letter to Wise, , April 22, 1944, AJA, 361 H293/3.
326 Weissman's telegram to Wise, May 6, 1944, AJA, 361 H296/3. On the JDC's anti-Zionist policy in the Portuguese context, see Weissmann's letter to Tartakower, January 19, 1944, AJA, 361 H296/2.
327 Weissmann's letter to the WJC's institutions in London, which included the names of five relevant children, September 7, 1944, AJA, 361 H296/4.
328 Telegram from Weissmann to Wise, including the names of children who arrived at the beginning of May, May 9, 1944, AJA, 361 H296/3. See also a letter from Weissmann to Ms. Spector of Philadelphia regarding her young sister who was on her way to the United States. Weissmann

In late October 1944, prior to his departure for America to participate in the WJC's emergency war conference in Atlantic City, Weissmann received a letter from Robert Dexter, the WRB's envoy in Lisbon. Dexter praised the WJC, and especially Weissmann, for having worked to ameliorate the living conditions of the refugees in Portugal, and for the rescue operation they had set up there. Toward the end of the letter he referred to the number of children who were rescued through Weissmann's efforts in Lisbon, as follows:

> It is not your fault that this number was not vastly greater, but the hundreds who did come through, whether under the auspices of your organization or in any other way, owe you and the World Jewish Congress a deep debt of gratitude. In view of the difficulties under which you have been laboring here, your accomplishment has been of an unusually high order.[329]

Dexter's praise was not offered without a context, and should be read against the backdrop of the severe criticism leveled at the mode of operation of the WJC, particularly its leadership, on the part of its rank and file delegates. This widespread dissatisfaction was unmistakably manifested during the debates at the Atlantic City conference. At the conference, the WJC leadership, as well as some of its ordinary members, described the overwhelming obstacles that confronted the organization in its attempts to rescue the Jews of Europe—from the restrictions the Allies placed on the transfer of food and money to Europe, to their refusal to attack the German death industry, to the cooperation of many of Europe's citizens with the Nazis. Alongside these explanations, they presented the brighter side of the picture as they related the practical steps taken by their organization on behalf of Europe's Jews. They told of the dispatch of food packages, the assistance rendered to refugees, political activity designed to ease the burden of Bulgarian and Danish Jews, and the rescue of children in Portugal. Yet despite the understanding shown toward the difficulties and the presentation of the organization's

---

added that, to his regret, he had no information whatsoever about the parents, and asked Ms. Spector to inform him of her sister's arrival in America, Weissmann's letter, June 19, 1944, AJA, 361 H296/4. See also Weissmann's report in the *Congress Weekly*, December 29, 1944. See, for example, a report on the voyage of the Portuguese ship Nyassa to Haifa with 750 Jewish refugees on board. Weissmann's letter to Kubowitzki, January 25, 1944, AJA, 361 H296/8. On the cooperation between the WJC and the Jewish Agency in the context of the voyage, see Weissmann's letter to Tartakower, January 7, 1944, AJA, 361 H296/8. The British embassy in Spain provided valuable assistance in arranging the voyage. See letter from Weissmann's office to the British ambassador in Madrid, January 16, 1944, AJA, 361 H294/5. On the voyage of an additional ship carrying 500 refugees from Portugal and Spain including 90 children, see Weissmann's telegram to Kubowitzki, October 24, 1944, AJA, 361 H295/9. Regarding the transfer of equipment, see Weissmann's telegram to the WJC executive in New York, September 19, 1944, AJA, 361 H296/4.

329 Robert Dexter's letter to Weissmann, October 24, 1944, AJA, 361 H296/4.

achievements, the Atlantic City conference was held amidst an atmosphere of failure and loss because American Jewry and the WJC had been unable to halt the murder of millions by the Nazis, or at least to curb it significantly.[330]

The Congress's rescue operation in Portugal was proudly mentioned several times during the debates at Atlantic City.[331] Yet, as is implied in Dexter's letter and in the testimony of Samuel Roth (a Jewish refugee who arrived in Lisbon and wrote to Kubowitzki about events there), contemporaries were aware that in spite of the vast financial and organizational effort invested in Portugal and the exceptional devotion displayed by all those involved in the operation, only relatively few children were rescued.[332] Over the intervening years this critical component of the assessment of the Congress's wartime comportment has been reinforced, and the story of the rescue operation has fallen by the wayside with regard to both the organization's official history and the public memory of its members. One may surmise that the WJC's official historiographers believed that emphasizing the rescue of hundreds of children in Portugal would simply exacerbate criticism of the Congress and its leadership for having saved "only" a handful. The downplaying of the Portuguese saga in the official historiography of the WJC led to its exclusion from scholarly research as well; the Congress archive was inaccessible until recently, so that scholarly debate on the endeavor of the WJC at the time of the Holocaust relied primarily on memoirs and various collections published by the Congress's institutions and functionaries. This state of affairs was evident in Wise's address at the WJC conference held in Montreux, Switzerland, in June 1948. While Wise, as president of the WJC, was undoubtedly involved in its rescue operation, he ignored it altogether in his address, in which he said, "We failed to save millions of Jews, but we helped to save, in however decimated a form, the Jewish people."[333]

The difficulty of integrating the story of the rescue in Portugal with the general scholarly discourse on the rescue of Jews during the Holocaust was significantly compounded by the fact that the WJC's operation in Portugal was totally excluded from the memoirs of activists in the other organizations that took part in the general Jewish rescue operation, especially those in the Iberian Peninsula. For example, Eliyahu Dovkin, head of the Jewish Agency's Aliya Depart-

---

330 See the summary of the Atlantic City debates, November 26–30, 1944, AJA, 361 A67/5. For harsh criticism of the Allies' failure to attack the German death industry, see the summary of the Congress's rescue operation submitted to the Atlantic City conference, November 26, 1944, AJA, 361 A68/2.
331 See, for example, a copy of Weissmann's report to the conference in Weissmann, *Colossi of Evil*, 127–30, and a summary of the rescue operation, November 26, ibid.
332 Samuel Roth's letter to Kubowitzki, June 12, 1944, AJA, 361 H296/4.
333 Wise's speech, June 27, 1948, AJA, 361 A5/9.

ment during World War II, wrote of the rescue activities conducted in Spain and Portugal in his book *Aliya and Rescue During the Holocaust Years*: "By contrast, the Jewish Agency authorized immigration permits for 700 of the 5,000 refugees who escaped to Spain and Portugal via the Pyrenees. Arrangements are currently underway for their voyage on a special ship to Palestine."[334] Dovkin's terse account totally ignores the efforts of the WJC in Portugal and in fact conceals the rich narrative set out in this chapter. The manner in which Dovkin glosses over the actions of the Congress in Portugal is particularly puzzling given that he himself, as the Jewish Agency's representative, signed the memorandum of understanding between the WJC and the JDC concluded in July 1944 at the American embassy in Lisbon. This proves beyond doubt that he was aware of the organization's operation in Portugal. A similar picture emerges from a book by Haim Barlas, head of the Jewish Agency's Rescue Committee in Constantinople, titled *Rescue at the Time of the Holocaust*. Barlas wrote on the book's title page: "In 1943 the Jewish Agency and the Joint set up rescue centers in Lisbon, Teheran and Shanghai, and emissaries from Palestine operated there too."[335] Further into the book he wrote, "At that time E. Dovkin was sent to Lisbon and Spain and he succeeded in arranging the aliya of Jewish refugees from France who were living in Spain, in particular the aliya of the children, and this facilitated the passage of further refugees to this country. Prior to this the refugees were regularly apprehended by the Spanish authorities, and ran the risk of being handed over to the Nazi border guards."[336] Like Dovkin, Barlas was aware of Weissmann's actions in Portugal, as evidenced by the contacts between the two men in 1943 regarding the fate of Turkish Jews living in France who were in grave danger. Weissmann and Barlas led the operation undertaken by the WJC and the Jewish Agency on behalf of these Jews, most of whom were saved. Further evidence of the contacts between the two can be found in the 1944 exchange of telegrams between Lisbon and Constantinople regarding the fate of 400 Spanish Jews who were living in Athens.[337]

As part of the attempt to shape Jewish historical memory and Israeli memory in particular, activists in the various bodies who had engaged in rescue sought to glorify the work of their own organizations while playing down that of their com-

---

[334] Eliyahu Dovkin, *Aliya and Rescue During the Holocaust Years* [in Hebrew] (Jerusalem, 1946), 53.
[335] Haim Barlas, *Rescue at the Time of the Holocaust* [in Hebrew] (Tel Aviv, 1975), 9.
[336] Ibid., 104–105.
[337] For a detailed account of the contacts between Weissmann and Barlas on the issue of Turkish Jews, see Weissmann, *Colossi of Evil*, 105–107; a telegram from Barlas to Weissmann on the matter of the Jews of Spanish citizenship living in Athens, April 5, 1944, AJA, 361 H296/3.

petitors. Examination of the books written by Dobvin and Barlas reveals that they chose to completely exclude the efforts of the WJC, but to mention the activity of the JDC, emphasizing its contribution in the Iberian Peninsula. This strategy may be read, as we have seen in earlier chapters, as resulting from the fact that the WJC was not defined as a Zionist organization (although it was not at all anti-Zionist), and that it was in effect competing with the Zionist movement. The JDC, on the other hand, was an entirely philanthropic organization and as such had no political or ideological quarrel with the Zionist movement. For this reason, mention of its contribution to the rescue operation during World War II could not constitute a propaganda or political tool that might detract from the reputation of the Zionist movement.

Despite the critical attitude toward the WJC and the tendency of nearly everyone—contemporaries, scholars, the organization's official historiographers, and activists belonging to other bodies—to ignore its rescue operation, from the perspective of over half a century of hindsight, a different evaluation emerges. The significance of the rescue of over a thousand children and parents who were smuggled into Portugal, and the thousands more who were concealed in France and conveyed to Switzerland by the WJC in 1943 and 1944 cannot be overstated. The episode of the rescue of the children by Congress officials in Lisbon sheds a different light on the WJC's entire operation at the time of the Holocaust. In this case the organization's leadership and its rank and file activists displayed initiative and determination, and altogether transcended the accepted boundaries of Jewish philanthropic activity prior to World War II and during its initial stages. True, this transformation took time, yet any assessment of the process should take into account the need for an organization that operated within the international political system, but conducted largely philanthropic work, to function in an entirely different arena. To make this transformation, it had to construct an organizational system that could work with espionage organizations, smugglers, underground groups, and a variety of governmental agencies. Notwithstanding the vital role that Weissmann played in setting up and running the rescue operation in Portugal, it was Riegner, representing the organization, who, realizing that it was essential to match the WJC's team of activists to the dramatic changes occurring for European Jewry since the outbreak of the war, had selected Weissmann for the position. The documents demonstrate that Weissmann could not have operated as he did without the organizational, financial, political and moral support of the World Jewish Congress.

From Denmark to Bulgaria: The Involvement of the World Jewish Congress in Further Rescue Operations in Europe

In Lisbon, Weissmann was primarily engaged in rescuing children and caring for the Jewish refugees in Spain and Portugal. Yet because of its strategic location, the WJC's branch in Lisbon served as a major center of additional rescue activities. Weissmann exploited his extensive network of contacts with political elements in the Iberian Peninsula and beyond in order to take action himself and to activate others on behalf of European Jews. Of particular interest is his endeavor to assist a group of Turkish Jews located in the region governed by the Vichy regime in France. On December 13, 1944, Weissmann learned of the immediate danger threatening thousands of Turkish Jews who had neglected to extend the validity of their Turkish passports and had thus lost their citizenship. As a result, the French regarded them as foreign nationals, but the Turkish consulates could not offer them protection. Weissmann began an international political campaign on their behalf. Making use of the singular lines of communication at his disposal, he turned to Haim Weizmann, president of the World Zionist Organization, to the Jewish Agency's envoys in Turkey, and to Stephen Wise. This international activity, particularly the pressure exerted by the United States, induced Laurence Steinhardt, the American ambassador in Ankara, to take resolute action to rescue them. Together with the Jewish Agency envoys, Steinhardt approached Turkey's foreign minister and was able to secure an audience for Haim Barlas, the Agency's representative, with Turkey's prime minister. The Turkish government eventually intervened with the Vichy government, which took the Turkish Jews under its wing and suspended their deportation from France.[338]

On another occasion in early 1944, Haim Barlas informed Weissmann of 400 Spanish Jews being held at the Haidari camp in the vicinity of Athens, pending deportation to the death camps.[339] Weissmann contacted Nicolas Franco, the Spanish ambassador to Portugal and the brother of the Spanish dictator, and arranged a meeting with him. Weissmann later related that the ambassador enquired of him whether the Jews arrested by the Germans were in fact Spanish

---

[338] On the activity on behalf of the Jews of Turkey, see Weissmann's report to Kubowitzki, September 15, 1944, AJA, 361 H296/4; a report on the same activity in the WJC's mouthpiece *Congress Weekly*, vol. 11, no. 18, December 29, 1944, AJA, 361 A68/3. Weissmann told of the events in his memoirs, Weissmann, *Colossi of Evil*, 105–107. On the deportation of Turkish Jews whose nationality was unclear and the release of Jewish prisoners who were able to prove their Turkish citizenship, see Renee Poznanski, *Being a Jew in France, 1939–1945* [in Hebrew] (Jerusalem, 1994), 344, 402.

[339] Barlas' telegram to Weissmann concerning the Jews of Spanish nationality in Athens, April 5, 1944, AJA, 361 H296/3.

citizens or perhaps were merely carrying documents certifying that they were entitled to the protection of the Spanish government. Weissmann assured the ambassador that these were indeed Spanish citizens. The ambassador then claimed that, contrary to earlier statements, Spain had only limited influence in Germany. Weissmann responded by asserting his view that in the case of the Jews of Spanish nationality who had been apprehended in Athens, Spain had a natural right to care for its citizens and required no "special relationship" with Germany in order to apply this right. As the meeting proceeded, the ambassador stated that the Spanish government would take action on behalf of the arrested Jews in Athens, maintaining that his brother General Franco and the Spanish regime in general were not implementing an anti-Jewish policy. On the contrary, General Franco was most concerned about the Jewish issue, especially about the fate of Spain's Jews. To illustrate his point, the ambassador reminded Weissmann of Franco's refusal to pass anti-Jewish legislation in Spain despite Germany's demand. Weissmann responded feistily, informing the ambassador of the insurmountable difficulties faced by Spanish Jews who sought entry to Spain and of the severe restrictions that the Spanish government imposed on the number of Jews it was prepared to accept at any one time. Weissmann further reminded the ambassador of the prolonged time Spain had taken in permitting the entry of 400 Spanish Jews from Thessalonica and the Spanish government's refusal to accept additional Jews until this group had left the country.[340] The ambassador promised Weissmann that he would telephone Foreign Minister Count Jordana immediately after their meeting to ensure that the Spanish Jews in Athens received immediate assistance. He also undertook to approach his contacts in the Spanish regime in an effort to amend Spain's overall policy toward its Jewish citizens living in countries occupied or controlled by Germany.[341] The minutes of the meeting suggest that while Weissmann did ask the ambassador to intercede in the matter, he did so not as someone meekly requesting assistance, but as a skilled and assured politician who did not hesitate to argue his case and forcefully censure Spain's policy regarding its Jewish citizens. Weissmann's manner is reflective of his considerable stature in Lisbon and of the broad network of political connections he had built there.

The revelation of Weissmann's involvement in this episode adds a further dimension to the narrative of the rescue of Spanish Jews in Greece. Once Italy had surrendered, the Germans took control of southern Greece and Athens and

---

[340] For an extensive discussion of the affair of the Jewish Spanish nationals in Thessalonica, see Avni, *Spain*, 147–163.
[341] Secret minutes of Weissmann's meeting with the Spanish ambassador in Lisbon, April 8, 1944, AJA, 361 H296/3.

prepared to exterminate the remnants of Greek Jewry. On October 7 and 8, 1943, on the eve of Yom Kippur, the Day of Atonement, announcements were posted in Athens ordering the Jews, including foreign nationals, to assemble at designated points to be registered. Some months later, on March 25, 1944, the Jews of Athens, including those of Spanish nationality, were sent to the concentration camp at Haidari; from there they proceeded by train northward through central Greece. Additional Jews from other towns that had previously been under Italian control joined them so that the train now comprised 80 freight containing over 5000 Jews. When the train reached Austria, the carriages carrying the Spanish and Portuguese nationals were detached and they were transferred to the transit camp at Bergen Belsen. From the time of the German seizure of Athens until the incarceration of its nationals at Bergen Belsen, the Spanish authorities failed to take decisive action to prevent the Jews' imprisonment and subsequently to release them. A single exception is the actions of Spanish Consul General to Greece Sebastian Romero Radigales, who made every effort to protect the Jews, but faced opposition on the part of his superiors. The Spanish government eventually altered its policy, took stronger action on behalf of its Jewish citizens in Bergen Belsen, ensured that they remain alive, and took steps to have them moved to Spain. Despite the change in Spain's policy, the turmoil in Europe during the final months of 1944 delayed their transfer to Spain, and they were eventually liberated at the last moment by front-line American forces on April 13, 1945.[342] Even though the Spanish government had taken steps some months earlier to have its citizens in Thessalonica released, Spain in fact refused to prevent the arrest of the Jews in the first place or to accept its Jewish nationals from Athens who had been held in Bergen Belsen. Nevertheless, on April 11, 1944, it did appear that the Spanish government was changing its policy when it approached the German foreign ministry through its embassy in Berlin to request that its deported nationals be handed over and that the Germans attend to the bureaucratic and technical aspects that this entailed. The reason for this change of heart is unclear. Scholars who have investigated the event speak of a dispute within the Spanish regime between those who advocated the absorption of the Jews and others who opposed it, which could have resulted in a change of Spain's policy and in the prolonged delay in implementing the decision. It is very likely that Germany's deteriorating military position and Spain's desire to prepare for the Allies' victory played a part in reshaping the regime's policy.[343] Nevertheless, it is noteworthy that this transformation in Spanish policy occurred two days after Weissmann's meeting with

---

342 Avni, *Spain*, 147–163.
343 Ibid.; Michael Molcho and Yosef Nehama, *The Holocaust of Greek's Jews, 1941–1944* [in Hebrew] (Jerusalem, 1965), 92–93, 146–147. For criticism on the part of one of the survivors toward

the Spanish ambassador in Lisbon. This meeting, held in the midst of an internal Spanish dispute concerning the fate of the Jews, must have reinforced the argument of those who favored taking action to rescue the Jews of Spanish nationality in Greece. Spain's willingness to accept the Greek Jews is all the more remarkable in that prior to the episode of the Thessalonica Jews, the Spanish government held a narrow definition of Jews considered to be Spanish nationals and thereby entitled to the its protection, so that many Jews of Spanish nationality did not receive that protection.[344]

The political endeavor of the WJC's Lisbon branch on behalf of Turkish Jews in France and Spanish Jews of similar status in Greece was a small-scale version of the political activity conducted by the Congress's New York office on behalf of the Jews of Denmark and Bulgaria. In early 1943 the WJC leadership in New York learned of the Bulgarian authorities' intention to expel the nation's Jews and, in effect, to deport them to the death camps.[345] The information that reached New York reflected these dramatic developments in Bulgaria. In the winter of 1943 Bulgarian authorities, in conjunction with German officials, had begun practical preparations for deportation of Jews. In early March of that year a decision was made to deport the Jews of Macedonia and Thrace without delay. These regions had been taken from Yugoslavia and Greece and annexed to Bulgaria in response to its support for Germany. Their legal status was unclear; although Bulgaria controlled them, the Jews living in them were not granted Bulgarian citizenship. The Jews of Macedonia and Thrace were assembled in designated locations and the great majority of them, over 11,000 individuals, were eventually deported to the extermination camps. Meanwhile, the Bulgarian authorities began to prepare for deportation of the Bulgara's Jewish citizens. Information regarding these intentions leaked out and sparked a political and public campaign within the country. At its peak, Deputy Speaker of Parliament Dimitar Peshev and 42 other deputies signed a petition protesting the deportation of the Jews and presented it to the prime minister. An order to cease the deportation was eventually issued, and although the Jews of Sofia were sent to provincial towns and Jewish leaders were imprisoned for varying periods, the danger of deportation to the death camps receded.[346]

---

the relatively late effort made by the WJC on behalf of Greek's Jews, see Michael Matsas, *The Illusion of Safety, The Story of the Greek Jews During the Second World War* (New York, 1997), 24–25.
344 Avni, *Spain*, 198–199.
345 Tartakower, a draft of his memoirs, undated, CZA, 6-C/32.
346 On the saga of the rescue of Bulgaria's Jews, see Binyamin Arditi, *The Jews of Bulgaria During the Years of the Regime, 1940–1944* [in Hebrew] (Tel Aviv, 1962); Nissan Oren, "A New Perspective on the Rescue of Bulgaria's Jews" [in Hebrew], *Yad Vashem Collected Studies* 7 (1968):116–177.

A comprehensive debate on the Bulgarian decision to halt the deportation of the country's approximately 50,000 Jews continues to this day. Scholars and contemporaries alike have offered various explanations. These include the opposition expressed by Bulgaria's King Boris to the expulsion; the endeavors of sections of the Bulgarian people and church to resist the deportation because of the Jews' close involvement in Bulgarian society; the protest in the Bulgarian parliament; the growing strength of the Allies in the war on Germany; and the intrepid stand taken by Bulgaria's Jewish community and its leadership. So far, scholarly study has failed to arrive at a definitive answer to the question of what led to the rescue of Bulgarian Jewry and it is widely agreed that no single answer exists; the decision most probably resulted from a complex assortment of influences.

Both scholars and contemporary observers have played down the significance of international pressure and have ignored altogether, or merely hinted at, WJC efforts as factors.[347] However, the papers of the WJC tell a different story. While the organization's store of documents fails to provide a comprehensive solution to this question that has occupied so many scholars and survivors, it does provide valuable additional information about the array of pressures exerted on the Bulgarian regime by the WJC. As soon as word reached the Congress that the Bulgarian government intended to expel the country's Jews, Stephen Wise approached high-ranking officials in the U.S. State Department and urged them to exert pressure on the Bulgarian regime to prevent their deportation. The organization's New York office received a stream of reports on events in Bulgaria and the WJC maintained intensive contact with organizations and figures in the United States and Europe that had dealings with Bulgaria. Christian lay and religious leaders recruited to the campaign approached the Bulgarian Church; contact was established with leaders of the Bulgarian diaspora community in neutral countries; in the United States, connections of former Ambassador to Bulgaria Henry Wharton Shoemaker, were called upon; and various Latin American countries approached the Bulgarian government at the request of the WJC.[348] I do not maintain that

---

347 This tendency is apparent in all the publications referred to above. See, for example, the passing reference to Wise's involvement in the campaign on behalf of Bulgarian Jewry in Oren, *A New Perspective*, 93. See also Haim Keshles, *The Annals of Bulgaria's Jews During the Holocaust Period, 1939–1944* [in Hebrew], vol. 3 (Tel Aviv, 1969), 194–196.

348 For information on WJC activity on behalf of Bulgarian Jews, see the attempt to persuade the International Red Cross to intervene on their behalf, minutes of the Emergency Committee for the Rescue of European Jews, July 21, 1943, AJA, 361 A70/7; Report on the WJC rescue effort, November 26, 1944, AJA, 361 A68/2; a lecture delivered by Leon Kubowitzki, November 26, 1944, AJA, 361 A68/2; a top secret report of the WJC Rescue Council, November 1944 (no precise date given), which addresses primarily the pressure exerted on the Bulgarian authorities through ecclesiastical figures in Bulgaria and around the world, AJA, 361 A68/2. See also Photostats of

WJC efforts within the United States on behalf of Bulgarian Jews constituted the weightiest factor in bringing about the change in Bulgarian policy, yet recognition of the organization's endeavor to rescue Bulgaria's Jews adds an important element to the assessment of the circumstances that brought about this rescue, and underscores the importance of applying international pressure— a significant contribution of the WJC. It is particularly important to acknowledge the substantial role played by the WJC in saving Bulgarian Jewry because scholarly works on this dramatic saga of rescue allude to the organization's contribution only in passing and somewhat vaguely, if at all.

Shortly after learning of the danger awaiting the Bulgarian Jewish community, the WJC received similar communications with reports that the Germans intended to deport the Jews of Denmark. This information was conveyed to Stephen Wise by Denmark's ambassador to Washington, Hendrich De Kauffmann. The ambassador shared with Wise information divulged by a senior German official posted in Denmark. The Swedish government was willing to accept the Jewish refugees, and the Danish government had agreed to fund the clandestine transfer of Denmark's Jews to Sweden.[349] The reports that reached the United States were mere indications of a complex process that had been set in motion following the German invasion of Denmark in April 1940. The country had been occupied by the Germans very quickly, even though it had declared itself neutral. The terms of surrender allowed Denmark to maintain its institutions of government, which enabled the regime to prevent implementation of Germany's racist policy toward the Jews. Hostile acts aimed at the Germans in Denmark became more frequent in the summer of 1943, leading the Germans to declare a state of emergency followed by dissolution of the government, and the imposition of military rule on August 29. This development enabled Nazi leaders to activate their plans for the expulsion of Denmark's Jews. The Germans' intention to implement the "final solution in Denmark" was leaked by Georg Ferdinand Duckwitz, a German diplomat at his country's embassy in Denmark. The information was conveyed to the Danish underground and to the heads of the Jewish community. Danish Jews went into hiding, and an operation to smuggle Jews out of the country by way of fishing boats to neutral Sweden commenced. In excess of 7,000 Danish Jews, some 90 percent of the community, were transferred to Sweden in this manner. The Germans managed to lay their hands on less than 500 Jews, whom they

---

Stephen Wise's telegrams and letters pertaining to the rescue of Bulgaria's Jews in the memoirs of Binyamin Arditi, *The Jews of Bulgaria*, 316–317.
349 On the WJC's efforts regarding Denmark's Jews, see the summary of the organization's activities submitted to the Atlantic City conference, November 26, 1944, AJA, 361 A68/2; Tartakower, Memoirs (undated), 27, CZA, C-6/352.

deported to Theresienstadt concentration camp. The Danish government continued to monitor the fate of the imprisoned Jews. Its representatives visited them and they were sent food and medication. By virtue of these actions, only some 150 Danish Jews were murdered in the Holocaust.[350] The papers of the WJC reveal that the information on the Germans' intention to activate their plan for the final solution in Denmark also reached Stephen Wise in America. Wise and his colleagues in the WJC leadership acted in conjunction with the Danish ambassador to the United States to ensure that Sweden did indeed accept the Danish Jews. Their objective was to encourage the administration to exert significant political pressure on Sweden, namely to inform the Swedish government that the United States fully supported the absorption of Danish Jews in Sweden, even if they entered the country without the Germans' permission. The Danish ambassador impressed upon Wise that the Roosevelt administration's intensive involvement in the matter was vital to encouraging the neutral Swedish government to absorb the Danish Jews despite Germany's opposition. On October 1, 1943 Wise and Goldmann met with Undersecretary of State Breckenridge Long, who accepted their suggestion that the State Department officially request the Swedish government to allow the entry of the Danish Jews to the country. Wise and Goldmann held a further meeting with Finland's ambassador to Washington, Dr. Hjalmar Procope.[351] The minutes indicate that this meeting was part of a concerted effort by Wise and Goldmann to secure Finland's agreement to accept the Jews of Denmark should the Swedish move fail. The ambassador's discussion with Wise and Goldmann reveals that the government of Finland was prepared in principle to absorb the Danish Jews, although the three men agreed that because of technical difficulties, Finland could only absorb a relatively small number of Jews. The Finish agreement is important primarily because it may have encouraged the government of Sweden to adopt a similar policy, particularly since the meeting's participants believed that there were similarities in the two nation's status of neutrality.[352] In her comprehensive study of the operation to rescue Denmark's Jews, Leni Yahil wrote that it did not commence until spring 1943, when, after Stalingrad, a change

---

350 On the rescue of Denmark's Jews, see a historiography survey of studies on this topic, Tatiana Bronstein Bernstein, "The Unsuccessful Attempt to Expel the Jews of Denmark in Historiographical Debate" [in Hebrew], *Yad Vashem Collected Studies* (1987): 17–18, 299–328; Vilhjalmur Orn Vilhjalmsson and Bent Bludnikow, "Rescue, Expulsion, and Collaboration: Denmark's Difficulties with Its World War II Past," *Jewish Political Studies Review* 3–4 (2006): 3–30; Leni Yahil, *The Rescue of Danish Jewry, Test of Democracy* (Philadelphia, 1969) .Leo Goldberger, ed., *The Rescue of the Danish Jews* (New York, 1987).
351 This meeting is mentioned in a report on the activity of Wise and Goldmann in Washington, October 16, 1943, AJA, 361 B1/6.
352 Ibid.

in Swedish policy toward Germany became apparent and instances of resistance to Germany within the country became more frequent. Yahil stresses that while Sweden's willingness to absorb the Danish Jews was a part of this process, the Swedish government had at first merely lodged a diplomatic protest of the Jews' expulsion with the German Foreign Ministry. The change in Sweden's policy and its willingness to accept the Jews who had fled clandestinely from Denmark was not a foregone conclusion, but was the result of an extensive public campaign. Yahil specifically cites the broad endeavor by Swedish public figures and intellectuals, and the Finish reaction condemning the intention to expel the Danish Jews as having been particularly persuasive. The efforts of Wise and Goldmann in the United States through the State Department and the Finish Ambassador to Washington are not mentioned at all in scholarly literature, although they were part of a comprehensive political endeavor that complemented the activity undertaken in Sweden. Its full importance is made clear by noting that when this issue initially arose, the Swedish government refrained from adopting a clear-cut position in favor of accepting the Danish Jews into its country.[353]

The WJC offices in New York and Europe were also involved in the complex struggle to rescue Hungarian Jewry. Unlike the cases of Denmark, with its few thousand Jews, and Bulgaria, which was home to several tens of thousands, this was a large community numbering some 800,000 Jews following the annexation of Slovak, Romanian, and Yugoslav territories to Hungary. The deportations from Hungary to Auschwitz-Birkenau commenced in May 1944. Some 437,000 Jews were murdered within a period of 56 days. After the Arrow Cross party had gained power in October 1944, thousands of Budapest's Jews were murdered on the banks of the Danube and tens of thousands were sent on death marches toward the Austrian border. In all, some 565,000 Hungarian Jews were murdered. The United States administration, particularly the War Refugee Board, was deeply involved in efforts on behalf of this community.[354] Here again I do not intend to address in full the complex issue of Hungary's Jews and the rescue of hundreds of thousands of their number during the Holocaust, but merely to offer fresh information regarding WJC activity in the rescue effort. In 1944, seeking to use the experience gained in Portugal and Spain, the WJC leadership decided to implement a similar operation to enable small groups of Hungarian Jews to move into territory controlled by the Tito-led partisans in Yugoslavia and to reach hiding places in Slovakia to be prepared by the local resistance movement. Congress emissaries

---

353 Yahil, *The Rescue of Danish Jewry*, 320–368.
354 We are unable here to present the rich scholarship on the Holocaust of Hungarian Jews. See, for example, David Cesarani, ed., *Genocide and Rescue: The Holocaust in Hungary 1944* (Oxford, 1997).

established initial contacts with underground activists in the various regions, and transferred substantial sums of money to them toward the preparation of a plan. The WJC emissaries in Europe later reported that despite concerted efforts to protect them, the escape groups had been apprehended by the Germans. The escape enterprise failed because of technical obstacles that impeded the crossing from Hungary into territories under partisan control, and because of the unwillingness of some partisan and resistance groups to offer active cooperation in support of the operation.[355] In conjunction with the attempt to organize escape groups, the WJC conducted a political effort in a number of countries urging them to publish announcements stating that the Jews of Hungary were citizens of their respective states and were thereby entitled to the protection of those states. The organization's leaders were aware that such a statement had only declaratory significance, but hoped that its very existence would impress upon the Hungarian authorities that the safety of its Jews was enormously important to the international community. As part of this endeavor, Leon Kubowitzki wrote to the Portuguese ambassador in Washington informing him of what he considered to be terrible instances of the massacre of Jews in Hungary and stressing that the lives of tens of thousands of Jews were in imminent danger. The letter reveals that Kubowitzki sought to broaden the terms of a previous understanding reached between the WJC and the government of Portugal, according to which Portugal's embassy in Budapest offered protection to a small number of Jews. In his letter Kubowitzki cites the activity conducted by Raul Wallenberg, Sweden's envoy to Budapest, who had been authorized by his government to issue documents affording protection to thousands of Jews who were to be accommodated in special houses under the wing of the Swedish government. He requested that the Portuguese government undertake a similar initiative, thereby becoming the vanguard of a broad political move by all the neutral countries to halt the murder of Hungary's Jews. Meanwhile, at the suggestion of Congress officials in Britain, WJC leaders in Washington approached the United States administration and the British government with a request to offer the protection of their countries to the Jews remaining in Hungary. Because they appreciated the legal obstacles involved in declaring these Jews to be citizens, they proposed the following wording: "This country would proclaim that it considers all Jews remaining in Europe as being under its protection as far as their physical safety is concerned, and that any infringement upon this safety (such as removal from their dwellings, subjection to starvation diets, etc.) will be dealt with as if American citizens were concerned." WJC leaders believed that a public pronouncement along these lines would gain wide attention, which might prevent or at least mitigate the persecution of Hungarian Jews

---

[355] Top secret report by the WJC's rescue committee, November 26, 1944, AJA, 361 A68/2.

as well as of any Jews who remained in German occupied territory in general. Unfortunately, this belief was not shared by the administration's Committee for the Rescue of Refugees or by the British government, both of which believed that their governments were not in a position to afford true protection to the Jews declared to be their citizens or under their protection, and that there was thus no point in making such a declaration.[356] Like the WJC's Lisbon operation to rescue children, its political activity aimed at rescuing Jews of Turkish-Spanish nationality, its endeavors on behalf of the Jewish communities of Denmark, Bulgaria and Hungary were conducted behind the scenes and clandestinely so that they did not clash with the policy of restraint that dictated the Congress's actions during World War II. Yet, as we have seen with regard to the operation to rescue the children, the fact that this activity was conducted in secret had a far-reaching implication that persisted long after the time of the action itself: The secrecy created the impression that the WJC had done nothing whatsoever. After the war the overwhelming sense of shock at the murder of the millions relegated the WJC rescue endeavor to the shadows; it was no longer possible for the Congress to correct the distorted picture that they themselves had created. Despite the tremendous effort the Congress made to rescue Jews, scholars and survivors alike have presented a united front in criticizing the WJC. To a certain extent, its success in rescuing the few in face of the murdered millions merely exacerbated the censure. Nowadays, with the perspective afforded by the intervening years, we are able to examine the WJC leadership's actions more objectively, and to conclude that in spite of the outward appearance of having engaged in rather feeble action, the Congress's leaders and institutions in fact conducted a broad-scale, significant, and successful rescue operation.

---

[356] Cited from a report on rescue and the difficulties involved in the Congress's rescue activity, November 26, 1944, prepared by Leon Kubowitzki, 19, AJA, 361 A68/2. For additional information on the WJC's rescue effort, see a report on the organization's rescue activity during World War II, ibid. See also a document submitted by the WJC's New York office to the Committee for War Refugees on the rescue activity which the Congress deemed vital to conduct in Europe, March 3, 1944, AJA, 361 A68/2.

Chapter 4
Diaspora Nationalism, The World Jewish Congress, American Jewry, and the Post-War Rehabilitation of Europe's Jews

The Rehabilitation of Europe's Jews

The historical narrative pertaining to American Jewry and the Holocaust, portrayed at length in the previous chapters is, for the most part, one of harsh criticism of the insubstantial effort made by American Jews with regard to the rescue of Jews during the Holocaust, while at the same time celebrating the contribution of the American Jewish community to the founding of the State of Israel. The conventional interpretation maintains that the individual and public shock induced by the Holocaust and the unease generated by the futility of their campaign to promote the rescue endeavor led American Jews and their leaders to summon all their energy to work for the establishment of a Jewish state as part of the international arrangements instituted after World War II. The willingness of American Jews to act as an ethnic group in pursuit of specific political goals is all the more noteworthy in that they were endeavoring to promote the establishment of the state in the face of opposition from the Democratic administrations of Presidents Franklin Delano Roosevelt and Harry Truman. In effect, they used the Jewish vote as a political tool to alter the policy of the administration with respect to the founding of a Jewish state in the Middle East.[357]

Previous studies have focused on the contribution of American Jews to the founding of the State of Israel in the wake of the Holocaust. As we shall see, the campaign on behalf of a Jewish state was but one element within the growing tide of post-war ethnic Jewish activity in the United States. This period also witnessed a fascinating trend toward shaping a Jewish nationality in the Diaspora that would exist alongside the State of Israel. Those who molded this process were not driven by an anti-Zionist outlook, but rather sought to constitute a Jewish community that would coexist with Israel.[358] While large-scale philanthropic activity consti-

---

[357] For a comprehensive study of the Jews within the US political system, see Peter Y. Medding, "Segmented Ethnicity and the New Jewish Politics," *Studies in Contemporary Jewry* 3 (1987): 26–48.
[358] On the contribution and importance of American Jewry to the founding of the State of Israel, see Alon Gal, *David Ben Gurion: Toward a Jewish State, Political Preparation vis-à-vis the White Paper and the Outbreak of World War II, 1938–1941* [in Hebrew] (Ben Gurion University in the

tutes a major element in the ethos of Jewish American elites, WJC leaders added a further dimension to it. In addition to the traditional welfare endeavor on behalf of displaced persons and survivors, they involved these people in the post-war rehabilitation processes conducted in Europe and shaped an ethnic way of life characterized by a Diaspora nationality. The leaders of the World Jewish Congress led the way to establishing a functioning and active Jewish Diaspora in the post-war world. Their mode of operation during the three decades that followed World War II was markedly different from the patterns of action that characterized other segments of American Jewry. Indeed, significant groups among American Jews sought to shape the relations between the State of Israel and American Jewry in such a way as to ensure the continued functioning of American Jews as American citizens intimately involved with the Jewish state. This aspiration is made plain in the agreement concluded between Israel's Prime Minister David Ben Gurion and Jacob Blaustein, chairman of the American Jewish Committee in the 1950s. The agreement recognized American Jews' commitment to remain loyal only to the United States, and Blaustein's commitment to support the young state. Abba Hillel Silver, America's foremost Zionist leader in the 1940s, also sought to shape the State of Israel and its relationship with American Jewry in such a way as to ensure that American Zionism would continue to flourish following the founding of the state.[359]

What set the WJC apart from other Jewish organizations was that its leaders sought not merely to institutionalize the relationship between Israel and American Jewry, but involved themselves in the Jewish world as a whole, particularly in Europe where they worked vigorously to rehabilitate the Jewish Diaspora and to assist those survivors wishing to reestablish their lives there. The cataclysmic event of the Holocaust served as a catalyst toward reinforcing the ethnic-national endeavor that the Congress leaders led in a wide range of spheres, from the inauguration of cultural and educational institutions in Europe to the construction of political and economic mechanisms designed to promote the restoration of Jewish property and the payment of appropriate compensation to survivors and to the entire Jewish world. At the same time, they actively pursued the indictment

---

Negev, 1985), 131–148; Ariel L. Feldstein, *The Gordian Knot, David Ben Gurion, the Zionist Organization, and US Jewry* [in Hebrew] (Ben Gurion Institute for the Study of Israel, Zionism, and Ben Gurion's Legacy) (Qiryat Sdeh Boqer, 2003), 1–66; Raphael, *Silver*, 135–164.

359 See Feldstein, *The Gordian Knot*, 67–105. For an in-depth discussion of Silver's activities in the context of the founding of the State of Israel, see my article, Zohar Segev, "US Zionists in Israel During the Fifties: Political Opposition and a Liberal Alternative" [in Hebrew], *Iyunim Bitkumat Israel, Studies in Zionism, the Yishuv and the State of Israel* 12 (2002): 493–519.

of war criminals and participated in shaping political arrangements in Europe to guard against a recurrence of anti-Jewish activity.

In a speech delivered to the WJC's European wing in 1945 Stephen Wise expressed the view that the WJC's existence alongside the Zionist movement was absolutely essential, and that the two movements must agree on a division of labor within the Jewish world.[360] As he had done on previous occasions, Wise maintained that the Jews of the world were a single people sharing a common belief and future. The two most pressing problems confronting the Jewish people after the war were the opening of Palestine to immigration and the renewal of Jewish life in the liberated countries. He noted that the WJC had made every effort to promote the opening of the gates of Palestine and had offered its services to the Zionist movement. Applauding the Zionist movement and the Jewish society in Palestine, he underscored the immense importance of maintaining the community of 600,000 Jews in Palestine as the base for the continued existence of the Jewish people. Yet despite the Zionist movement's importance in the Palestine context, when it came to restoring Jewish life in Europe the WJC was the only body willing and able to undertake the task. Wise impressed upon his audience that the WJC's parallel activity on behalf of both these objectives—the establishment of a Jewish state and the restoration of Jewish life in Europe—was of utmost importance, and presented a challenge to those who regarded Zionism as the sole solution to the Jewish dilemma and who opposed the reconstitution of Jewish life in the Diaspora. He expressed the opinion that his Zionism did not stand in the way of engaging, as a Jew, with the problems of Jewish existence not only in Palestine, but worldwide. Throughout his speech Wise drew parallels between the Zionist movement and the WJC, explaining that many within both the Jewish and non-Jewish worlds believed there was no room for both movements. As the importance of the Zionist movement had become apparent to all in the early twentieth century, so too would the Jewish masses come to appreciate the undeniable need for the WJC. The parallels Wise traced between the Zionist movement and the Congress indicate his desire to shape the WJC in the image of the Zionist movement as a worldwide establishment boasting a streamlined set of institutions, representing world Jewry in its entirety, and gaining international recognition.[361]

---

360 Wise's speech at the conference of the WJC's European wing (no location given), August 19, 1945, AJA, 361 A9/10.

361 Ibid. The fact that Wise chose to draw a parallel between the Zionist movement and the WJC indicates that in 1945, both Wise and his audience regarded the Zionist movement as a successful venture that could be held up as a model whose major components were known to everyone. Wise's outlook found practical expression in an official publication that set out the Congress's working program for 1946, which underlined the organization's singularity vis-à-vis the Zionist movement. See The WJC work program for 1946 (no precise date specified), AJA, 361 A5/6. The

The founding of the State of Israel in 1948 reinforced the need to grapple with the problems that had surfaced in the past regarding the WJC's role and status regarding the Jewish state. Wise addressed this issue in his opening speech at the Congress's conference in Montreux, Switzerland, in June 1948.[362] He declared that despite the founding of the state, the heads of the WJC represented the large majority of world Jewry, and was the conduit through which they could make their concerns known. The founding of the state required that the WJC reshape Jewish life in the Diaspora. The Congress would work to ensure that Israel and the Diaspora cooperated productively, and that future Jewish life in the Diaspora would be thought out according to a predefined objective, rather than haphazardly.[363]

The Israeli wing of the Congress published an action program in 1949 clarifying the WJC characterization as the representative of Diaspora Jewry: The WJC leadership thought of the organization as the sole representative not just of Jews in its member countries, but of all Diaspora Jews, and would advocate on their behalf in dealings with Israel's government vis-à-vis international bodies and United Nations institutions, and with respect to the Israeli government itself. By virtue of its status, the WJC intended to maintain ongoing contact with Israel's foreign ministry regarding the fate of Jews in Arab countries, and to cooperate with the Israeli government and the Jewish Agency on this and any further issues requiring its involvement. The WJC would systematically expose the problems of Diaspora Jewry, present them to the Israeli public, and gather information from those migrating to Israel about their communities.[364]

Both Wise's speech and the action plan demonstrate the belief of Congress functionaries that the establishment of the state had not rendered their organization redundant. The Holocaust and the failure to rescue significant numbers of Jews reinforced their conviction that only Jewish unity allied with a worldwide organizational structure would stand world Jewry in better stead in the future. This need for a Jewish nationality in the Diaspora to which the State of Israel would not constitute an alternative was one of the most important implications

---

view that the WJC should combine the goals of Palestine and Diaspora Jewry had surfaced even earlier. See the memorandum of the WJC executive to the League of Nations, which clearly presents this integration: memorandum of the organization's executive to the League of Nations, December 16, 1936, AJA, 361 A1/2.

362 Wise's inaugural address to the WJC congress in Montreux, Switzerland, June 27, 1948, AJA, 361 A9/10. Wise returned to this theme in an article in Congress Weekly, August 20, 1948, AJA, 361 A29/1. For the complete resolutions adopted at the Montreux conference, see the Collected Resolutions, June 6–27, 1948, AJA, 361 A3/12.

363 Wise's inaugural address, ibid.

364 Action plan of the WJC's Israeli wing, November 4, 1949, AJA, 361 A28/8.

to be drawn from the Holocaust. Moreover, Wise declared that the significance of the WJC transcended the boundaries of the Jewish world. As he viewed it, "justice for the Jews," and their integration with the world that was emerging in the wake of World War II were not purely Jewish objectives because their realization would assure "world peace."[365]

The desire both to maintain a significant Jewish Diaspora alongside the State of Israel and to reinforce Jewish identity were expressed in practice during the 1940s in WJC efforts to rescue Jews from the horrors of the war in Europe and to care for them. The organization's sincere concern for the fate of Jewish survivors in Europe became blended with their recognition of the rehabilitation process as transcending the sphere of individual solutions and shaping the post-war Jewish world. The matter of the survivors was of major concern to the WJC as early as 1942, as evidenced by a two-day clandestine meeting convened to discuss the establishment of an advisory committee on European Jewry.[366] Committee members were to work both to create a constructive welfare apparatus that would address the immediate needs of the refugees such as food and well-being, and to develop strategies toward rehabilitating Jewish life in Europe and reintegrating the Jews with Europe's economic fabric. This was to be a long-term task, implemented gradually, that would go beyond the scope of conventional philanthropic endeavors. Attention would initially focus on the most pressing needs, but once conditions had been stabilized, the work would enter the second stage: Those refugees who wished to do so would be assisted in returning to their countries of origin and an efficient migration and support apparatus would be set up for those who wished to rebuild their lives elsewhere. Participants at this discussion believed that returning Jews to their original countries was the simpler stage of the rehabilitation process.[367] They foresaw that the process of restoring Jewish property and the payment of compensation would be prolonged and complex,

---

365 This suggests that the integration of Jews with the new world order was a touchstone of the capacity to realize a policy of reconciliation and peace in the post-war. See Wise, June 27, 1948, AJA, 361 A9/10. For a further example of the necessity for a worldwide representative organization for the Jewish people, see the resolutions on the post-war action plan adopted by the executive committee (undated), AJA, 361 A1/8. Beginning in 1948, the WJC placed concern for the fate of the Jewish communities in Arab countries at the top of their agenda. See, for example, the letter written by Charles Malik, head of the UN consultative committee with non-governmental organizations, to Leon Kubowizki regarding the WJC's application to UN bodies. The letter refers to a prolonged correspondence between the organization and UN departments that handled NGOs regarding the fate of the Jews in Arab lands. The writer concludes that no emergency action is required on this issue, despite the WJC demand to undertake such steps. See the letter from Charles Malik to Leon Kubowizki, June 2, 1946, AJA, 361 B104/3.
366 Minutes of meeting of the committee, June 6–7, 1942, AJA, 361 D104/6.
367 Ibid.

both technically and legally, yet regarded this as vital to the reintegration of Jews in Europe. They stressed that the rehabilitation of Jewish refugees must be undertaken as part of the overall process of European rebuilding and rehabilitation. The heads of the WJC foresaw that an intensive effort would be required if the Jews were to secure justice through the rehabilitation process. Their rights would have to be enshrined by law; they could not rely solely on the generosity and goodwill of governments and international organizations. The Congress leaders noted that prior to World War II only Jewish organizations had operated welfare and aid programs for European Jews, especially those in Eastern Europe. This solution was no longer tenable. Furthermore, Jewish wellbeing should be the concern of the various governments as part of the national tasks that confronted them. In pointing out those governments' obligation to ensure the welfare of their Jewish citizens, Congress leaders stressed that addressing the welfare and rehabilitation of Europe's Jews was primarily a Jewish task that should be undertaken by Jewish organizations through dedicated fundraising appeals among Jews throughout the world.[368]

This document indicates the WJC's belief that its contribution to the process of rehabilitating European Jews was more important than its engagement in matters of wellbeing. As a democratic Jewish organization, the WJC must contribute decisively to the development of an all-encompassing bureaucratic apparatus whereby Jews around the world—particularly those in Europe—could be organized into a democratic political force.[369] In the estimation of the Congress leadership, the integration of the Jewish people in the Diaspora to the reemerging fabric of European life could be assured only by means of democratic Jewish-led political activity, a marked departure from earlier patterns of philanthropic endeavor.

It should be noted that the efforts of the Congress leadership in the United States in reshaping Jewish existence in Europe in the long term were conducted alongside a similar endeavor within the American arena to care for the survivors in liberated Europe. As early as November 1944, Arieh Tartakower was engaged in intensive discussion with officials and military personnel in the Department of Defense to impress upon them the singular situation of Jewish displaced persons and survivors among the general refugee population.[370] Tartakower spoke of the terrible suffering endured by European Jews, stressing in particular that while some of the Jewish displaced persons were nationals of Germany or its satellite states, they must be considered citizens of the Allies rather than of enemy states.

---

[368] Ibid.
[369] Ibid.
[370] On these contacts, see Tartakower's letter to J.H. Hilldring, Head of the Civil Affairs Division at the Department of Defense, November 13, 1944, AJA, 361 D68/14.

He was particularly concerned by reports that the Allies were preparing to house the refugees in temporary camps until a long-term solution was found, and that assignment to the various camps would be based on country of origin. Tartakower demanded that a separate constellation of camps be set up for Jews. He explained to the Defense Department officials that many of the non-Jewish refugees, including citizens of non-enemy countries, came from communities that had a long history of hostility toward the Jews and had on occasion collaborated with the Germans in persecuting and murdering Jews. It would be unthinkable to accommodate Jews alongside their murderers, which would result in ongoing tension and violence. Moreover, Tartakower sought assurances that were the Allies and the American occupation administration to adopt an overall strategy ordering refugees to return to their countries of origin, Jews would be exempted from the requirement. Here again, Tartakower had to explain to his interlocutors that the Jews could not be forced to return to countries such as Poland, Hungary, Austria, and Romania because a considerable section of the population of these countries had collaborated with the Nazis in persecuting and murdering Jews. If such a return were to take place, it would require careful preparation and could only be implemented on a voluntary basis.[371] Tartakower was not content merely to present the needs of the Jewish displaced persons; he requested and obtained from Hilldring a commitment that the Department's recognition of the singular situation of the Jewish displaced persons would take the form of orders, memoranda, and written instructions, rather than merely oral agreements between the Congress representatives and their Defense Department and U.S. Army interlocutors.[372]

The WJC's desire to gain recognition of the Jewish displaced persons' singular condition and its attempt to influence policy toward them is also apparent in its endeavor to become involved in shaping the policy of UNRRA (the United Nations Relief and Rehabilitation Administration). The organization was founded in 1943 and became a part of the United Nations after 1945. It operated as an international agency until 1947 initiating, administering, and implementing welfare programs in Europe. The WJC involved itself in UNRRA's activity from its inauguration by submitting memoranda to the body's various branches and seeking to place Jews, especially Congress representatives, on its staff in Europe.[373] In September 1944 Wise and Goldmann submitted a signed memorandum to UNRRA. In it they applauded the body's policy of conducting welfare activity directed at

---

371 Ibid.
372 See letter from Hilldring to Tartakower, November 29, 1944, AJA, 361 D68/14.
373 On attempts to involve Jews and Congress activists in UNRRA activity, see Tartakower's report on his activity in London, AJA, 361 A1/4.

Europe's entire population, irrespective of origin, religion, or race, without differentiating between those in need of assistance who were nationals of enemy states and citizens of countries liberated from Nazi occupation. They added, however, that "those discriminated against by the Nazi oppressors must be given the same opportunities of recovery as the others. Thus, the Jews should be given equitable priorities in the distribution of food, medical aid and shelter, as well as in the return, repatriation, and resettlement of displaced persons."[374]

These attempts to influence the activities of the administration and UNRRA were accompanied by a supreme fundraising effort among WJC member nations to provide the money required to finance welfare and rehabilitation. The Congress raised ten million dollars during 1944. At the same time, it criticized other Jewish organizations, particularly the Joint Distribution Committee, for raising considerable sums of money but continuing to conduct only philanthropic activity rather than engaging in broad, politically significant rehabilitation efforts. An opinion piece in the December 1944 *Congress Weekly* addressed the issue: "On this need for centralized Jewish authority is based the decision adopted by the War Emergency Conference of the WJC to raise a fund of $100,000,000 for rehabilitation and reconstruction. Unlike other organizations which attempt to separate Jewish relief work from political activities the WJC, primarily a political organization, realized from its inception that the two are inseparable parts of a single task."[375]

In preparation for the reconstruction of the communities, the Congress established a training facility on the outskirts of Paris to teach personnel, primarily women, how to operate within European bureaucratic systems; in March 1946, 30 young women were selected to commence the study program.[376] They received training in a variety of areas, including education, community organization and action, Jewish festivals, selected issues pertaining to Jewish tradition, Zionism, and the Palestine problem. While all of this was going on, the WJC was also investing considerable effort in cultural rehabilitation within the communities. Hundreds of thousands of books were dispatched to Europe: basic textbooks on Jewish issues, Yiddish and Hebrew literature, prayer books, and Bibles. Particular emphasis was placed on the dispatch of more than 60 Torah Scrolls, most of them donated by communities in New York and Chicago, with the express intention of reviving the religious life of European Jewry.[377]

---

[374] WJC memorandum submitted to UNRRA, September 1944 (no precise date given), AJA, 361 C98/6.
[375] Editor's opinion piece in *Congress Weekly*, December 29, 1944, AJA, 361 A68/3.
[376] Report on the WJC's Cultural and Educational Division, March 20, 1946, AJA, 361 E10/14.
[377] Ibid.

In subsequent years the WJC continued to regard itself as being responsible for the overall cultural life in the communities. Its institutions sought to encourage Jewish youth in Europe to choose a career in Jewish education, and actively promoted the establishment of teacher-training institutes. In the papers of the Congress's European bodies there is documentation of programs for the preparation of textbooks on Jewish history between 1848 and 1938; for the founding of scientific journals addressing Jewish culture; and for adult education activities using the modern technology of the day such as radio, gramophone and movable displays.[378]

Engagement in the economic and cultural aspects of rehabilitation was accompanied by a debate pertaining to the political, legal, and juridical problems of Jewish life in post-war Europe. This discussion began with the assumption that the Allied victory would not offer an immediate resolution to the issue the Congress had termed the "Jewish problem," and that a considerable effort would be required to ensure the continuation of Jewish life in Europe.[379] Among the major problems mentioned in the report were: abrogation of the anti-Jewish legislation promulgated by the Nazis; restoration of Jewish property confiscated by the authorities; and resolution of issues intrinsic to the process of restoration of Jewish property including the creation of machinery for calculating the economic damage suffered by the Jews, recognition of the right of displaced persons to return to their homes, and establishment of a judicial apparatus that would prevent discrimination against Jews in the process of rehabilitation. The ongoing debate conducted by the Congress's institutions reveals that its leaders sought to go far beyond ameliorating the pressing privation that the Jewish refugees would surely experience after the war. Provision of health services, food, and temporary accommodation was only an intermediate objective. Rather, the Congress leadership sought to restore the Jews of Europe not only as individuals, but also as functioning, democratic Jewish communities. They were convinced that this model of the Jewish Diaspora was correct from an ideological standpoint, and would likewise ensure the maintenance of post-war Jewish life worldwide.[380]

However, the meager Jewish presence in the spheres of industry and agriculture severely impeded the rehabilitation process. The heads of the WJC foresaw

---

378 See a memorandum of the WJC's Paris office pertaining to future cultural activity, September 24, 1948, AJA, 361 E10/14. On the primacy and importance of the cultural aspect of processes of national crystallization, see John Hutchinson, "Cultural Nationalism and Moral Regeneration," in John Hutchinson and Anthony D. Smith (eds.), *Nationalism* (Oxford, 1994), 122–131.

379 Secret discussion on the preparations for post-war welfare activity among the Jews, June 6–7, 1942, AJA, 361 D104/6 .

380 Ibid.

these areas as the main thrust of economic growth, and recognized that the integration of Jews to Europe's economic structure required the establishment of a vocational training system. In addition, participants at the secret meeting placed special emphasis on the topic of housing. They believed that post-war Europe would suffer extensive destruction, and that a supreme effort would have to be made to ensure adequate accommodation for millions of Jews. This optimistic estimate of the number of survivors may be attributed to the fact that the discussion was held at an early stage of the war, before the WJC's European outfit had conveyed the first reports of the final solution to the United States.

The minutes of the meeting indicate the development of a detailed plan for caring for Holocaust survivors in which Palestine did not figure as the preferred destination for those to be rescued. Migration to Palestine is mentioned in a single paragraph noting that this issue would remain within the domain of the Jewish Agency. Meeting participants expected that migration to Palestine would increase because of the large number of refugees, but did not present Palestine as a preferred destination, leaving the implied suspicion that they were dissatisfied with the manner in which the Jewish Agency was addressing the issue. Discussion of the topic of welfare led to engagement with the political and legal aspects of post-war Jewish life in Europe. Those present assumed that while the Allies would win the war, the victory would not bring about an immediate solution to the Jewish problem. Such a solution would require an effort aimed specifically at ensuring the future of Jews after the war. The freedom of Jews to live in security wherever they chose was the supreme goal of WJC activity in the post-war period, and the participants stressed that this objective would not be easily met.[381]

In caring for the survivors and displaced persons, the WJC placed particular emphasis on the children. The importance of the issue of caring for children within the Congress's overall rehabilitation endeavor is clearly evident. Archival material testifies to the impressive apparatus set up by the Congress to address the needs of Jewish children in Europe. Educational facilities naturally played a major role in this respect, and the examination of this material provides a richer understanding of the WJC perspective regarding their desired configuration of the Jewish people following the war. As early as 1943 they had identified the need for a special deployment to care for children once the war was over; consequently, a Children's Division concerned primarily with Jewish orphans in Europe began operation in 1944. This arm of the Congress coordinated the fundraising effort on behalf of Jewish orphans and planned an array of related actions to be coor-

---

[381] Ibid. For a similar assessment of the rehabilitation process of European Jews, see the address delivered by Jacob Robinson, head of the WJC's Institute of Jewish Affairs, to the Peace Research and Study Committee in New York, January 25, 1943, AJA, 361 D104/6.

dinated by a committee, headed by Stephen Wise, charged with overseeing the rehabilitation of orphans.[382]

The endeavor on behalf of the children was manifested in two ways. The first involved setting up and operating an adoption procedure for Jewish children in both the United States and Palestine. The Congress encouraged adoption by families living in Palestine, stressing that the adopted children would subsequently participate in the building of the Land of Israel. Yet it nevertheless noted that it would also respond to applications for adoption submitted by American families.[383] The adoption issue is an indication of the WJC's dualist policy during the late 1940s. While it engaged in an intensive effort to rehabilitate Jewish life in Europe, it actively promoted the founding of a Jewish state in Palestine. One may surmise that by directing candidates for adoption to Palestine, the WJC leadership was intentionally applying this dual policy. The adoption process in Palestine was only peripherally associated with the rehabilitation of Jewish communities in Europe, and not likely to impede it. Moreover, migration to the United States was a highly complex undertaking, and delivering children for adoption in Palestine eased the Congress's burden of contending with bureaucratic complexities in the finding of appropriate and rapid solutions for a greater number of children.[384]

---

382 In discussions on the deployment required to care for the children after the war, it was estimated that over 150,000 children would need support. See Niva Ashkenazi, "The Youth Movements' Children's Homes in the US Occupation Zone in Germany, 1946–1948" [in Hebrew] (M.A. thesis in the Humanities, Tel Aviv University, 1996), 42. The numbers with which the WJC would in effect have to deal were regrettably lower. See a discussion held by the Peace Research and Study Committee in New York, January 25, 1943, AJA, 361 D104/6. The Congress papers contain no information on the precise date on which the division responsible for caring for the children was established. Evidence of its activity is to be found from 1944 onward. See a letter pertaining to fundraising for the children, July 10, 1944, AJA, 361 D71/2. See also an official pronouncement by the WJC on the topic of welfare and rehabilitation that underscores the privations suffered by the children and the unique nature of engagement with this issue: official declaration by the WJC on the topics of relief and rehabilitation, Novemeber 1944 (no precise date given), AJA, 361 C98/7. On the American Committee for the Care of Orphans, see Wise's letter to the American Council of Voluntary Agencies in which he requests that the committee receive official recognition by the council: Wise's letter, November 26, 1946, AJA, 361 D71/6. For a wide-ranging discussion of the issue of Jewish children in Europe, see Yehudit Tidor Baumel, "The Rescue and Settlement of Jewish Refugee Children from Europe in the USA during the Years 1938–1945" [in Hebrew] (Ph.D. dissertation, Bar Ilan University, 1985).

383 Stephen Wise, minutes of meeting of the Planning Committee for the Care of Children, January 25, 1946, AJA, 361 D71/7. For a similar view regarding the importance of adoption in Palestine, see a memorandum (name of author not given) on the WJC's activity in Belgium, January 25, 1946, AJA, 361 D71/7.

384 The Congress heads were aware of the problems inherent in the US immigration laws and sought to amend these laws in the late 1940s and to resist the proposed changes in legislation,

The WJC leaders proceeded along a parallel track by establishing orphanages in Europe and offering financial and pedagogical support to existing orphanages as well as those run by other Jewish organizations. While WJC children's homes were defined as orphanages, they also accepted children from single-parent families unable to look after them adequately in the conditions of post-war Europe. The heads of the WJC were aware of the onerous nature of this task and of the extreme complexity of caring for children who had undergone traumatic experiences during the war. They believed that the best way of rehabilitating these children and educating them to become good citizens was to have them adopted by Jewish families in Europe. The Congress leaders knew, however, that only few such families were able to undertake this task, and therefore made a point of setting up an educational and psychological support system in the orphanages.[385]

The Mizrahi movement, the Jewish Agency, and various Orthodox organizations chose to transfer responsibility for their orphanages in Europe to the WJC, signifying the Congress's commitment to caring for the orphans and the financial and organizational power it wielded that enabled it to assume responsibility for the orphanages run by other organizations. The relevant documents reveal that by taking these additional orphanages under its wing, the WJC agreed to bear a large part of the cost of their operation, in addition to taking responsibility for their ongoing administration. While the pedagogical elements of the curriculum would be suited to the nature of each of these institutions, they would adhere to a broad educational program set out by Congress bodies. In 1946, the WJC took care of over 1,600 children, who were placed in 13 children's homes.[386] The estab-

---

which they considered even worse, in the early fifties. See the statement made by WJC President Irwin Miller, March 17, 1950, AJA, 361 D68/4; Miller's press announcement, February 10, 1950, AJA, 361 D68/3.

385 See a report on the founding of an orphanage in Antwerp, Belgium, which includes a detailed survey of the candidates for enrollment: Memorandum on the Founding of an Orphanage in Belgium (no author specified), October 25, 1945, AJA, 361 D71/10. Regarding the dimension of the task facing the WJC in caring for the children and the preference for arranging for adoption by families, see a report by Leon Kubowizki, the official responsible for the Congress's rescue effort in Europe, April 26, 1945, AJA, 361 D71/6.

386 Post-War Work Plan of the WJC's Child Care Division (no date specified), AJA, 361 D71/11. In 1945 the WJC operated eight orphanages of its own, and was involved in administering and funding five others. The organization took care of over 1,400 children in Europe. See classified minutes of meeting of the WJC's Children's Affairs Committee, January 15, 1945, AJA, 361 D71/12. The number 1,600 was noted for 1946 in a letter written by Robert Marcus. See Letter from Marcus, November 5, 1946, ibid. Regarding the WJC's administration of the orphanages of other Jewish organizations, which provides an indication of its greater financial and organizational capacity, see, for example, a memorandum on the transfer of Ha-Mizrahi's orphanages to the care of the WJC, which refers to seven orphanages, the maintenance of which cost in excess of $70,000

lishment and maintenance of the orphanages presented a complex challenge to Congress institutions, as exemplified by Leon Kubowizki's April 1945 letter to Dr. Jacob Helman, a WJC activist from Buenos Aires in Argentina.[387] The letter tells of the founding of an orphanage by the organization for Italian Jewish children in Switzerland. The orphanage was built by virtue of Dr. Helman's donation, but the amount donated covered the operation of the orphanage only until July 1945. Kubowizki wrote that the orphanage had begun to function in December 1944 and that before entering the orphanage, most of the children had been in the care of the International Red Cross or Swiss philanthropic organizations. He emphasized that, because of the many difficulties involved in caring for them, the various welfare organizations were less than enthusiastic about taking responsibility for the children, whose condition was far from satisfactory. The WJC made a concerted effort to assemble 55 children between the ages of eight and sixteen who had been distributed among various institutions and in private homes. The organization rented a former high school building to house the children's home and adopted a pedagogic curriculum suited to Italian schools. The home was administered by an executive committee whose members included Dr. Gerhardt Rieger and a representative of the International Red Cross. The staff included a rabbi, who performed the function of a spiritual advisor, as well as a female spiritual counselor. Among the varied activities conducted in the orphanage, Kubowizki singled out the regular issue of an internal newspaper.[388]

The introduction of a curriculum suited to the requirements of the Italian Education Ministry is of particular interest, and lends support to the view, to be discussed later in this chapter, that one of the major goals of the educational program used in the Congress's children's homes was to prepare the pupils for a life in Europe. Apart from a small sum provided by the International Red Cross, the orphanage's budget, estimated to be between 6,000 and 7,000 Swiss francs

---

per annum. See a memorandum on this subject, February 18, 1947, AJA, 361 D71/12. In addition, special children's homes for the orthodox were established. These would be partly subsidized by the relevant orthodox organizations, but administered by the WJC. See minutes of meeting of the Child Care Planning Committee for Children's Affairs, March 6, 1946, AJA, 361 D71/11. See also the agreement between the WJC and the Jewish Agency according to which the Congress would assume exclusive responsibility for running the Agency's orphanages in Europe. The Jewish Agency undertook to consult with WJC functionaries with regard to all educational matters. A WJC representative would, moreover, join the Agency's administrative bodies that dealt with the topic of orphanages. See the agreement between the Jewish Agency and the WJC, 1945 (no precise date given), AJA, 361 D71/11. See also a report on the orphanage that formally belonged to the Aliyat Ha-No'ar organization but was in fact wholly administered by the WJC: minutes of meeting of the Planning Committee for Children's Affairs, January 25, 1945, AJA, 361 D71/25.

387 Letter from Leon Kubowizki to Joseph Helman, April 16, 1945, AJA, 361 D71/2.
388 Ibid.

per month, was funded primarily by donations from WJC members. Kubowizki wrote the letter with the intention of obtaining additional funding for the orphanage, which was in danger of closing unless more money was forthcoming.[389]

This letter requesting a donation from Argentina constitutes part of a wider effort to fund the care of children in Europe As part of this endeavor, American Jewish families and organizations undertook to cover the cost of maintaining a child in the WJC's children's homes in Europe. The amount requested was $300 per annum in addition to food parcels that the donor dispatched to the selected child. With a view to enhancing the donors' commitment, Congress leaders made a point of sending each donor family a photograph of their supported child, as well as information pertaining to the child's life story. Families that wished to do so could contact the child directly.[390] Another way in which American families could support the children was to send food parcels to Europe on a regular basis. In this instance too, the American families accepted a long-term commitment to send food parcels to the child with whom they had been paired by the WJC. During 1946 some 7,000 such parcels were dispatched monthly.[391]

The WJC effort to rehabilitate Jewish children in Europe did not stop at founding and operating orphanages. Those at the head of the organization were aware that many children had been separated from their parents during the course of

---

389 Ibid.
390 In order to obtain an idea of the sums raised, one may note that in 1945 a total of $300,000 was collected for the orphans. See minutes of meeting of the Children's Affairs Committee, January 15, 1945. See also a report on the collection of $134,000 in 1946. See the report by Robert Marcus, the outgoing chairman of the Children's Adoption Committee, January 30, 1946, AJA, 361 D71/11. The WJC's emissary to Switzerland wrote to a Congress activist by the name of Jacob Zucker about the importance of creating links between the Jewish orphans in Europe and Jewish children in the United States. See the letter from Riegner to Zucker, January 10, 1946, CZA, C-3/204.
391 Cited from a top secret letter from Robert Marcus, chairman of the Children's Adoption Committee, to Stephen Wise, November 5, 1946, AJA, 361 D71/7 . The full significance of WJC willingness to care for the European children and to take steps to have them adopted in the United States may be appreciated by reading a letter from Meta Flanter to Y. Golan, the Jewish Agency representative, which states: "I strongly wish to reiterate that one must take great care in forming the groups, particularly with regard to the children's health. No-one who is disabled or who suffers from tuberculosis should be included in the transport. And certainly not defective children. Letters on this topic arrive regularly from Jerusalem, explaining that there are after all no beds for tuberculosis sufferers in the land and there is no money to maintain—ever—disabled or mentally ill children. If you were able to send us a precise list with the transport and even a doctor's certificate if available, that would be most beneficial to our Italian office." Letter from Meta Flanter, representative of the Aliyat Ha-No'ar department, Paris, to Y. Golan, representative of the Jewish Agency in Austria, April 17, 1947, CZA, L-58/454. The WJC's operation in Europe facilitated the care of children who, because of their mental and/or physical condition, were unable to cope with life in Palestine.

the war and handed over to gentile families or to Christian religious bodies in the hope of saving their lives. The WJC engaged in legal wrangles throughout Europe in order to return these children to their parents, their relatives, or in the last resort, to the Congress's children's homes dotting Europe.[392] Its institutions, in addition, provided financial support to parents and to relatives who accepted the children into their families. Congress leaders declared that financial support for the children's families was one of the organization's primary missions in Europe.[393]

The fact that WJC senior functionaries endeavored to rehabilitate the orphans both in Europe and in the United States indicates that, alongside their support for the founding of a Jewish state and their efforts to bolster the Jewish community in Palestine, they were prepared to assist the survivors to rebuild their lives in the Diaspora. This outlook also found expression in the curriculum prepared for the pupils in the European orphanages. The topics of study and enrichment stressed the unique status of Palestine as the home of the Jewish people as well as a variety of subjects that prepared the pupils for the continuation of Jewish life in Europe and created a basis for establishing communities there. Among the topics addressed were observance of *kashrut* (Jewish laws pertaining to the consumption of food), Sabbath customs, and the study of prayers, in the belief that an acquaintance with Jewish tradition and observance of its customs were a necessary condition for the future functioning of Jewish communities. It is worth noting that rabbis served as the major spiritual guides in the orphanages, and that the kashrut laws were observed in all the educational institutions; the Sabbath was likewise strictly observed. In addition, the curriculum in the orphanages included Jewish history, Jewish customs and the teaching of the Yiddish language. The desire to teach Yiddish is of particular significance in light of the opposition on the part of the Zionist establishment in Palestine and subsequently in Israel toward the Yiddish language, which was a symbol of Jewish life in the Diaspora in contrast to Hebrew, which symbolized the revival of Jewish life in the Land of Israel. Since the use of Yiddish was clearly irrelevant to life in Palestine, it is clear that those who planned the curriculum sought to maintain Jewish life in Europe.[394] The creators of the curriculum created a cultural and educa-

---

392 This is a broad and fascinating issue deserving of a separate article. See, for example, a report on Catholic institutions in France and in Belgium which refused to return Jewish children to their parents, relatives, or to the WJC's orphanages: report on the situation of the Jewish Children in France and Belgium, November 26, 1945, AJA, 361 D71/6.
393 Post-War Work Plan of the WJC's Child Care Division (no date specified), AJA, 361 D71/11.
394 See a meeting of the Planning Committee for Children's Affairs, January 25, 1946, AJA, 361 D71/11. The resolutions of the WJC's Montreux conference in Switzerland in 1948 likewise included a declaration to the effect that the teaching of Yiddish was one of the Congress's fundamental

tional mélange that combined religious and traditional components with modern aspects of Jewish life in general and in Europe in particular. Such integration constitutes a powerful tool for the reinforcement of nationalist sentiments, as many scholars of both Jewish and worldwide issues of nationality have observed.[395] While WJC activists appreciated the significant position that the Jewish center in Palestine occupied in post-war Jewish life, they actively engaged in shaping a new ethnic reality in Europe in which Palestine was an important element, but was not the singular goal.[396]

The revival of Jewish life in Europe was a complex undertaking that involved activity in a wide range of areas and required the construction of new organizational systems that integrated ideology with practice. A prime example of such a structure was a special program for the training of American Jewish social workers to operate in Europe. Preparations for the commencement of training began in late November 1944, with a view to sending the program's graduates to Europe as soon as the political and security situations allowed.[397] The training program was to be run by the WJC in conjunction with the New School for Social Research. The curriculum and selection of lecturers was prepared with the assistance of Prof. Horace M. Kallen. The position paper attached to the curriculum reveals the WJC leaders' world view regarding the configuration of the Jewish people after the war, and the tasks they expected to confront at that time. The need for a special training program for social workers stemmed from the singular problems that would confront the Jewish people after the Holocaust. Among the tasks that they foresaw was the need to rescue hundreds of thousands of Jews from famine and

---

goals. See the collection of conference declarations, June 27, 1948, AJA, 361 A3/12. On the Zionist and Israeli establishment's attitude toward Yiddish, see Rachel Rojanski, "Ben-Gurion's Attitude to Yiddish in the 1950s" [in Hebrew], *Studies in Israel's Independence* 15 (2005): 463–82.

395 See, for example, Benedict Anderson, *Imagined Communities, Reflections on the Origin and Spread of Nationalism* (London, 1983), 17–40.

396 Post-War Work Plan of the WJC's Child Care Division (no date specified), AJA, 361 D71/11. The full significance of the educational and pedagogical program instituted in the WJC children's homes becomes evident in relation to the very different programs adopted in the children's homes run by the youth movements, the chief objective of which was to prepare the children for migration to Palestine. On the programs of the youth movements' children's homes, see Ashkenazi, *The Children's Homes*, 87–92.

397 Proposal for a training program for social workers, submitted to the WJC's emergency conference in Atlantic City, November 16, 1944, AJA, 361 C69/1. An estimation of the need for training a professional cadre of functionaries that would care for the refugees after the war had been made in 1942. See a meeting of the advisory committee on European Jews, June 6–7, 1942, AJA, 361 D104/6. No evidence suggesting that this program was in fact implemented is to be found in the WJC's papers, yet the intention to run this program is in itself of considerable importance to our discussion here.

illness, the urgent need to direct the mass movement of the Jewish refugees, and the raising and administration of the vast sums required to resettle the Jewish displaced persons in Europe. The document's authors, members of the WJC Aid and Welfare Committee, particularly underscored the social and economic challenge of planning and implementing the process of reintegrating the Jews into Europe's wider social fabric. The document presents the training of a significant group of social workers who would engage in welfare and rehabilitation as one of the most important factors in facilitating the restoration of European communities. European Jewry's network of social support had failed to survive the Holocaust, and the only way of training a skilled workforce that could cope with the enormous tasks was to institute a special program to train Jewish social workers in New York.[398]

The curriculum and syllabus provide an additional perspective on the program's objectives and the world view of its compilers. They include courses that address the problems of citizenship in the context of welfare; discussions on the rehabilitation of Jewish community life; and lectures on how to conduct welfare activity while maintaining contacts with governments, international organizations, and the private sector. The program's basic principles outlined at the beginning of the document and the list of topics studied indicate that those who devised the program sought to revive Jewish life in Europe. The challenge was all the more difficult given the desire to operate not only among Western European Jewish communities, but also in Central and Eastern European countries, whose Jewish communities had been almost completely annihilated, and in which the local populations resisted the return of the Jews.[399]

Perusal of the proposed syllabus indicates that while Congress leaders took note of the singular position occupied by Palestine as a refuge for the displaced persons, it constituted only a peripheral component of the curriculum, which demonstrates the tremendous importance that the organization's senior echelon attached to the process of rehabilitating the survivors in post-war Europe.[400]

The Institute of Jewish Affairs

The WJC's endeavor to shape a national identity in the Jewish Diaspora following World War II was not confined to addressing intra-communal dynamics. In posi-

---

398 Proposal for a training program for social workers, submitted to the WJC's emergency conference in Atlantic City, November 16, 1944, AJA, 361
399 Ibid.
400 Ibid.

tion papers, speeches, and letters its leaders portrayed the organization's status in terms of its role as representing the great majority of world Jewry in the wake of the Holocaust. Consequently, in order to integrate the Jews into the new world structures that were emerging after the war, the heads of the WJC worked within the international arena to establish a research operation that would provide data pertaining to world Jewry to the organization's institutions, to international organizations, and to governments.

The research effort was conducted by the Institute of Jewish Affairs, a research center founded by Dr. Jacob Robinson in 1941 in New York. Robinson was a jurist, legal advisor to the Jewish Agency, and the WJC representative at the United Nations who played a decisive role in the institute's research projects. Established during World War II, the institute played a pioneering role in collecting data on the fate of Europe's Jews during the Holocaust. Its scholars strove to set up a research infrastructure to serve as a foundation for discussions among both Jewish and non-Jewish international leadership on what should become of the Jews following the war. Congress papers indicate that the institute's importance transcended its scholarly endeavor; it was intended to serve as a vital tool in their effort to shape post-war Jewish existence according to their world view.

Robinson's life story and his activity within the WJC encapsulate the transformations and developments in the organization's status during the war years, as well as its leaders' views on the appropriate manner in which their organization should become involved in Jewish activity during the war, in the post-war period, and in the context of the founding of the State of Israel. Born in Lithuania in 1889, Robinson graduated from the law school of the University of Warsaw, was conscripted into the Russian army at the outbreak of World War I and was held as a German prisoner until the end of the war. His inclination toward public activity became evident in the prisoner of war camps, where he frequently served as spokesman for the Jewish prisoners, as well as for the Russian prisoners in general. Upon returning to Lithuania after the war, he combined his law practice with public activity. He was elected to the Lithuanian parliament and served as legal advisor to Lithuania's foreign ministry, devoting much of his time to Lithuania's intricate status problems stemming from the peace agreements concluded after the war.

In 1940, after the outbreak of World War II, Robinson and his family managed to enter the United States where he immediately became active in the WJC. After founding the Institute of Jewish Affairs with his brother Nehemia, he continued his research within the institute and published his first study in English, *Were the*

Minorities Treaties a Failure?, in 1943.⁴⁰¹ The work, which cast a critical eye on the minorities treaties to be signed as part of the peace agreements concluded after World War I, was an element of the institute's research aimed at developing solutions to the distress suffered by European Jews after the war from a broad historical Jewish and non-Jewish perspective. Robinson was a member of the Congress delegation to the San Francisco Conference, held from April to June 1945, at which the United Nations Charter was drawn up. The delegation attended as observers and campaigned on behalf of the cause of human rights, thereby assisting the Jewish Agency. The next stage of Robinson's public activity was closely associated with the Nuremburg Trials, where he advised Justice Robert H. Jackson on Jewish topics. Jackson led the American prosecution team and was instrumental in highlighting the Jewish aspects of Nazi criminality.⁴⁰² The experience he gained at the Nuremberg Trials and the extensive information he had gathered regarding the fate of the Jews during the Holocaust while working at the institute would later lead him to join the prosecution team at the Eichmann trial in 1960.

In 1947, in the wake of the British government's decision to relinquish its mandate in Palestine and turn the country's fate over to the United Nations, Robinson joined the Jewish Agency's delegation in New York as a legal advisor, continuing in his role as part of the Israeli delegation until 1957. Robinson was involved in the founding of the Yad Vashem institution in Jerusalem in 1953, and played a central role in shaping the reparations agreement between Germany and Israel, which was signed by both governments on September 10, 1952. During these years, he was also appointed advisor to the Claims Conference, which had been founded by the envoys of 23 Jewish organizations throughout the world. The Conference is a joint body that represents the Jewish people in its dealings with the German government, according to its separate agreements with the governments of West Germany and Israel.⁴⁰³ A survey of Robinson's extensive public

---

401 Jacov Robinson and Oscar Karbach, M. Laserson, Nehemia Robinson, Marc Vichniak, *Were the Minorities Treaties a Failure?* (New York, 1943).

402 Mark A. Lewis, "The World Jewish Congress and the Institute of Jewish affairs at Nuremberg: Ideas, Strategies, and Political Goals, 1942–1946, *Yad Vashem Studies* 2008 (36), 181–210. WJC functionaries were extremely critical of the Jewish Agency's activity in the context of the Nuremberg Trials. See, for example, a letter from Stephen Wise to the US Department of Defense regarding the dispatch of WJC representatives to Nuremberg: Wise's letter to the US Department of Defense, October 17, 1945, AJA, 361 B1/8. See also Robinson's secret report to the team at the Institute of Jewish Affairs engaged in the Nuremberg Trials, December 6, 1945, AJA, 361 C14/16.

403 For further information on Robinson and the Institute, see the press statement distributed by the Congress in the wake of Robinson's appointment to the position of Advisor to the UN Committee on Human Rights in 1947 (no precise date given), 26/14-C 361. See also an article by Shabtai Rosen, Professor of International Law and an Israeli diplomat, "The People of Israel's Great Advocate, in Memory of Jacov Robinson" [in Hebrew], *Gesher* 1978 (3,4): 91–101.

activity beyond the confines of the various WJC bodies reflects the objectives toward which he and the WJC leadership strove when they founded the Institute for Jewish Affairs. The juridical, historical, and political knowledge that Robinson and his associates acquired through their research work served to underscore the world view expressed in the range of activity undertaken by the WJC during the course of World War II and thereafter. Robinson and his colleagues sought to involve themselves wholeheartedly in the process of shaping the post-war Jewish world. They supported the establishment of a Jewish state as part of the political arrangements that were to be put in place after the war. At the same time, they strove to assure the continued existence of a Jewish Diaspora displaying unique ethnic characteristics, as part of an overall international process of reinforcing minority rights and protecting human rights in general. Thus, although Robinson invested efforts toward the founding of Israel within the sphere of the United Nations, he did not regard the birth of the state as the main objective. He campaigned at the UN for minority rights for all people, while seeking to ensure the status of Diaspora Jewry through his activity in the Claims Conference.

In 1941 Robinson introduced the Institute of Jewish Affairs to the readers of the *Congress Weekly*.[404] He explained that every European power had established a dedicated research institute whose role was to conduct studies and collate factual data in order to enable decision makers to operate more effectively. By contrast, world Jewry's 17 million members had not succeeded in creating similar research institutes, despite the complex existential problems that they faced. The Jews' overwhelming existential hardship and the complexity of Jewish life in the world in general, and in Europe in particular, warranted the founding and operation of a research institute charged with providing vital information to the leaders of the Jewish people and to the international bodies that would attempt to find solutions to the Jewish problem after the war. Robinson was, of course, aware of the existence of academic research institutions in Palestine and the Jewish world, but argued that these had not provided the required data in the past, nor would they be able to act as information providers for the Jewish people's decision makers in the future. Robinson preempted those who favored establishing the institute in the Land of Israel rather than the United States by arguing that since the Institute was to operate in the sphere of the Jewish Diaspora, it was both ideologically and practically preferable to locate it in New York. In New York the Institute could more easily obtain research data and maintain ongoing contact with international institution. Furthermore, this location would allow the Institute to maintain a direct link with the Jewish Diaspora, which constituted its field

---

[404] Jacob Robinson in *Congress Weekly*, February 21, 1941, AJA, 361 C86/1.

of research and whose leaders it was expected to serve.[405] Robinson emphasized that the Institute's research work would not be confined to the theoretical level. Its team would examine day-to-day developments in Europe, later proposing practical programs for the rehabilitation of European Jews and world Jewry as a whole. To this end, research departments within the organization would explore a variety of topics ranging from Jewish history during the past 25 years, through examination of the juridical, political, and economic aspects of Jewish existence in the present, to proposing solutions to the issues of migration and rehabilitation.[406]

Robinson's presentation is fascinating and reveals the significance of the founding of the Institute. It was not by chance that he invoked the research institutes of European powers in explaining the need for his institute. While the Jewish people had no European state of its own, it did possess national attributes and a well-developed political and bureaucratic system, justifying the establishment of a research body similar to those of the European states. The Institute of Jewish Affairs was important not only because of its status as a symbol of Jewish nationality in the Diaspora, but also because of its activity, and because the data it collected added tangible content to the abstract notion of Jewish nationality in the Diaspora.[407] European Jewry's sorry plight in the early 1940s did not deter WJC leaders from going ahead with their plans for the Institute of Jewish Affairs. On the contrary, the emergency situation and the burgeoning anti-Semitic propaganda reinforced their awareness of the pressing need for such a body. The crisis made it imperative to provide the most reliable data possible and to prepare contingency plans for the period that would follow the elimination of Nazism. Moreover, they believed that it was precisely the ideological and physical attacks on world Jewry that necessitated the establishment of an academic research institute that could contribute to the reinforcement of a national identity in the Diaspora and respond in a structured, effective and rational manner to the enemies of Jewry.

---

[405] A secret document compiled by Robinson on the Institute of Jewish Affairs, April 29, 1939, AJA, 361 A9/6.
[406] Jacob Robinson in *Congress Weekly*, February 21, 1941, AJA, 361 C86/1.
[407] Anthony Smith has written about the importance of national symbols and representation of the nation and its images, which confers practical and tangible meaning to the spread of nationalism. See Anthony D. Smith, *The Nation in History, Historiographical Debates about Ethnicity and Nationalism* (University Press of New England, 2000), 52–76. Benedict Anderson has stressed the important contribution of national censuses to the emergence of nationalism in countries that had been subjected to colonial rule. See Anderson, *Imagined Communities*, 141–147. Arieh Tartakower underscored the institute's "national character." See Arieh Tartakower, unpublished manuscript of a book on the institute (undated), CZA, C-6/352.

In 1941 Robinson set out a work plan for the Institute in a secret document that provides an important indication of the reasons for founding the research institute and the areas it would address.[408] He was aware that the establishment of a Jewish research institute in 1941, in the midst of the war, could be regarded as a superfluous luxury given the travails of the war and the dire plight of European Jewry. He therefore stressed even though the war was now at its fiercest, it behooved the heads of the WJC to display the responsibility demanded of them as leaders of world Jewry by preparing for the post-war period. He maintained that it was the Jews, who were suffering most during the war, who must prepare for the war's conclusion in order to ensure their continued existence. The ongoing Jewish distress served to underscore the WJC leadership's responsibility to present the Jewish cause adequately and correctly in the international arena within the new world order that would emerge after the war. The research to be undertaken by the Institute of Jewish Affairs was to provide the bodies of the WJC with the data, statistics, and work plans necessary to enable the organization's heads to present the Jewish perspective to international bodies and governments in the most effective manner possible. Robinson emphasized that victory over Germany would eventually be achieved and that this assumption was the only one that facilitated any sort of planning for the future. Yet from the Jewish point of view, victory was neither the sole nor the overriding objective. Victory alone would not ensure protection of Jewish rights after the war. Robinson termed it "naïve" to assume that an end to the terrible suffering endured by the Jews of Europe would "automatically" result in a solution of the Jewish issue. Jewish leadership had to be prepared to confront the nations of the world to ensure the destiny of the Jews. This would require painstaking preparation that took into account the dramatic transformation in the status of world Jewry that had occurred over the preceding 25 years, as well as careful study of the mistakes made by Jewish organizations that had represented the Jews in the international arena in the past.[409]

Robinson noted that the proposal to establish the Institute for Jewish Affairs had been initially floated in April 1939, and had been authorized by the relevant bodies of the WJC. The original intention had been to found the Institute in Geneva, but at the outbreak of World War II the enterprise was transferred to New York, where it began operation on February 1, 1941. The Institute was granted an annual budget of $100,000 and a team of four researchers was assembled. Its primary objective was the collection of facts and data pertaining to the

---

408 Robinson, Work Plan for the Institute of Jewish Affairs, 1941 (no precise date given), AJA, 361 A5/3. See also the founding document of the Institute of Jewish Affairs, including a list of functionaries and departments, 1941 (no precise date given), AJA, 361 C68/1.
409 Ibid.

condition of European Jewry since 1914, with particular emphasis placed on the destiny of European Jews under the Nazi regime. The Institute's scholars were to establish an extensive archive and library to contain relevant literature, journals, newspapers, government publications, and economic and statistical data on the Jews in the various communities, with emphasis on those countries that had imposed economic restrictions on the Jewish minority. In addition, the Institute's scholars would assemble any other written material that might contribute to an understanding of the situation of the Jews, or that provided information pertaining to European Jews. The Institute's scholars would analyze and process this information, and present their findings in the form of publications and position papers. The researchers would focus on examining the juridical and political status of European Jews in light of the sweeping changes experienced since the Nazis' accession to power in Germany and the consequent outbreak of war. Robinson was most concerned about the juridical status of the Jews and its impact on their right to participate, through representative organizations, in the political process that would begin once World War II had ended. Two years after the Institute of Jewish Affairs was founded, Robinson stressed that even the Jews' possible self-identification as a separate group would be insufficient to guarantee their representatives could participate in the political process that would shape the post-war world order. He maintained that affording the Jews appropriate international juridical expression and finding a singular formulation that would incorporate both their uniqueness and their judicial right to participate in international processes would entail elaborate and delicate action by the Institute of Jewish Affairs. Robinson believed that neither such a legal solution nor an organizational structure capable of applying the legal principles were yet in place, since the Jewish Agency, grounded in international law, represented the Jewish people only with regard to the Palestine issue.[410]

Apart from their research work, the Institute's scholars would monitor the discussions and preparations conducted by governments and international organizations in anticipation of the international agreements to be concluded in the post-war period. A practical example of this aspect of their endeavor are the attempts by WJC leaders to foster cooperation between the Institute and the research arms of the State Department, as manifested in a meeting between Nahum Goldmann, Stephen Wise and Undersecretary of State Sumner Welles,

---

[410] See Robinson's memorandum in response to the contention by Louis Lipsky that the very definition of the Jews as a group would facilitate their integration within international affairs following the conclusion of World War II, August 3, 1943, AJA, 361 B95/8.

who promised that the State Department's research facilities would maintain an ongoing, formalized working relationship with the WJC's research institute.[411]

The work plan of the Institute of Jewish Affairs devotes considerable attention to its projected research on the issue of migration and colonization, about which Robinson wrote:

> The Institute, therefore, proposes to study the records of migration during the past twenty-five years and the experiences of that period, especially in connection with the refugee problem. It will study the attempts by governments, free organizations and individuals to bring order and system into an unplanned migration. Open spaces throughout the world and limits of city and country settlement will be carefully studied. Closely related to the migration question is that of colonization. Efforts at Jewish colonization in the past will be studied and a plan for Jewish colonization formulated in addition to the rehabilitation of the Jewish National Homeland in Palestine. Looking ahead the Institute will study all available data relative to the form which the post–war Europe is to take, such as greater units (Federations), etc. The opportunities for Jews in this new world order will be considered in detail.[412]

The plan, with its emphasis on the issue of migration and colonization represented the world view of the WJC leadership during the 1940s and reinforced the impression that the Congress did not regard the establishment of Jewish sovereignty in Palestine to be its overriding mission, but sought to integrate Jewish migration to Palestine with the rehabilitation of Jewish life in Europe. The importance of the Institute of Jewish Affairs, however, goes further than this. Its founding during the harsh years of crisis in the early forties and the breadth of the tasks with which it was charged indicate the belief of the WJC leaders that they and their organization were called upon to play a decisive role in shaping world Jewry as an ethnic minority in the wake of World War II. Robinson and his associates came to realize that the collection and analysis of so great a variety of data and the preparation of appropriate work plans required wide-ranging research activity and extensive organizational effort that were beyond the capability of any other body in the Jewish world at the time.

The dramatic reports of the mass murder of the Jews of Europe and the Nazis' plan for the final solution prompted a fundamental change in the Institute's research program. Beginning in 1942, its researchers ceased to focus on the preparation of position papers and work plans for the post-war period and engaged instead in collecting, verifying, cataloging, and editing information per-

---

[411] Minutes of meeting between Wise and Goldmann and Welles, February 17, 1941, AJA, 361 D16/6.
[412] See Robinson's memorandum, August 3, 1943, AJA, 361 B95/8.

taining to the fate of European Jews, and then disseminating it to the public at large and to the Allied decision makers.

Locating the Institute of Jewish Affairs in New York created a singular situation. Although the Institute and its researchers were far removed from the horrors of the war, they received regular reports of occurrences in Europe by virtue of the intensive contacts between the Congress leadership in New York and the organization's bureaus in Europe. Robinson addressed these developments and the transformation in the Institute's pattern of activity in 1946:

> When the Institute was established for the purpose of postwar planning, its primary concern was *European* Jewry. At that time Europe was still the greatest center of Jewish life both in number and in importance. The initial assumption was that, after the war, we should have to deal with approximately the same number and distribution of Jews as prior to the war. In the course of 1941–1942, the situation changed radically. It became obvious that it would be useless to continue planning on the basis of the pre-war Jewish community in Europe. Furthermore, since current information was both vague and contradictory, it was imperative that our organization take the lead in establishing the facts. Although we did not for a single moment discontinue our thinking and planning with regard to postwar problems, inadvertently the emphasis shifted to a realistic appraisal of the situation as it appeared at any given moment.[413]

Robinson's remarks alluded to a large-scale research effort that, for the first time, had revealed comprehensively and systematically the Nazis' overall anti-Jewish activity in Europe. A summary of the Institute's research was published during the war in several voluminous books. The activities that the Nazis had directed against the Jews from their rise to power in 1933 until 1943 were presented in three volumes produced by an Institute team headed by Robinson: *Jews in Nazi Europe* (November 1941); *Hitler's Ten Years War on the Jews* (August 1943); and *Starvation Over Europe* (1943). During the same period, two other Institute scholars, Arieh Tartakower and Kurt Grossmann, also published research on the refugee problem, titled *The Jewish Refugee (1933–1944)*.[414]

The research conducted on the condition of the Jews of Germany and the rest of Europe prior to and during World War II not only served documentation and commemoration purposes, but also allowed for the creation of a base of evidence to be used for the indictment of war criminals. By 1943 the various WJC bodies had begun to discuss the issue of bringing Nazis and their European collaborators to trial for the murder of Jews. These discussions addressed the problems

---

413 See Robinson's summary of the activity of the Institute of Jewish Affairs during the forties, December 1946 (no precise date given), AJA, 361 A5/6.
414 Ibid.

involved in appointing Jews to the international war crimes tribunals, and the danger that any Jewish activity directed against war criminals would generate an anti-Jewish atmosphere in Europe that would impede the return to their countries of origin of those Jews who wished to do so. Questions were subsequently raised as to the status of the international prosecutor, and an attempt was made to define the uniqueness of Nazi crimes against the Jews while seeking to merge them into the general body of Nazi criminality. The interlocutors did not hesitate to raise provocative questions. They deliberated on how to prosecute members of the Reichstag who had passed anti-Jewish legislation and how to treat Hitler, who, in fact, had himself not bodily harmed a single Jew.[415] The Congress leadership believed that prosecuting Nazi war criminals following the war was an essential procedure, not only because of the wish to punish those who had committed crimes against Jews, but also as a symbolic expression of the shaping of a new world order that was fundamentally different from that which the Nazis had tried to impose. Nahum Goldmann vented such sentiments in his speech to the WJC's Atlantic City conference in November 1944:

> Another demand is the punishment of the criminals who have committed the crimes against the Jews. This is not a question of revenge. To teach the world that crimes such as those committed by the Nazis and their allies cannot remain unpunished, is a necessary condition for the restoration of the moral balance of the world of tomorrow. And we note with satisfaction that the leaders of the United Nations have time and again proclaimed this principle and their determination to carry it through.[416]

As may be gathered from Goldmann's address, Congress leadership assiduously monitored the level of commitment displayed by Allied leaders to the prosecution of the war criminals, and was well informed of the disagreements and arguments among the Allies over the process whereby this prosecution should be implemented. While the WJC request to participate in the work of the UN War Crimes Committee (established in October 1943) was rejected, the Congress continued to campaign for the definition of war crimes to be expanded to include Nazi persecution of the Jews prior to the outbreak of war in 1939.[417]

---

[415] See the following minutes of meetings of the team of the Institute of Jewish Affairs: March 28, 1943; September 24, 1943; October 12, 1943, AJA, 361 C68/6.
[416] Citation of Goldmann's speech in the *Congress Weekly*, December 1, 1944, AJA, 361 A68/3.
[417] Regarding the information on the juridical steps taken by the Allies, see the minutes of a secret meeting on this issue held at Kubowizki's home, January 5, 1944, AJA, 361 C68/6. For a further discussion of this matter, see the minutes of the second meeting of the WJC's War Crimes Committee, March 28, 1944, AJA, 361 C68/6. For a comprehensive study of the international activity leading up to the Nuremberg Trials, see Ariel J. Kochavi, *Prelude to Nuremberg, Allied War*

Moves toward prosecution of the war criminals found practical expression in 1945 when the Institute's scholars prepared and publicized what Robinson termed a master list of the war criminals responsible for crimes against Jews. Meanwhile, the Institute's research team, headed by Robinson, provided valuable preliminary information on the Nazis' crimes against the Jews to the American team engaged in preparing the Nuremberg Trials. The heads of the Institute of Jewish Affairs felt that the Institute and the WJC were virtually the only organizations campaigning for the prosecution of the Nazi war criminals following the war. As Robinson stated at a meeting of the Institute's team in late 1944:

> It is worthwhile to stress one point of political, not scientific character. While the WJC in its activities has a great number of competitors in every field, in the realm of war crimes it is left alone, without any competition, research or political. This imposes a tremendous responsibility on the WJC which will be held responsible for our failure in this field, and rightly so. The work of our political bodies is limited by the extent of our preparatory work, which in turn increases our responsibility.[418]

Later during the same meeting, Robinson stressed that research activity geared primarily to juridical use had required the Institute's scholars to adopt different modes of operation. He presented the fruits of their research in a manner designed to facilitate the prosecution and conviction of the war criminals, explaining that "the writing should be done in a manner different from *Hitler's Ten Years War*. Now we are not only historians, we are primarily attorney generals [sic]. Here we must have a source for every statement, fact, names, date."[419]

Perusal of the minutes of the meeting reveals that the need for a clear presentation of the research findings, with a view to contributing to the prosecution of the war criminals, led to a sharper formulation of questions that would continue to engage Holocaust scholars far into the future. The Institute's scholars noted, for example, that the mass murder of Jews was conducted only in Eastern Europe and that the extermination camps were built on Polish territory rather than in the west of the continent, but they failed to agree on the reasons why. Some asserted that the Germans had refrained from carrying out mass extermination in Western Europe because they feared the reaction of the local population, while others believed that the Jews had been deported from Western to Eastern Europe with the intention of employing some of them in a system of forced labor that could

---

Crimes Policy and the Question of Punishment, Chapel Hill and London, 1998. On the resistance to including WJC representatives on the UN War Crimes Commission, see ibid., 150–151.

418 Minutes of meeting of the Institute of Jewish Affairs' team, December, 28, 1944, AJA, 361 C68/6.

419 Ibid.

be set up only in Eastern Europe. Moreover, Institute scholars joined together to formulate the array of concepts they were to use to define and describe the range of Nazi action against the Jews. They decided that the most appropriate way to portray Nazi crimes was to employ the Nazis' own terminology. In light of the future involvement of the Institute of Jewish Affairs with the Nuremberg Trials, as well as Robinson's role in these trials and in the Eichmann trial, it is clear that the research patterns shaped by the Institute in 1944 influenced the future historical and juridical debate on the Holocaust. Subsequent use of concepts such as "the final solution" should be read against the 1944 decision made by the Institute's researchers to employ the Nazis' own definitions when describing the events of World War II in the Jewish context.[420]

The importance that the Institute of Jewish Affairs and the WJC's other arms attached to shaping Holocaust memory among Jews was demonstrated in Atlantic City at the Congress's November 1944 conference by an exhibition addressing the fate of the Jews during the Holocaust period. The Institute staff determined the content of the exhibit and set it up, making it the first exhibition of its kind—predating the founding of museums and Holocaust commemoration centers in the United States.[421] The deliberations prior to the opening of the exhibition reveal the major dilemmas that occupy those engaged in shaping public memory and in founding Holocaust commemoration institutions to this day. The scholars of the Institute of Jewish Affairs portrayed the historical sphere that the exhibition was to address as "the Jewish catastrophe" during the World War II period. Exhibits of the documents, data, and photographs related to the fate of European Jewry were based on material assembled in the Institute's archive.[422] Participants in the discussions maintained that although non-Jewish institutions such as Yale University, the Department of State, the Library of Congress, and the Herbert Hoover Library at Stanford University maintained a base of primary sources pertaining to World War II, the archive maintained by the Institute of Jewish Affairs was of a different order. Robinson referred to this archive's singularity during the preparations for the exhibition. Like the archives of the non-Jewish institutions, this archive too was called the War Archives. Robinson explained that, despite the shared definition, the Institute's archive concerned itself predominantly with

---

[420] Ibid.
[421] Hasia Diner conducts an important debate on this issue, contending that the State of Israel's desire to maintain control over the designing of Holocaust museums and remembrance centers was one of the factors that delayed the establishment of such institutions in the USA. See Diner, *We Remember*, 24–44.
[422] Minutes of a meeting of the team that prepared the exhibition, March 1, 1944, AJA, 361 C89/2. For a subsequent discussion that addressed similar issues, see minutes of meeting, March 20, 1944, AJA, 361 C98/2.

those aspects of the war related to the Jews, and at the time was the only archive administered by a Jewish organization.⁴²³

It is a fair assumption that the designation of the archive maintained by the WJC as the War Archives, without mention of its specifically Jewish aspect, was a part of the policy of restraint adopted by the Congress during World War II in order to play down the Jewish perspective on the war within the American arena. The title "War Archives" thus avoided any allusion to the fact that the data collected referred primarily to the Jewish war experience. Yet the Institute's scholars and the archive staff did, in fact, focus mainly on the collection of primary material directly relevant to the fate of the Jews during the time of war.

The purpose of the data presented at the exhibition was to highlight the information contained in detailed portfolios to be handed out to convention delegates. The information and data pertaining to the fate of the Jews of Europe during the war was intended to serve both as a basis for analysis of Congress activity during the war and as an introduction to the debates on the post-war process of rehabilitation. Preparation of the exhibition and the information portfolios presented Institute scholars with a formidable challenge. The team working on the preparations was well aware that a number of those receiving the portfolios and visiting the exhibition would be survivors and refugees who had experienced the horrors of the war first-hand. This meant that the team had to take great care to ensure that the material contained in the portfolios and presented at the exhibition was accurate and reliable, but that it would not offend its audience.

The North African portion of the display presented a particular problem. As described in previous chapters, the Congress leadership and the Institute's researchers received much reliable information about the fate of Europe's Jews under the Nazi occupation, yet only scant information was collected on the plight of the Jews of North Africa during that time. The Institute staff determined that they could not obtain the necessary information and would have to seek the assistance of the conference delegates from North African in order to gather the missing data.⁴²⁴

The staff members engaged in preparing the exhibition held intensive discussions on its structure and content. The average length of time visitors would spend at the exhibition was estimated to be about 25 minutes, and the exhibits would be built with the intention of transporting them to other cities once the

---

423 See the minutes of meeting of March 1, 1944, AJA, 361 C89/2.
424 Ibid. Scholars and Jews of North African origin believe to this day that insufficient attention has been paid to the Holocaust of North African Jewry in both scholarly and public discourse. For discussion of this issue, see Hanna Yablonka, "Oriental Jewry and the Holocaust: A Three-Generational Perspective," *Israel Studies* 14, no. 1 (2009): 94–122.

conference had ended.⁴²⁵ These restrictions on the design of the display meant that it could not include exhibits on every issue related to the fate of the Jews during the war. The planning team decided that the exhibition would address only issues concerning the harshest aspects of the Jewish experience. In the words of the planners, "[The exhibition] is not intended to give the whole picture of the situation of the Jews, nor all of what we are doing—just highlights. It will be an exhibit only of the dark side of the picture, and will not contain anything on relief, etc."⁴²⁶

The exhibition was to fill six small rooms, which the planners deemed more attractive than placing all the exhibits in two larger spaces. Between ten and twelve exhibits would hang on the walls of each room, and two or three exhibits would be placed in display cabinets in each room. Given the physical layout of the exhibition and the need to select a limited number of exhibits, the Institute staff began to deliberate over which topics would be addressed. It was agreed that the exhibition should present what they termed "the war on the Jews, in Europe," rather being limited to the activity of the World Jewish Congress, combining a portrayal of the daily lives of Jews in occupied Europe with a presentation of the means employed by the Nazis to disseminate their anti-Semitic ideology. Because of the space limitations, the planners decided to display only the most essential information about the Jews of Europe prior to the Nazis' rise to power in Germany and the anti-Jewish and anti-Semitic trends in Europe from the Middle Ages to the modern era. Conversely, they sought to cover Jewish resistance during the Holocaust period and the participation of Jews in the Allied fighting forces as extensively as possible. The exhibits and the relevant background material would be arranged chronologically according to the following categories:⁴²⁷

A. Rise: From the Middle Ages to World War I
B. Crisis: from the end of World War I to 1933
C. Catastrophe: from 1933 to the present

This division into three chronological periods presented Institute scholars with a significant historiographical challenge. The major problem was the difficulty of defining the boundaries of the "Catastrophe" period. Several of the scholars felt that the category should be extended to begin with the Nazi rise to power in 1933, while others believed that it was more appropriate to the begin the period with the outbreak of war in 1939. A compromise was eventually reached: The period

---

425 Minutes of meeting of the Institute of Jewish Affairs team, March 8, 1944, AJA, 361 C98/2.
426 Ibid.
427 Minutes of meeting of the Institute of Jewish Affairs team, March 13, 1944, AJA, 361 C98/2.

would be defined differently relative to each of the various geographic zones. The concept of catastrophe would include Germany from the year 1933, but would apply to the condition of the Jews in the countries occupied by the Nazis beginning in 1939.[428]

The planners envisioned that most of the visitors would be Americans who were routinely exposed to high quality visual information of the sort common to Hollywood. Therefore they sought to comply with the highest technical standards and to ensure that only original materials be presented. They believed that any attempt to provide illustrations or reenactments would end in abject failure because they would not meet the exacting technical standards American audiences expected and would therefore be perceived as inauthentic. Instead, the condition of the Jews under Nazi rule in Europe would be conveyed using the prohibitions placed on Jews to use telephones and to travel on public transportation, along with citations from speeches delivered by Nazi leaders, excerpts from the Nazi party press, and books that expounded on the party's anti-Semitic ideology. The exhibits were to comprise a blend of photographs, documents, maps and tables. Included would be photographs of Jews engaged in forced labor, a map on which synagogues that had been destroyed throughout Europe were marked in red, tables presenting the rates of death in the various ghettos, data pertaining to the starvation of Jews, documents testifying to anti-Jewish legislation in Germany and in the occupied countries, and other similar material. German-language documents would be exhibited in the original and in English and Yiddish translations.[429]

During the course of the discussions, Robinson, as the Institute's Chairman, clarified that the financial and technical constraints that pertained in 1944 would force the organizers to resign themselves to producing a restricted exhibition at the moment, but that they should consider building a Jewish War Museum in the future. It behooved the WJC to play a leading role in founding such a museum in the United States, but the size and complexity of the task called for cooperation with other Jewish organizations and institutions. Robinson felt that Jewish bodies in America were not yet ready to engage in cooperation of this kind; for foreseeable future the WJC would have to confine itself to presenting an array of temporary exhibitions rather than establishing a permanent museum.[430]

---

[428] Ibid.
[429] Minutes of meeting of the Institute of Jewish Affairs team, March 8, 1944, AJA, 361 C98/2.
[430] Ibid. Upon conclusion of the war Robinson would stress the need to found a historical center that would engage in the documentation of the fate of the Jews in the context of World War II. See Robinson's comments at a meeting of the Institute of Jewish Affairs team, September 19, 1946, AJA, 361 C68/8.

The discussions culminated in a decision to prefer the inclusion of visual exhibits rather than written material in order to attract the wider public and to make the exhibition more accessible. The team charged with setting up the exhibition was instructed to create a blend of exhibits that would be of interest both to the public at large and to scholars, and to maintain a high academic standard that would enhance the stature of the Institute as a leading research body engaged in documenting the fate of the Jews during World War II.[431] It was eventually decided to house the exhibition in six rooms, each devoted to a particular theme. The designations were:[432]

Room 1 – Anti-Jewish Legislation
Room 2 – Uprooting (migration, deportation)
Room 3 – Forced Labor
Room 4 – Ghetto Life
Room 5 – Atrocities, Concentration Camps
Room 6 – Extermination (including starvation).

An array of commemoration museums would not be established in Israel, Europe and America until several years after the war. The most prominent of these to date are the first permanent exhibition at the Yad Vashem Museum created in Jerusalem in 1958, the the permanent structure housing the museum inaugurated at Kibbutz Lohamei Ha-Geta'ot in 1959, the Holocaust Museum in Washington founded in 1993, and of the *Jüdisches* Museum in Berlin, which opened in 1997. (Although the name of the Berlin museum does not indicate that it is devoted exclusively to the Holocaust, it is considered by the public to be a Holocaust museum.)[433]

The exhibition in Atlantic City was designed many years before the first museums were founded. In 1944 the Nazi extermination machine was still operating in Europe and those engaged in planning the exhibition still deliberated over an appropriate title for the fate of the Jews during World War II. Nevertheless, it is fascinating to observe that the contours shaped in 1944 and the topics deliberated by the construction team in Atlantic City have continued to inform

---

431 Meeting of the Institute of Jewish Affairs' Exhibition Committee, March 21, 1944, AJA, 361 C98/4.
432 Ibid.
433 For an extensive discussion of the establishment of museums to commemorate the Holocaust, see Stephanie Rotem, "Holocaust Remembrance Museums, the Role of Architecture in Constructing the Collective Memory of the Holocaust" [in Hebrew] (Ph.D. dissertation, Tel Aviv University, 2010).

those engaged in erecting Holocaust museums to this day. The ongoing deliberations among historians, architects, community leaders, educators, and exhibition designers reflect an important historiographical debate on the appropriate way to present the impact of the Holocaust on the fabric of Jewish life in Europe prior to the Nazis' rise to power in Germany and thereafter by means of displays in museums. Considerable thought has also been devoted to how much attention should be paid to the issue of Jewish resistance and the operation of Jewish underground organizations in occupied Europe as part of wider Jewish life under the Nazi yoke. Construction team records indicate that the staff of the Institute of Jewish Affairs realized that the exhibition would play a part in shaping American Jewry's ethnic and communal identity and therefore made a point of presenting anti-Nazi Jewish activity in Europe and Jewish participation in the Allied combat forces.[434] This combination enhanced the sense of Jewish pride, particularly given the somber mood among the conference delegates, and positioned the Jews as an integral part of the public and political fabric of the Allies engaged in fighting the Nazis. Many scholars have similarly noted the importance of the Holocaust Museum in crystallizing the ethnic identity of American Jewry, and have observed that the organized visits to Yad Vashem by schoolchildren and soldiers likewise constitute a significant element in the formation of a national identity among the Jewish population of the State of Israel.[435]

Despite the similarity between the design and construction processes of the 1944 exhibition and those of the subsequent Holocaust museums, there is a significant difference between these enterprises. The heads of the Institute of Jewish Affairs devoted their exhibition to Hitler's war on the Jews and sought to name the museum they planned to erect in the future the Jewish War Museum. It is this author's belief that using the term "war" in both cases, as well as the fact that the WJC gathering in Atlantic City was termed "the war conference," did not stem solely from confusion in choosing the precise term to describe the process of extermination of the Jews of Europe. Like the emphasis placed on the aspect of resistance in portraying the annals of the Jews under Nazi rule, using the concept

---

434 Minutes of meeting of the Institute of Jewish Affairs team, March 8, 1944, AJA, 361 C98/2. For an examination of museums as institutions that impart values and national identity, see C. Duncan and A. Wallach, "The Universal Survey Museum," *Art History* 3 (4) (1980): 447–69. On theories that address the construction of collective memory, see, for example, M. Halbwachs, *On Collective Memory*, trans. L. A. Coser, (Chicago, 1992).

435 Stephanie Rotem, *Holocaust Remembrance Museums*, 54–141, 142–218. See also D. E. Lipstadt, "America and the Memory of the Holocaust, 1950–1965," *Modern Judaism* 16 (1996): 195–214; A. Mints, *Popular Culture and the Shaping of Holocaust Memory in America* (Seattle, 2001). For an additional and controversial discussion of this issue, see P. Novick, *The Holocaust in American Life* (Boston and New York, 1999).

of war to label the events initiated by the WJC positions the Jews as an active element that shaped its own destiny and resisted those who afflicted it, even though its foe enjoyed overwhelming advantage. Depicting the fate of the Jews during World War II in this manner takes issue with their conventional image as passive victims and underscores their struggle against the Nazis and those who collaborated with them.

Using the concept of war to describe the manner in which Jews confronted the Nazis served the WJC in yet another way. As will become clear later in this chapter, in the latter half of the 1940s the WJC leadership sought to reinforce the ethnic identity of Diaspora Jewry and of American Jewry in particular, and to enhance nationalist components within the fabric of Jewish life in the Diaspora. Wars in the modern era are generally waged between nations, or between groups of nations possessing a national identity and various characteristics of a sovereign political entity. Although the Jews did not operate as a separate sovereign entity during World War II, because wars are waged by at least two sovereign groups, the very definition of the final solution as a war introduces nationalist characteristics to Jewish existence during the forties and contributes to the enhancement of ethnic identity consistent with the outlook of WJC leaders during the second half of the 1940s.

Diaspora Nationalism

During the 1950s and '60s, community leaders and rabbis sought to establish the Warsaw Ghetto Uprising as a major component of Holocaust memory and commemoration among the American Jewish community. The minutes of WJC meetings reveal that as early as 1944—prior to the conclusion of the war and while the Nazi extermination machinery was still operating—Congress leaders deliberately emphasized the Warsaw Ghetto Uprising and other instances of Jewish resistance in the Atlantic City exhibition. They were, in fact, creating an initial foundation for intensive and far-reaching activity by the WJC and other Jewish organizations to make the Warsaw Ghetto Uprising an integral part of Jewish public memory in the United States and the Jewish world at large.[436]

In 1951, the WJC head office in New York dispatched a memorandum to all the organization's branches in the United States and around the world. The document was part of the preparation for the eighth anniversary of the Warsaw Ghetto Uprising and traced the main outlines of a commemoration event to be held in Congress branches worldwide. It included the following passage:

---

[436] See, for example, the minutes of the meeting held on March 8, 1944, AJA, 361 C98/2

> In all parts of the world, wherever there exists a nationally conscious Jewry, this great national day of mourning should be observed with becoming dignity and impressiveness. At large public gatherings an appraisal should be given of those cruel days and of the valor and self-sacrifice of the heroic Jewish men and women of the Warsaw Ghetto uprising. Those heroes of ours[s] bequeathed a mission to future generations, namely to safeguard Jewish existence and to fight for Jewish rights ... This year, more than ever before, we must make it clear to the whole world that our brothers and sisters of the Warsaw ghetto and elsewhere *did not die for our people only, but for all mankind* in the battle against forces which are preparing to rise up again not only against our people, but against the triumph of morality and humanity in general.[437]

The memorandum sent out from New York in 1951 elaborates on the tendencies that surfaced during the preparations for the 1944 conference. The events held to commemorate the Holocaust, especially those pertaining to the Warsaw Ghetto Uprising, held broader significance than similar events conducted to commemorate victims of the Holocaust. These ceremonies were part of a broad organizational and ideological strategy promoted by the WJC, the practical significance of which was to create an ambience of nationalism among the Jews of the Diaspora in the wake of World War II. The memorandum deliberately defines the anniversary of the uprising as a national day of commemoration, and emphasizes the universal aspect of the struggle. In keeping with the world view espoused by the Congress leaders, it proclaims that the ghetto fighters' war against the Nazis was waged not only on behalf of the Jews, but also as part of an all-encompassing endeavor in the interests of morality and humaneness.

The WJC's New York office continued its effort to turn the Warsaw Ghetto Uprising into a major component of Holocaust memory among Jewish communities in the United States and around the world throughout the 1950s. The organization's emissaries were instructed to ensure that commemoration ceremonies marking the outbreak of the uprising be held not only in the capital cities, but in regional cities and in small communities as well. A circular dispatched from New York in 1955 declared that the commemorations were meant to ensure that the memory of the uprising would become etched forever among wide swathes of the Jewish people. WJC offices in Europe and in the United States were required "to send to our office not later than the end of April all material which may serve as a report about what was done in your community as a dignified link in Jewry's world girdling chain, in order that this anniversary may become a perpetual memorial to the greatest manifestation of sacrifice and heroism in our history."[438]

---

437 Memorandum dispatched from the WJC's head office in New York titled "Eighth Anniversary of Warsaw Ghetto Uprising: An Appeal to All Our Affiliates," February 19, 1951, AJA, 361 H294/2.
438 Memorandum from the New York head office on the occasion of the twelfth anniversary of the Warsaw Ghetto uprising, January 25, 1955, AJA, 361 H294/2.

The memorial ceremonies were to become part of a broad educational endeavor among Jewish communities and schools including lectures, distribution of background material on the uprising, and discussions on the topic, with the intent to ensure that the memory of the Holocaust would pass from one generation to the next, and also to use the event as a means of empowering Jewish life in the various communities, as denoted by the slogan "Reconstruction after the *Churban* [devastation]."[439]

The circulars constituted part of a comprehensive effort by the WJC to establish the Warsaw uprising as a central component in the historical memory of Jewish communities in the United States and worldwide. As part of this process, in 1955 the New York office produced a lengthy document titled "Warsaw Ghetto Uprising: "Remembering and Rebuilding," which had two major sections.[440] The first contained a report on a comprehensive survey of the Warsaw Ghetto Uprising memorial ceremonies and commemoration activities conducted in large Jewish centers and in small communities in 47 countries. The surveys presented data pertaining not only to the ceremonies themselves, but also to ongoing educational and community projects relating to the uprising. The second section of the document offered an analysis of the findings, as well as guidelines for future activity designed to merge commemoration of the Warsaw Ghetto Uprising with its use as a reinforcer of Jewish identity, as stated in the introduction to this section:

> In the light of the facts brought out in this survey, the anniversary of the Warsaw Ghetto uprising will remain a permanent national or world Jewish Memorial Day. As the time goes on, the element of mourning will tend to become suffused with a spirit of contemplation and marked by an element of education and the building up of new cultural strongholds. But never will the element of mourning vanish altogether. This will be, as it should, the affirmative answer of a people with thousands of years of history behind it to the uprising of its heroic sons and daughters in the Warsaw Ghetto.[441]

The discussion in the second section of the document on shaping the patterns of memory of the uprising took the form of 14 questions and answers composed by the authors. These addressed a number of issues ranging from the involvement of the Orthodox sector of world Jewry in memorial ceremonies to information about countries in which no such ceremonies were held at all. Of particular interest is the question concerning the status of memorial ceremonies in the State of Israel:

---

439 Ibid.
440 "Remembering and Rebuilding, Survey and Analysis of the Twelfth Anniversary Commemoration of the Warsaw Ghetto Uprising," July 1955 (no precise date specified), AJA, 361 H294/2.
441 Ibid.

Question: Is it true that in Israel the commemoration of the Warsaw Ghetto Uprising receives little attention because of an alleged indifference to Jewish affairs outside Israel and owing to a tendency not to have the struggle for today impaired by mourning for yesterday?

Answer: According to our observation, the reply is clearly no. It is simply not true. It may be true in some measure that the commemorations of the Uprising in the Warsaw Ghetto are of a less pensive character in Israel than in the Diaspora. They are more focused on the idea of rebuilding than of mourning, and this is only natural.[442]

This question indicates that many WJC members believed there were significant differences between the status of the Warsaw Ghetto Uprising in the collective memory of Diaspora Jews and the meaning attributed to it in the Israeli society of the 1950s. This impression is reinforced by the answer to the question. The authors begin by declaring that there was no truth in the assumption that the uprising was not accorded a fitting status in Israel, yet the continuation of the answer shows that its preamble was no more than a statement of political correctness and that the authors indeed felt that the State of Israel had not accorded the uprising the status it deserved and that there were significant differences between the patterns of commemoration that had evolved in Israel and among Diaspora Jewry.

Determining whether the belief that the Warsaw Ghetto Uprising was not accorded a meaningful place in Israel's collective memory was correct goes beyond the scope of this book.[443] For our purposes it is important to note simply that the WJC leadership in New York believed there were significant differences between the patterns of Holocaust memorialization in the Diaspora and those in Israel, and that they and the organization's members were the champions of empowering the status of the uprising in the individual and public memory of Diaspora Jews. They felt that they were creating a singular pattern of remembrance that enhanced the memory of the Warsaw Ghetto Uprising as opposed to the relatively marginal status that the uprising occupied in the patterns of Holocaust memory that had emerged Israel in the 1950s.

With a view to disseminating knowledge of the Warsaw Ghetto Uprising among Jews worldwide and among WJC members in particular, in 1956 the WJC's Organizational Division issued a wide-ranging essay written in English and

---

442 Ibid.
443 For a different perspective on the place of the Warsaw Ghetto uprising in Israel's public memory and a discussion of the founding of the Ghetto Fighters House on Lohamei Ha-Geta'ot kibbutz as a museum that accords the uprising pride of place, see Rotem, *Holocaust Remembrance Museums*, 72–75.

Yiddish titled "The Warsaw Ghetto Revolt: Climax of Jewish Heroism and Resistance in the Last 1800 Years." [444]

The essay's title is self-explanatory: It establishes the authors' intention to use events commemorating the Warsaw Ghetto Uprising to shape the ethnic identity of Diaspora Jews into that of a Jewish community fighting for its existence rather than one functioning as a purely passive entity. This perspective is also reflected in the introductory remarks to the essay penned by Isaac I. Schwarzbart, Chairman of the WJC's Organizational Division:[445]

> This Year the WJC again addressed itself to Jewish communities the world over to observe this national memorial day. In this connection the Congress urged that the story of the Warsaw Ghetto Uprising be told this year as part of the glorious record of Jewish deeds of valor which adorn the pages of our long history. That the Warsaw Ghetto Uprising is not an isolated Jewish history which has frequently repeated itself, is clearly demonstrated in the accompanying survey entitled "The Warsaw Ghetto Revolt: Climax of Jewish heroism and Resistance in the Last 1800 Years." It is intended to serve first and foremost, our youth in our homes and schools. It might strengthen the ties between our youth and the spirit of Modin, Jerusalem, Masada, Beythar and Warsaw.

The WJC's mouthpiece *Congress Weekly* played its part as well in turning the Warsaw Ghetto Uprising into a major component of Holocaust memory among Diaspora Jews. The issues of the weekly that appeared close to the memorial date carried testimonies and recollections of the uprising and encouraged readers to make the day of remembrance an integral part of public events related to the Passover festival. An editorial column in the March 1953 issue reads: "As we honor the memory of the Ghetto victims in this season of our Festival of Freedom, let us recall their invincible faith in the inevitable coming of liberation and in the ultimate triumph of justice. That is their legacy to us and to generations to come."[446]

The deep sense of responsibility felt by Robinson and his associates with regard to the fate of the Jews during World War II and thereafter can be clearly seen in the efforts made by the WJC leadership to cultivate the memory of the Warsaw Ghetto Uprising, in the arguments and debates concerning the design of the appropriate space in which to display the exhibit on the Holocaust, in the minutes of the various meetings, and in Robinson's own comments. This outlook was also clearly manifested during the prosecution of war criminals after the war.

---

444 1956 publication (no precise date given), AJA, 361 H294/2.
445 Ibid.
446 The WJC's weekly publication, *Congress Weekly – Tenth Anniversary of the Warsaw Ghetto Revolt*, March 30, 1953, AJA, 361 H294/2. The weekly's editorial board continued to devote special issues to the topic of the Warsaw Ghetto in later years. See, for example, *Congress Weekly*, April 1, 1963, AJA, 361 H294/2.

Congress functionaries believed that the mission of bringing the war criminals to justice was of utmost importance both to Jews and to the world in general. They felt that the other Jewish organizations, especially the Jewish Agency, were not investing sufficient energy in this endeavor to ensure that the issue of crimes committed against the Jews was accorded the attention it deserved during the forthcoming trials. Robinson's efforts and WJC involvement in the prosecution of war criminals were part of the trend that had begun with the organization's rescue operation in Europe that Congress activities had altogether exceeded the conventional parameters of a philanthropic organization primarily concerned with welfare and health-related interests. It is important to emphasize that, despite the enormous challenge presented by collecting and editing the information pertaining to the Holocaust of European Jewry, the Institute of Jewish Affairs and the other institutions within the WJC consistently involved themselves in shaping a system of international post-war arrangements that would ensure the maintenance of human rights within a climate of political and cultural freedom. A practical expression of this commitment can be found in Robinson and the WJC's response to a request from the United Nations to prepare the scholarly foundation for UN discussions of this issue. This appeal to Robinson indicates not only that the WJC and Robinson personally were committed to the notion of human rights, but that the international community recognized their significant contribution to the struggle for human rights in the post-war period. Robinson related the following:

> You probably know that both the WJC and the Institute of Jewish Affairs are committed to work in the field of the internationalization of human rights and fundamental freedom. You know too, that in the United Nations there was a nuclear commission on human rights which met in New York in April and May, 1946. Parts of its decisions were adopted on June 19, 1946, by the Economics and Social Some Council. On January 27, the first session of the permanent Commission on Human Rights is to take place. When the Secretariat of the United Nations started to prepare for this first session, they felt that they are not fully equipped for this work. They sent an S. O. S. to the Institute and to congress to "loan" me out for ten weeks to the United Nations in order to prepare for this session.[447]

The endeavor to enhance a Jewish identity in Europe and to protect the rights of the Jews living there was not confined to the realms of academic scholarship and jurisprudence. WJC papers tell of a campaign on behalf of restitution of Jewish

---

447 Minutes of a meeting of the Institute of Jewish Affairs team, November 27, 1946, AJA, 361 C68/8. Robinson's work in the UN institutions during 1946 was part of a broader involvement on the part of the WJC in the UN's engagement with this issue. See, for example, Memorandum of the World Jewish Congress on the Forthcoming Third Session of the Human Rights Commission, March 28, 1948, AJA, 361 C68/10.

property and protection of the rights of Jews and other minorities under the postwar political arrangements. It should be stressed that the process of registering pre-war private and communal Jewish property was conducted not only for the sake of reparations, but also in order to establish a foundation for the reconstruction of Jewish communities in Europe. The process of collecting data pertaining to pre-war Jewish property in Poland was a complex matter that required extensive research in both the United States and Europe. The rationale underlying the discussions concerning the property was that the overriding objective the WJC was to revive the communities in Europe, in Poland in particular, despite the total destruction of Jewish life there.[448] Special attention was devoted to establishing a mechanism of reparations for individual survivors and for the Jewish people as a whole. The reparation money would be channeled into cultural institutions, community bodies, and educational interests according to well-thought-out guidelines derived from the view that because the entire Jewish people had been afflicted by the Holocaust, the process of rehabilitation required huge resources that could be attained only through reparations. The WJC regarded itself as the representative of the section of the Jewish people that resided outside Israel and of the major Jewish organizations. Thus, following the founding of the State of Israel, the WJC demanded that substantial amounts of money be made available to it rather than to the government of Israel for the rehabilitation of the Jewish people and its continued existence in the Diaspora. The WJC leadership, particularly Nahum Goldmann, would play a vital role in fashioning the reparations agreement between Germany and the State of Israel. Of particular interest are the efforts of the WJC leadership and its delegates to the Claims Conference to reach a compensation agreement on behalf of those forced to produce Zyklon B gas in the plants of the German chemicals company I. G. Farben, which exploited tens of thousands of forced laborers in its German and European plants during World War II. WJC representatives assisted in the submission of claims by surviving laborers, accusing the company's management of raising the issue of non-Jewish forced laborers merely in order to undermine the negotiations between the

---

448 On the view that regarded community property as the basis for rehabilitating the communities in Poland, see the discussions of the WJC's Committee for the Restitution of Communal Property in Poland, November 26, 1944, AJA, 361 A68/1. Participants in these discussions noted that the WJC's research body had created a file of information regarding 1053 communities numbering at least 5,000 individuals. In addition, data had been collected on all the Jewish schools that had operated in 1936. The data retrieval and research work was conducted in Europe and in archives in the USA.

parties, and threatened to initiate a public campaign against the company in the United States if no agreement could be reached.[449]

An example of the WJC's independent activity in the international arena is its attempt to gain official status at the United Nations. Various committees of the Congress submitted papers, distributed memoranda, and presented data to the UN addressing the issues of minorities and welfare. Stephen Wise voiced harsh public criticism of the view that Zionism was the sole constituting force of Jewish life following the Holocaust. In a 1948 speech, Nahum Goldmann stressed that the WJC, rather than the government of Israel, should be the official spokesman of Diaspora Jewry. In this vein, a Congress report on its activity within the UN emphasized not only the role played by the organization in presenting the perspective of the Jewish Diaspora to world bodies, but also its status as the only organization dedicated to protecting the rights of Jews around the world. This outlook was clearly expressed in a report submitted in 1948 by Dr. Robert Marcus, chairman of the WJC's political committee, to the United Nations Commission on Genocide. Marcus maintained that the organization's proposals to the commission should be given serious consideration since the WJC represented all of world Jewry. He added that the experience of the world's Jews as a minority group that had resisted the attempts to annihilate it during the Holocaust and was now struggling for its rights lent added weight to the WJC outlook on the issues of genocide and minority rights. On the strength of his Jewish experience, Marcus proposed that several measures be taken including: passage of international legislation designating the infringing of minority rights as a crime; creation of an international system of intervention in the case of infringement of minority rights; and formation of a reparations mechanism to facilitate the rehabilitation of victims.[450]

Through their endeavors at the United Nations, the heads of the WJC again expressed their conviction that they were the representatives of the Jewish people. In 1947 they requested and received recognition as a non-governmental organization with advisory status, thereby gaining judicial, public, and international authorization of their singular status.

---

449 See the discussions of the WJC's Committee for the Restitution of Communal Property in Poland, ibid. For an extensive discussion of this issue that focuses on Goldmann, see Ronald W. Zweig, "'Reparations Made Me,' Nahum Goldmann, German Reparations and the Jewish World," in Raider, *Goldmann*, 233–253. On I. G. Farben, see Joseph Borkin, *The Crime and the Punishment of I. G. Farben* (New York, 1978). For WJC documents relating to this issue, see March 2, 1956; March 9, 1956; April 6, 1956, AJA, 361 C45/6.
450 Memorandum submitted by Dr. Robert Marcus, Chairman of the WJC's Political Committee, to the UN Commission on Genocide, March 6, 1948, AJA, 361 B104/3.

While Congress leaders attributed great importance to the international recognition they received through the UN, their involvement in its activity stemmed from their overall support of the organization. WJC papers indicate that the organization's leaders called upon its members and on the general American Jewish public to actively support the UN. They maintained that as an intellectual collective upholding a progressive world view, the Jews were obliged to support the UN, and emphasized that international peace and cooperation as manifested by the UN were particularly vital to Jews, given the suffering and catastrophe they had experienced during World War II. Nevertheless, Jewish support of the United Nations did not stem from narrow self-interest, but emanated from a sense of mission that recognized the importance of the organization to the entire world. Jews should commit themselves both to support the founding of the UN and to reinforce it, so as to ensure that the ideals underlying its establishment should not remain only within the realms of utopia. The WJC leadership in New York also endorsed the Bretton Woods Agreement, concluded during the course of an international economic summit held in July 1944 in the town of Bretton Woods in New Hampshire, which comprised a series of trade agreements determining the exchange rates of currencies among the developed countries. The 44 countries attending the conference established the International Monetary Fund and the World Bank. WJC representatives participated in public activity in the United States to promote the agreements; the organization's American members were called upon to lobby their representatives in Congress to support the agreement; and its institutions distributed information pertaining to the agreements to the members and conveyed their support of the agreements and the financial arrangements concluded in their wake.[451]

The prospect of establishing the State of Israel and its subsequent founding did not deter the WJC from promoting the existence of a Jewish Diaspora possessing nationalist characteristics; in fact, it provided an impetus for it. The found-

---

[451] See Nehemia Robinson, *The United Nations and the World Jewish Congress* (New York, 1955). On support of the United Nations, see a memorandum to the WJC conference at Atlantic City, November 17, 1944, AJA, 361 A68/3. On the participation of WJC representatives in related activity in Washington and their support for the Bretton Woods agreements, the World Bank, and the International Monetary Fund, see an article written by Nehemia Robinson in the *Congress Weekly*, April 20, 1945, AJA, 361 B95/3. See also a memorandum by Robinson, undated, AJA, 361 B95/1; a telegram from the US Treasury Secretary Henry Morgenthau Jr. inviting the WJC to send a representative to the consultations in Washington regarding the Bretton Woods agreements, February 17, 1945, AJA, 361 B95/3. On the request to lobby Congressmen to support the Bretton Woods agreement, see the action guide of the WJC's Women's League, February 5, 1945, AJA, 361 C68/5. On the agreements and their significance, see John Maynard Keynes, *Activities 1941–1946: Shaping the Post War World: Bretton Woods and Reparations* (London, 1980).

ing of the state challenged the leadership of Diaspora Jewry, which was Zionist in outlook, to find fresh ideological causes. During the years when a supreme effort was required to establish the state and protect its independence, an equally complex and exacting endeavor was being made to revive Jewish life in post-Holocaust Europe and to enable those survivors wishing to do so to merge into the fabric of European life. Because the Zionist movement had focused primarily on founding the Jewish state, Congress leaders felt that Diaspora Jewry had not been accorded the attention it deserved during the latter half of the 1940s. The heads of the Congress thus felt compelled to step into the breach and engage energetically in the rehabilitation of the Jews of Europe.[452]

The large number of survivors and the terrible destruction wrought on the European communities did not dissuade the WJC leaders or cause them to reduce their efforts to strengthen Jewish ethnic identity. On the contrary, they viewed the wartime events conclusive proof of the need for an international Jewish organization devoted to two main tasks: first to protect the rights of world Jewry and to represent it in the international arenas that were taking shape after the war; and second to foster an ethnic identity comprising nationalist characteristics among the world's Jews. Such a step would ensure the continued existence of the Jewish people in the Diaspora both as individuals and as communities, and would contribute to molding a better world that would safeguard the rights of minorities, particularly the Jews, in the post-war period.

The activity of the World Jewish Congress in post-war Europe adds a further dimension to the historical discourse on Diaspora nationalism. This aspect denotes a complex condition whereby a scattered minority that shares ethnic and economic attributes is either unable or unwilling to integrate fully with the wider society and therefore constitutes a quasi-national cultural, political, and social population that lacks a sovereign territorial base. The configuration of a number of national groupings, such as Greeks, Kurds and Armenians, may be defined as Diaspora Nationalism.[453] Scholars of the annals of nationalism broadly agree that modern patterns of Jewish existence constitute a prime example of Diaspora Nationalism. This broad consensus notwithstanding, the debate concerning the meaning of the concept in Jewish history is still going on. Two major trends can be discerned here, the differences between which are linked to the wider discussion regarding the place of modernity in the definition of nationalism in general and Jewish nationalism in particular. The first approach assumes that the concept is vital to understanding the patterns of Jewish existence in the Diaspora, and that

---

[452] On the efforts of the WJC on behalf of the Jews of the Diaspora, see Goldmann, *The Jewish Paradox*, 38–63.

[453] Anthony D. Smith, "Zionism and Diaspora Nationalism," *Israel Affairs* 2 (1995): 9–10.

nationalist trends can be identified throughout the ages of Jewish life in the Diaspora. The foremost proponent of this view is Anthony Smith. Smith emphasizes the singular nature of Jewish existence in the Diaspora, maintaining national characteristics while lacking a clear national center. Despite the spiritual bond to the Land of Israel, the national elements are intrinsically linked to prolonged existence in Diaspora rather than in the Land of Israel. Smith stresses that the Jews' historical existence within a Diaspora nationalism was necessary for the creation of the Zionist movement and for the capacity to realize Jewish nationalism in the modern age. He maintains that Zionism is an example of a successful Diaspora nationalism, not in the political sense (in which the development of Zionism depended on international circumstances that were largely beyond its control) but rather in light of Zionism's impressive spiritual victory gained by virtue of the Jews' lengthy existence in a state of Diaspora nationalism.[454]

By contrast, the second approach restricts use of the concept to the period during which modern Jewish nationalism crystallized as part of the process that led to the founding of the State of Israel. This outlook is clearly manifested in the work of Ernest Gellner, who asserts that the patterns of national existence in the modern world impelled minority groupings to construct political and social patterns of organization that facilitated their concentration in a particular territory. He maintains that Diaspora nationalism did not exist in the pre-modern age and thus constitutes merely an intermediate stage in the process of territorial concentration, and that its success is to be gauged by the ability to realize national aspirations in a particular territory.[455] Gellner emphasizes the negative and threatening aspects of Diaspora nationalism, especially its Jewish manifestation. He asserts that a group's existence in a condition of national dispersion is a dangerous condition that could lead a minority choosing this path to endure hardships ranging from genocide to deportation and, in some cases, to preserving a certain unstable and uncomfortable equilibrium.[456]

It is not the purpose of this study to resolve the complex debate concerning the place of Diaspora nationalism in the annals of nationalism or of Israel, but to show that it was precisely in the context of the Holocaust and the founding of the State of Israel that the WJC leaders wished to shape the structure of the Jewish people according to the model of Diaspora nationalism, in parallel to the Jewish state rather than in its place.[457] While the heads of the WJC did not make use of

---

454 Ibid., 7–8.
455 Ernest Gellner, *Nations and Nationalism* (Oxford, 1983), 101–109.
456 Ibid., 138.
457 It is beyond the scope of this book to survey the vast literature on the roots of nationalism. In addition to Gellner's above-mentioned work, see Smith, *The Nation in History*; Anderson,

the Diaspora nationalism model in presenting the essence of their post-war activity in Europe, their ideological explanations and activity in effect expressed this notion. Whereas both scholars and contemporaries looked askance at the idea of Diaspora nationalism, the heads of the WJC regarded Jewish existence in the Diaspora favorably and argued that such an arrangement could and should be maintained alongside the State of Israel. They believed that this was the correct way to preserve Jewish existence in the world, both from an ideological standpoint and given the impracticality of the notion that Jews the world over would migrate to Palestine.

As has been shown, the desire to fashion an active, democratic Jewish Diaspora possessing representative institutions was demonstrated by the wide range of activity conducted in Europe and in international bodies. Activity of this nature transcends the boundaries of American Jewry's traditional philanthropic endeavors. The impressive scope of the philanthropic post-Holocaust effort of the Joint Distribution Committee on behalf of the displaced persons and remnants of European Jewry notwithstanding, that enterprise was devoid of the nationalist elements that characterized the activities of the WJC. It is possible to surmise that the WJC endeavor to shape a democratically oriented Diaspora nationality presented the major obstacle to cooperation between it and the American Jewish Committee, whose leadership rejected the nationalist elements of WJC ideology and practice. The heads of the American Jewish Committee issued public declarations critical of the WJC at the time of its establishment and the two organizations were adversaries in the public sphere for many years, even though they maintained clandestine contacts, as in the case of the Jewish response in the United States to the Holocaust.[458]

The heads of the WJC themselves pointed to the significant differences between philanthropy and the patterns of activity undertaken by their organi-

---

Imagined Communities; Elie Kedourie, ed., *Nationalism in Asia and Africa* (London, 1971); Eric Hosbawm, *Nations and Nationalism Since 1780* (Cambridge, 1990); Hugh Trevor-Roper, *Jewish and Other Nationalisms* (London, 1961).

458 On the Joint's work in Eastern Europe, see Yosef Litwak, "The Joint's Contribution to the Rehabilitation of Survivors in Poland," in Binyamin Pinkus, ed., *East European Jewry Between Holocaust and Revival 1944–1948* [in Hebrew] (Ben Gurion Heritage Center, Ben Gurion University, 1987), 344–388. On the relations between the American Jewish Committee and the WJC and the Committee's response to the founding of the WJC, see Cohen, *The American Jewish Committee*, 219–226. It should be noted that the American Jewish women's organization Hadassah conducted impressive and important philanthropic activity, but unlike that of the WJC, most of its effort was invested in Palestine. On the work of Hadassah in Palestine, see Erica B. Simmons, *Hadassah and the Zionist Project* (New York, 2006).

zation.⁴⁵⁹ A clear indication of the WJC leaders' perception of the singular status of the organization is found in their use of the term "parliament" to portray the concept of the Congress's desired democratic system of operation. From its inception they strongly asserted that individual organizations could not resolve the problems of the Jews around the world. This was a mission that only a *parliament of world Jewry* (the original wording) could confront. This parliament was to be democratically elected by the Jews of the world and would seek to achieve a comprehensive solution to the plight of Jews wherever they lived and to engage in specific campaigns directed at ameliorating the condition of Jews in those countries where it was necessary. Independent Jewish action undertaken by means of a parliament would confer added validity to the demand that the organization be accepted into the sphere of international politics. The authors of the WJC's inaugural letter stressed that it was, in fact, a Jewish parliament operating independently of other organizations. The founding of the Congress was a supremely important historic event that ushered in a new age in Jewish existence and expressed in practice the cooperation among Jewish communities based on recognition of their shared national identity.⁴⁶⁰

As expected, the notion of establishing a Jewish parliament raised questions about dual loyalty and the degree of independence enjoyed by the various communities vis-à-vis the organs of the WJC. During the latter half of the 1930s and throughout the 1940s, WJC leaders did indeed make a point of asserting that their organization aspired neither in practice nor in theory to function as a government of Diaspora Jewry. While "parliament" is a juridical concept, Diaspora Jews had no state of their own and were full citizens of the various states in which they resided. The WJC was merely a democratic organization working toward a common goal, namely the welfare of the Diaspora Jews.⁴⁶¹

The heads of the WJC viewed the organization, founded in 1936, as a direct extension of the Committee of Jewish Delegations established in 1919. They regarded the activity of that committee to have constituted a turning point in modern Jewish history by campaigning not only for individual Jewish rights, such as civil and political equality and freedom of worship, but also for collective

---

459 Nahum Goldmann at the WJC conference, November 1941 (no precise date given), AJA, 361 A5/3.
460 Letter of the founding committee, October 26, 1933, AJA, 361 A40/4. Recent studies question the characterization of migration to Palestine as having been ideologically driven. See, for example, Gur Elro'i, *Immigration: Jewish Migration to Palestine in the Early Twentieth Century* [in Hebrew] (Jerusalem, 2004).
461 See Wise's address at the inaugural convention of the WJC, August 8, 1936, AJA, 361 A40/8. See also a publication of the WJC's women's league, March, 1946 (no precise date given), AJA, 361 A5/6.

rights that called for recognition of the right of Jews to internal autonomy within their countries of residence with regard to their culture and national existence.[462] The view that the Jews were a people whose national life should be conducted throughout the world and not in a separate territory is expounded extensively in the works of Shimon Dubnov, a writer and historian and founding member of the autonomist movement.[463] Like Dubnov, the heads of the WJC regarded Jewish existence in the Diaspora as a legitimate part of Jewish life, unlike him, however, they did not seek to establish Jewish autonomy, but actively engaged in integrating Jews within their countries of residence while underscoring their cultural characteristics and the need for an organizational structure that would ensure the rights of Jews in particular and of all minorities.

The concept of Diaspora nationalism has underpinned a wealth of studies in the general sphere of nationalism. For the most part these studies deal with the minority that resides in the Diaspora and its links with the mother country, or with an alternative territorial concentration in which the minority conducts its sovereign national life.[464] The actions of the WJC in Europe and the United States during the 1940s and '50s point to a different view of the essence of Diaspora nationalism. These activities present an alternative to the assumption that the

---

[462] See Natan Feinberg, "The Committee of Jewish Delegations 1919–1936" [in Hebrew], *Gesher (A Quarterly on the Issue of the Life of the Nation), published by the Israeli executive of the WJC*, 63–64 (1970): 15–16. See also Nahum Goldmann, "Fifty Years of Struggle for Jewish Rights," ibid., 7–12; A. Bein, "The Role of A. L. Motzkin in the Struggle for Jewish National Rights in the Diaspora and in the Founding of the Committee of Jewish Delegations," ibid., 30–38.

[463] On Dubnov, see, for example, Sophie Dubnov-Erlich, *The Life and Work of S. M. Dubnov, Diaspora Nationalism and Jewish History* (Bloomington, 1991), 1–33. This book presents archival sources relating to the ideological origins of the WJC's leaders' advocacy of the existence of a Jewish Diaspora Nationalism. For a general discussion on the ideology of the American Jewish reform movement on this issue, and its preference for integrating Jews among the nations of the world, see Ofer Shiff, *Integrating Jews: American Reform Universalism vis-à-vis Zionism, Anti-Semitism and Holocaust* (Tel Aviv, 2001), 129–168.

[464] For a discussion of this issue in the American Jewish context, see, for example, Jasmin Habib, *Israel Diaspora and the Routes of National Belonging* (Toronto, 2004) 27–36. Simon Rabinivitch, (ed), *Jews and Diaspora Nationalism* (Waltham, MA, 2012). David N. Myers, *Between Jew and Arab: The Lost Voice of Simon Rawidowicz* (Waltham MA, 2008). James Loefler, "Between Zionism and Liberalism: Oscar Janowsky and Diaspora Nationalism in America," *AJS Review* 34 (2010): 289–308. Noam Pianko, *Zionism and Roads Not Taken: Rawidowicz, Kaplan, Kohn* (Bloomington Indiana 2010). See also David Mittelberg, *The Israel Connection and American Jews* (London, 1999), 21–35. Regarding other ethnic groups, see, for example, Michael Doorley, *Irish-American Diaspora Nationalism: The Friends of Irish Freedom, 1916–1935* (Dublin, 2005). For a discussion on the reciprocal relations between Diaspora, nationalism, and geographic borders, see Smadar Lavie and Ted Swedenburg (eds.), *Displacement, Diaspora, and Geographies of Identity* (London, 1996), 1–25.

link to the mother country constitutes a major component in the ideology and practice of Diaspora nationalist life. This view proclaims that the Jewish people is unique only because of its bond to the Land of Israel. While they recognized the importance of the Land and the State of Israel to modern Jewish existence, the WJC leaders believed that this bond was not the sole dominant factor, and that it was imperative to create an ideological infrastructure and an organizational structure that would facilitate Jewish life in the Diaspora, within which the link to the Land of Israel would be but one component of ethnic Jewish identity throughout the world.

The WJC documents referenced in this chapter show that the heads of the organization were aware of the complex challenge posed by the attempt to revive Jewish life in Europe. Apart from the day-to-day distress faced by the people of Europe following World War II, the Jewish population confronted anti-Semitism, xenophobia, seizure of their property by their neighbors, pogroms, the total destruction of the communities' physical infrastructure, and a severe demographic crisis brought about by the dimensions of Nazi mass murder.[465] It is safe to assume that the fraught and complex reality in Europe, particularly among Jews, as well as the evolution of the Cold War and the growing rift between East and West, restricted the capacity of the organization to act within the Jewish communities of Eastern Europe and impeded the realization of the notion of Jewish Diaspora nationality in Europe.

By contrast, WJC activity in the American arena, together with that of other elements of the Jewish community there such as the American Zionists, contributed to the emergence of components of Diaspora nationalism among American Jewry. The dramatic triangle of the Holocaust, the survivors, and the State of Israel constituted not only a catalyst for the processes leading up to the founding of the state and integration of the survivors into it, but also a framework for enhancing the national identity of European and American Jews. The WJC was indeed focused on Europe, but its endeavors there compelled it to enhance and streamline its philanthropic machinery in the United States in order to create the organizational and economic infrastructure that would facilitate its European effort. This intensive ethnic activity directed toward objectives beyond the United States thus influenced developments within American Jewry. This process served to heighten American Jews' sense of responsibility toward their brethren around the world as well as their sense of ethnic identity. Meanwhile, a Jewish-American national identity in which the State of Israel played only a specified part was

---

[465] See Pieter Lagrou, "Return to a Vanished World: European Societies and the Remnants of their Jewish Communities, 1945–1947," in David Bankier, ed., *The Jews Are Coming Back, The Return of the Jews to their Countries of Origin After WW II* (New York and Jerusalem, 2005), 1–24.

taking shape. However, the WJC's success in enhancing ethnic Jewish activity in the United States was not entirely due to what had occurred in Europe. It was also facilitated by the process of integration of Jews into the fabric of American life, the gradual improvement in the socio-economic status of American Jews, and acceptance by American society of the Jews as an ethnic community with its own distinctive characteristics.[466]

---

[466] On the growing sense of responsibility on the part of US Jews toward the distress of Jews around the world, see Henry L. Feingold, *Saving the Jews of Russia, The American Jewish Effort, 1967–1989* (Syracuse, N. Y., 2007). For discussion of the role of the State of Israel in US Jewish identity, see, for example, Steven M. Cohen and Charles S. Liebman, "Israel and American Jewry in the Twenty-First Century: A Search for a New Relationships," in *Beyond Survival and Philanthropy: American Jewry and Israel*, eds. Allon Gal and Alfred Gottschalk (Cincinnati, 2000), 3–24. For discussion of similar processes that occurred in the context of US Jewry's campaign for the founding of Israel, see Melvin I. Urofsky, *We Are One: American Jewry and Israel* (New York, 1978).

Summary

In November 1946 a document titled "The Program of the World Jewish Congress" was published in New York. It began by presenting the principles underlying the founding of the WJC, as well as the constellation of political circumstances that had prevailed at the time the organization was established in 1936. The following passage appears in this document:

> The isolated efforts of single Jewish organizations in individual countries could not meet the needs of the entire Jewish people. And so international Jewish associations for the attainment of specific objectives came into being. In 1897 the World Zionist Organization was formed for the purpose of establishing a legally secured, publicly recognized Jewish homeland in Palestine. The creation of an organization to look after the needs and interests of Jews throughout the world waited for a later opportunity to materialize.[467]

Couched in official language, this brief statement alludes to a political and ideological endeavor of great importance, which the World Jewish Congress announced at its inception and which its leadership led and promoted throughout the Jewish world during the first half of the twentieth century. It sought to found an international Jewish organization that supported the establishment of a Jewish state, but also acted to reinforce life in Jewish communities around the world under the format of "Diaspora nationalism."

The full significance of this process may be appreciated by examining the world view of Stephen Wise, the founder of the WJC, regarding Theodore Herzl and Jewish nationalism. In the summer of 1929, Wise delivered a lecture at a gathering in commemoration of Herzl. He began by stressing that the Jewish people had been reshaped by Herzl, who had transformed the public modes of operation of the Jewish elites.[468] Wise explained that in the pre-Herzlian era Jews whom he described as powerful were accustomed to assisting other Jews solely by way of philanthropy, but never in conjunction with the wider Jewish public. Herzl had changed this by initiating joint activity on the part of Jews of different socio-economic strata in order to establish patterns of Jewish life. Wise's portrayal suggested that by doing this Herzl had created genuine Jewish solidarity that rested upon robust foundations and constituted an essential part of a reemerging Jewish national existence in the modern age. Wise further asserted that in the era prior to Herzl, problems concerning Jewish existence had been aired for discussion by

---

467 The Program of the World Jewish Congress, New York November, 1946, AJA, 361 A5/6.
468 Wise's lecture on Herzl at a gathering in commemoration of him, New York, July 18, 1929, CZA, A-246/164. For a further lecture in the same vein, see Wise lecture, The Epochal Herzl, (no precise date or location given), CZA, A-243/163.

non-Jews, who had also proposed the solutions. These solutions were frequently imposed upon the Jews, who could only attempt to minimize the damage they caused. Wise defined this situation as "tragic," noting that the Jews had never examined what they themselves could do to resolve what he had previously termed the "Jewish questions."[469]

Wise believed that this situation had been completely once Herzl had turned the "Jewish question" into an issue that the Jews themselves had addressed as they identified the problems and sought to resolve them as Jews. Prior to Herzl's time, anti-Semitism had been the moving force of Jewish life; the Jews had merely reacted to the distress it had caused them and had frequently been convinced by the anti-Semites' arguments, which had induced them to try to modify their Jewishness and to downplay their singularity as Jews. By turning Zionism into the major element that initiated and motivated the life of Jews, Herzl had transformed their condition, refusing to respond to anti-Semitic acts and facilitating Jewish pride. Wise compared Herzl's importance and significance to that of the Messiah, claiming that the self-initiated transformation that had occurred among the Jews in the wake of Herzl's activity was the most genuine and wonderful miracle of all.[470] In his lecture Wise maintained that Herzl's tremendous importance to Jewish history stemmed not only from having succeeded in creating an ideological infrastructure and organizational platform for the founding of a Jewish state, but also from having created new forms of Jewish existence around the world. A by-product of the enormous effort made by world Jewry to build a national home was the unification of the worldwide Jewish community as a political force seeking common goals and administering active institutions.

As the above citation indicates, the dramatic crisis that confronted the Jews of Europe from the latter half of the 1930s reinforced the conviction of Wise and his colleagues that it was essential to express the world view expounded in his 1929 lecture by founding a representative international Jewish organization. They maintained that it was necessary to found the WJC because the Zionist movement was primarily occupied with the affairs of Palestine, and this additional organization would thus be preoccupied with addressing the needs of world Jewry. The great majority of the founders of the WJC considered themselves to be Zionists, and some holding senior positions in the Zionist movement. They saw no contradiction between their Zionist leanings and activity within the WJC. They fought diligently for the establishment of a Jewish state, while at the same time striving to empower the ethnic identity of Diaspora Jews. As documented throughout this book, the organization's founders were well aware of the existence of Jewish philanthropic

---

469 Ibid.
470 Ibid.

organizations that devoted their efforts toward the Jews of the Diaspora. Yet the founders of the WJC and its activists during the 1930s, '40s, and '50s believed that since these organizations operated as philanthropies they were unable to confront the Jews' existential crisis that began in the 1930s. Thus, in contrast to other organizations, from its inception in 1936 to the outbreak of World War II the WJC involved itself in world and European politics worldwide, at the League of Nations, and with representatives of European governments as it attempted to ameliorate the condition of European Jewry and to create solutions for long-term migration.

The outbreak of war and reports of the extermination of Europe's Jews induced WJC leadership and its operatives in neutral European countries to adopt modes of operation that were very different from the conventional patterns of philanthropic work in the Jewish public sphere. In this spirit they created a streamlined system for gathering information on the acts of murder and extermination in Europe, and set up a clandestine operation in neutral countries and in those under German occupation in order to rescue Jewish children and to facilitate the survival of Jews who had gone into hiding.

The discussion in this book of World Jewish Congress activities during the Holocaust reveals the complex and daunting challenges that the organization's leadership encountered during this period. The material presented here demonstrates that the WJC leaders did all that they could to rescue Jews during the Holocaust. This conclusion is at odds with the trenchant criticism, also described in this book, on the part of contemporaries and scholars alike, of the allegedly muted effort made by American Jewish leaders in general and the WJC leadership in particular to effect the rescue of Jews. As mentioned above, examination of the WJC program reveals that by 1946 its leaders were aware of this criticism and sought to make public the variety of actions taken by the organization on behalf of Europe's Jews during the war years. The Congress maintained that these activities would only gain the recognition they deserved at some point in the future.

> During the war years, the World Jewish Congress was the tireless representative in the free world of the Jews of the Axis-occupied countries. Its chief concern was to save Jewish lives from imminent death at the hands of the Nazis. It is too early to enumerate all the manifold and dramatic endeavors in this field. Suffice it to say that the Congress engaged in rescue work by ransoming and smuggling Jews out of Nazi-held areas. It prevailed upon the Swedish Government to permit the entry of Jews from Denmark. It marshaled its connections and influences to prevent the mass deportation of Jews from Bulgaria and Hungary. For those and other activities which the future historian will relate with pride, the World Jewish Congress mobilized the Jews of the New World, where it has always had a large and devoted following, especially in Latin America.[471]

---

471 The Program of the World Jewish Congress, New York November, 1946, AJA, 361 A5/6.

The explanation of these diverse assessments calls for an examination of the activities of Stephen Wise, Nahum Goldmann, and their colleagues in the leadership of the WJC within the American arena. Their activities should be appraised not merely as the actions of Jewish leaders, but also as those of American Jewish leaders who operated within the political and social milieu of the United States. While they were dissatisfied with the level of the Roosevelt administration's commitment to the rescue of European Jews, they understood that it was subject to the constraints inherent to American politics in the first half of the 1940s. They believed that it would be unwise to exert excessive public pressure on President Roosevelt to take action to rescue European Jews, and sought to understate the president's engagement in the Jewish dilemma. Their intention was to protect Roosevelt from being presented as a friend of the Jews and as having led the United States into the war in response to Jewish pressure rather than out of concern for American interests. Wise, Goldmann, and their colleagues sought to create a durable association between the issue of Jewish rescue and the inevitable American victory in the war; thus they downplayed the presence of the Jewish issue in the American public sphere. They believed that there was no need to intensify Jewish activity by, for example, convening press conferences and demonstrations designed specifically to promote the rescue of European Jewry. The operation to rescue children orchestrated from Lisbon and the political steps taken on behalf of the Jewish communities of Denmark, Bulgaria, and Hungary were thus conducted clandestinely behind the scenes, in keeping with the policy of restraint that dictated the Congress's actions during World War II.

The correspondence between the WJC offices in the neutral countries and its New York headquarters, the minutes of its various committee meetings, and the reports on events in Europe are all written in dry, formal language. Nevertheless, they provide a clear indication of the deep distress felt by the WJC leaders at the time of the Holocaust. From the information gathered by the Congress's European bureaus they learned first-hand of the horrors of the Holocaust, but realized that they could rescue only a small number of individuals and were powerless to halt the murder of European Jewry. In an academic work such as this it is difficult to depict the dreadful circumstances under which Stephen Wise came to the conclusion that he must delay publication of the information he had received via the Riegner telegram. It is similarly difficult to portray the depth of emotion that Nahum Goldmann experienced as he declared in his letter of April 1943 to Yitzhak Gruenbaum, chairman of the Palestine Rescue Committee, that he assumed with a heavy heart that most of Europe's Jews living in the areas under Nazi occupation would be murdered.[472]

---

[472] Letter from Goldmann to Gruenbaum, April 5, 1943, CZA, Z-6/2755.

The policy of restraint pertaining to the response of American Jewry to the Holocaust that Wise, Goldmann and their colleagues followed in the American public sphere is extensively addressed in this book. The correspondence between Wise and Goldmann during World War II and thereafter reveals the personal and public price that the two men paid for directing this policy of restraint. While they remained convinced of the wisdom of the path they had chosen, the secrecy inherent in administering a policy of this sort and the need to conceal it from the wider ranks of WJC delegates and from the American Jewish public in general, considerably diminished their stature as leaders during World War II and thereafter, and their public standing suffered. Wise and Goldmann's personal and public distress cries out from the archived material. This is particularly evident in the case of Wise, who was among the most prominent Jewish leaders in the United States during the 1940s. A clear manifestation of his predicament is seen in his efforts to cancel the April 1943 press conference arranged to address the fate of European Jewry. Wise did cancel the event, but only with much painful soul searching and a deeply held conviction that by so doing he was fulfilling, to the best of his ability, his duty as a Jewish leader during World War II. He wrote to Goldmann that it was very easy to convene press conferences and public meetings, but that one must also take their possible ramifications into account. He believed that such activities would contribute nothing to the rescue effort; on the contrary, they would severely harm it, and would ultimately detract from his ability as leader of the American Jewish public to rescue Jews. Wise added that although Roosevelt had not acted on behalf of the Jews of Europe with the vigor that he, Wise, had expected, the president should nevertheless be thought of as a friend who had done all he could to help rescue Jews.[473]

The narrow confines within which Wise was obliged to maneuver are also evident in the restraint shown by the WJC in its campaign for a Jewish state. There are significant differences between the issue of rescue and the struggle for a Jewish state. Wise and Goldmann believed that although Jewish American activity on behalf of founding a Jewish state that challenged Roosevelt's administration was undesirable, such activity did not resemble the attempts to lobby aggressively for assistance to European Jewry. The issue of Palestine was close to the heart of the Jewish public and occupied decision makers in the administration, but did not have the public and political significance of the rescue issue. Unlike the war in Europe, the question of the founding of a Jewish state was not at the top of the national agenda, did not personally engage every American, and therefore was not potentially harmful to the president, since his political opponents could not significantly exploit the issue in order to denigrate him. Despite these differences,

---

[473] Letter from Wise to Goldmann, April 22, 1943, CZA, Z-6/18.

Wise also took steps to moderate the Jewish campaign in the United States with regard to the establishment of a Jewish state. He wholeheartedly supported the cause, but opposed the submission of the pro-Zionist resolutions to Congress in 1943 and 1944 and, unlike Reform rabbi and Zionist leader Abba Hillel Silver, took steps to prevent the use of the Jewish vote as a tool in the American Zionist struggle against the administration.

Wise's letter to David Niles in early 1945 reveals that he knew his support for Roosevelt was undermining his stature as a Jewish leader in the United States.[474] In this letter he requested a public meeting with Roosevelt before the president left to attend the Yalta Conference. This was a political stratagem designed to strengthen Wise and his associates in American Zionist circles and among American Jewry in general. Such a meeting would enable Wise to appear to enjoy free access to the president, who would be seen as consulting with him prior to attending a political event of the utmost importance. Indeed, Wise's stature as a Zionist leader was seriously damaged by his policy of restraint in the United States, and he was, in effect, deposed from every official Zionist post that he held in the United States and the wider Zionist movement during the latter half of the 1940s.

The significance and repercussions of the policy of restraint continued to reverberate beyond the 1940s, affecting the personal fate of Wise and his colleagues in the WJC leadership. The clandestine nature of the policy created an impression of total ineffectiveness. Conscious of this, at the 1944 WJC Atlantic City conference Nahum Goldmann tried to convey to the delegates the nature of the difficulties that confronted him and his colleagues in the leadership during the war, and to explain the reasons for their policy of restraint. In addition, he and other senior WJC functionaries reported at length on the rescue efforts conducted by the organization from the outbreak of the war up to that time. Yet all of this was to no avail. The assessment regarding WJC inactivity during the Holocaust period has been etched into historical memory. This book tells an altogether different story, one of concern and action. But the successful rescue of relatively few Jews pales in the face of the enormity of the tragedy and the horrific extent of the loss, and to some extent have only served to exacerbate the perception of failure and inactivity.

Despite the considerable harm to his public stature, Wise continued to serve the WJC until his death in 1949. His policy and that of the organization after the end of World War II clearly manifested the sense of responsibility the leaders felt

---

[474] Wise's letter to Niles, January 8, 1945, CZA, A-243/39. Roosevelt responded to Wise's request, and prior to leaving for Yalta held two meetings with him at which the issue of Palestine was discussed.

toward world Jewry and their conviction that it was their privilege and obligation to act on behalf of the Jewish people. They accordingly founded the Institute of Jewish Affairs, which was to provide the scholarly infrastructure in support of Jewish existence throughout the world in the wake of World War II; they promoted the indictment and trial of war criminals; they campaigned to set up an equitable reparations system for survivors and for the Jewish people collectively; and they carried out a complex policy designed to restore Jewish life to post-Holocaust Europe, while at the same time supporting the founding of the State of Israel.

The wartime papers of the World Jewish Congress provide valuable information on the organization's activity related to the Holocaust and the founding of the State of Israel during the forties. Their importance, however, exceeds the mere presentation of facts. They reveal an unusual and singular Jewish ethnic mix that offers an alternative to the conventional patterns of Jewish existence in the modern era. While the leaders of the World Jewish Congress supported the establishment of a Jewish state in Palestine, they did not regard it as their foremost objective. They saw themselves as representatives of the Jewish world on the eve of World War II, during the course of the war, and thereafter. And as such they labored for the establishment of a Jewish state and for the revival of Jewish life in the Diaspora as twin goals that complemented rather than contradicted each other.

Afterword

The importance of the founding and evolution of the Jewish community in the United States reaches far beyond the borders of that nation. The migration of millions of Jews to America in the past centuries is among the most significant episodes in the annals of the Jewish people in the modern age. This migration, which comprised many Jews from Eastern Europe, totally transformed the complexion of the Jewish people and generated a new reality in its politics, economy, and spiritual life.

The story of the World Jewish Congress during the 1940s is part of an organizational, political and ideological process whereby American Jewry gained ever increasing importance in the Jewish world. This development became all the more apparent following the Holocaust and the loss of the Jewish communities in most of the European regions overrun by the Nazis.

The bibliography that follows will demonstrate that leading early and contemporary academics who have engaged in the study of American Jewish history have made an important contribution to scholarship in this field. There are numerous groundbreaking studies on the history of the American Jewish community: the modes whereby Jews integrated with American society; the singular characteristics of the Jewish way of life in the United States; and Jewish political activity in the general American arena and in the context of World War II and the Holocaust of European Jewry. By contrast, only relatively few studies underscore the importance of the activity of American Jewry beyond the borders of the United States or address the far-reaching effects of the development of the Jewish community in the United States on Jewish life throughout the world. The examination of the World Jewish Congress activity offered in this book demonstrates that such a discussion is of particular importance because the activity undertaken by American Jewish organizations outside the country's borders—and particularly in Europe and in Palestine—transcended the confines of traditional philanthropic work, however important that work may have been. American Jewish leaders were imbued with a deep sense of mission and responsibility for the fate of world Jewry. They promoted activity directed at supporting and assisting the various Jewish communities, while striving to mold the Jewish world according to their views as American Jews. I hope that this book will contribute to enriching the discourse on the significance of American Jewish activity beyond the borders of the United States.

Another issue that emerges from the bibliography is directly linked to the debate about American Jewish activity during the Holocaust. Both scholars and contemporaries stress that the American Jewish community enjoyed extraordinary political and economic power during the 1930s and '40s. This phenomenon was not merely the outcome of the improved economic and political condition of Jews in the United States. The crisis of European Jewry and the political weight carried by the United States in the context of World War II both contributed to the enhanced standing of the American Jewish community among world Jewry. The fact that the American Jewish community remained unharmed by the horrors of the war and the Holocaust despite the major contribution of American Jews to their country's war effort has led many scholars to level trenchant criticism at the allegedly muted activity undertaken by American Jews in general and their leadership in particular toward rescuing Jews during the Holocaust.

The story of the World Jewish Congress presented here indicates a far more complex reality. Perusal of the organization's archive reveals that the Congress leadership conducted extremely significant rescue activity on behalf of European Jews during the 1940s. The full significance of the rescue efforts emerges against the backdrop of the restrictions and difficulties that confronted the Jewish leadership in the United States within the country at a time of world war.

I have sought to add a further stratum to the corpus of studies of the American Jewish leadership during the Holocaust through the diversity of sources cited in the book's chapters. I believe that this work demonstrates that sweeping censure of the patterns of activity conducted by the American Jewish leadership during the 1940s fails to consider the significant rescue efforts in spite of the difficulties encountered by American Jewish leaders during their campaign on behalf of European Jews during World War II.

As an Israeli scholar engaged in the study of American Jewry, I take particular interest in the activity that the World Jewish Congress directed toward shaping the Jewish Diaspora in Europe and rehabilitating the Jewish communities there following World War II. Most studies done during the initial decades after the founding of the State of Israel addressed the various contexts of this dramatic event. The discussion among American Jewry became a part of this trend, and their political and economic contribution to the establishment of the state was underscored by the criticism leveled at the limited success of their contribution to the rescue of Jews during the Holocaust. As the defining impact of the founding of the State of Israel gradually receded into the past, historical discourse began to address broader issues relating to the essence of Jewish existence following World War II as well as to the establishment of Israel. In this book I examine the attempt by WJC leaders to reestablish and rehabilitate Jewish communities in postwar Europe and to operate within the United Nations Organization as a representative Jewish organization. Rather than conducting this effort from an anti-Zionist worldview, they emphasized that the recovery effort would function alongside their public, economic and political support for the young state.

The efforts of the World Jewish Congress at rehabilitating the Jewish communities of Europe reinforce the conclusion that the founding of the State of Israel was but part of the process of shaping the postwar Jewish world. It behooves us as scholars to broaden the scope of the study and discussion of this issue within academia, and to contribute to the evolution of the discourse on this topic within the State of Israel, in the United States, and throughout the Jewish world.

Bibliography

Archives

American Jewish Historical Society (by collection)
Lipsky Louis Papers, P-672 Wise Stephen Papers, P-134

Central Zionist Archive Sin Jerusalem (CZA) (by record group)
Aliyat Ha-No'ar European Office, L-58 American Zionist Emergency Council/Committee, F-39 Felix Frankfurter Felix Papers, A-264 Nahum Goldmann Papers ,Office, Z-6, Personal, S-80 Jewish Agency Executive's meetings in Jerusalem (Protocols), S-100 Jewish Agency Office London, Z-4 Jewish Agency, Child and Youth Aliya Department, S-75, The Europen Office of the Youth Aliya Department L-58 Emanuel Neumann Emanuel Papers , A-123.
Stephen Wise Papers, A-243.
World Jewish Congress Geneva Office, C-3.
World Jewish Congress Israel Office, C-6. Zionist Organization of America, Z-5

The Jacob Rader Marcus Center of the American Jewish Archives, Cincinnati, OH. (AJA), collection 361: World Jewish Congress Records. 1918 – 1982.
Series A. Central Files. 1919-1976.
Series B. Political Department/Department of International Affairs and United Nations. 1919-1977.
Series C. Institute of Jewish Affairs. 1918 – 1979.
Series D. Relief and Rescue Department. 1939 – 1969.
Series E. Culture Department. 1943 – 1978.
Series H. Alphabetical Files. 1919 – 1981.

The American Jewish Joint Distribution Committee Archives, New York and Jerusalem (JDC)
Rescue activities in Portugal, Sections 1933/44

Microfilm edition of the Abba Hillel Silver Archive in Cleveland, Ohio (Silver Archive) (by rolle number and file number).

Yad Vashem Archives, Jerusalem (by record group)
Yad Vashem Collection of Testimonies O3.

Survivors of the Shoah – Visual History Foundation, established by Steven Spielberg Testimonies Collections O93.
War Refugee Board (WRB) Documents in Dr. Chaim Pazner Papers at Yad Vashem Archives, Section P-12

Published Documents

Adler, Selig. "Franklin D. Roosevelt and Zionism: The Wartime Record." In *American Zionism, Mission and Politics (American Jewish History, vol. 8)*, by Jeffery S. Gurock. New York, 1998, 209–220.

Alroey, Gur. *Immigration: Jewish Migration to Palestine in the Early Twentieth Century*. [in Hebrew] Jerusalem, 2004.

Anderson, Benedict. *Imagined Communities: Reflections on the Origin and Spread of Nationalism*. London, 1983.

Arad, Yitzhak. *Belzec, Sobibor, Treblinka: The Operation Reinhard Death Camps*. Bloomingtion and Indianapolis, 1987.

Arditi, Binyamin. *The Jews of Bulgaria During the Years of the Nazi Regime, 1940–1944*. [in Hebrew] Tel Aviv, 1962.

Arendt, Hannah. *Eichmann in Jerusalem: A Report on the Banality of Evil*. New York, 1963.

Ashkenazi, Niva. "The Youth Movements' Children's Homes in the US Occupation Zone in Germany, 1946–1948." M.A. Thesis. [in Hebrew] Tel Aviv University, 1996.

Avizoha, Meir, ed. *David Ben Gurion: Stepping toward a State, Memoirs from the Legacy*. [in Hebrew] Tel Aviv, 1993.

Avni, Haim. *Spain, the Jews and Franco*. Philadelphia, 1982.

Barlas, Haim. *Rescue at the Time of the Holocaust*. [in Hebrew] Tel Aviv, 1975.

Bauer, Yehuda. *My Brother's Keeper: A History of the American Jewish Joint Distribution Committee, 1929–1939*. Philadelphia, 1974.

Baumel Tidor, Yehudit. "The Rescue and Settlement of Jewish Refugee Children from Europe in the USA during the Years 1938–1948." Ph.D. Dissertation. [in Hebrew] Bar Ilan University, 1985.

Bernstein Bronstein, Tatiana. "The Unsuccessful Attempt to Expel the Jews of Denmark in Historiographical Debate." [in Hebrew], *Yad Vashem Collected Studies*. (1987): 299–328.

Bickerton, J. Ian. "President Truman's Recognition of Israel." *American Jewish Historical Quarterly*, 58 (1968): 173–240.

Bierbrier, Doreen. "The American Zionist Emergency Council: An Analysis of a Pressure Group." *American Jewish Quarterly* (1970): 82–105.

Bishop, James. *F. D. R.'s Last Years*. New York, 1974.

Bohler, E. Charles. *Witness to History, 1929–1969*. New York, 1973.

Borkin, Joseph. *The Crime and the Punishment of I. G. Farben*. New York, 1978.

Breitman, Richard and Allan J. Lichtman. *FDR and the Jews*. Cambridge and London, 2013.

Brubaker, Roger. *Ethnicity without Groups*. Cambridge, MA, 2004.

Campbell, Angus and Philip E. Converse, Warren E. Miller, Donald E. Stokes. *The American Voter*. New York, 1960.

Chalk, Frank and Kurt Jonassohn. *Genocide Analyses and Case Studies*. New Haven, CT, 1990.

Cohen, M. Steven and Charles S. Liebman. "Israel and American Jewry in the Twenty-First Century: A Search for New Relationships." In *Beyond Survival and Philanthropy: American Jewry and Israel*, edited by Allon Gal and Alfred Gottschalk. Cincinnati, 2000, 3–24.

Cohen, W. Naomi. *Not Free to Desist: The American Jewish Committee 1906–1966*. Philadelphia, 1972.

Cesarani, David, ed. *Genocide and Rescue: The Holocaust in Hungary 1944*. Oxford, 1997.

Diner, R. Hasia. *The Jews of the United States*. Berkeley, 2004.

Doorley, Michael. *Irish-American Diaspora Nationalism: The Friends of Irish Freedom 1916–1935*. Dublin, 2005.
Dovkin, Eliyahu. *Aliya and Rescue During the Holocaust Years*. [in Hebrew] Jerusalem, 1946.
Duncan, C. and A. Wallach. "The Universal Survey Museum." *Art History* 3 (4) (1980): 447–69.
Eddy, a. William. *F. D. R. Meets Ibn Saud*. New York, 1954.
Eilat, Eliyahu. *The Struggle for the State*. [in Hebrew] Tel Aviv, 1979.
Encel, Jean. *The Annals of the Holocaust: Romania*. Vol. 1. [in Hebrew] Jerusalem, 2002.
Erlich-Dubnov, Sophie. *The Life and Work of S.M. Dubnov: Diaspora Nationalism and Jewish History*. Bloomington, IN, 1991.
Feinberg, Natan. "The Committee of Jewish Delegations 1919–1936." *Gesher (A Quarterly on the Issue of the Life of the Nation)* (WJC Israeli Executive) (1970): 15–16.
Feingold, L. Henry. *Saving the Jews of Russia: The American Jewish Effort, 1967–1989*. Syracuse, NY, 2007.
Feingold, L. Henry. "Was there Communal Failure?: Some Thoughts on the American Jewish Response to the Holocaust." *American Jewish History* 81 (1993): 60–80.
Feldstein, L. Ariel. *The Gordian Knot: David Ben Gurion, the Zionist Organization, and US Jewry*. [in Hebrew] Qiryat Sdeh Boqer, Israel: Ben Gurion Institute for the Study of Israel, Zionism, and Ben Gurion's Legacy, 2003.
Ferrell, H. Robert. *Harry S. Truman*. Columbia, 1994.
Figowitz, Mordechay. "The American Jewish Background to the Founding of the World Jewish Congress: Shaping Policy and Organizational Patterns Between the Zurich Convention in 1927 and the Geneva Convention in 1932." M.A. Dissertation. [in Hebrew] Haifa University, 1977.
Friedrich, J. Carl. *American Policy Toward Palestine*. Washington DC, 1944.
Friling, Tuvia. *An Arrow in the Fog: Ben Gurion, The Yishuv Leadership, and Attempts at Rescue During the Holocaust*. [in Hebrew] Jerusalem, 1998.
Gabler, Neal. *An Empire of Their Won: How the Jews Invented Hollywood*. New York, 1988.
Gal, Alon. *David Ben Gurion: Toward a Jewish State, Political Preparation Vis-à-vis the White Paper and the Outbreak of World War II, 1938–1941*. [in Hebrew] Ben Gurion University, 1985.
Ganin, Zvi. "The Debate Between Activists and Moderatesin the US Zionist Leadership During the 1940s: The Stephen Wise and Abba Hillel Silver Dispute." [in Hebrew], *Ha-Tsionut* 9 (1984): 342–343.
Gellner, Ernest. *Nations and Nationalism*. Oxford, 1983.
Goldberger, Leo , ed. *The Rescue of the Danish Jews*. New York, 1987.
Goldmann, Nahum. "Dr. Stephen Wise." In *On the Paths of My People*, by Nahum Goldmann. [in Hebrew] Jerusalem, 1968.
—. *The Autobiography of Nahum Goldmannn: Sixty Years of Jewish Life*. New York, 1969.
—. *The Jewish Paradox*. London, 1978.
Gottheil, J. Richard. *Zionism*. Philadelphia, 1914.
Guttman, Israel, senior editor. *Encyclopedia of the Holocaust*. [in Hebrew] Vol. 2. Tel Aviv, 1990, 459–480.
Habib, Jasmin. *Israel Diaspora and the Routes of National Belonging*. Toronto, 2004.
Halbwachs, M. *On Collective Memory*. Translated by L. A. Coser. Chicago, 1992.
Halperin, Samuel. *The Political World of American Zionism*. Detroit, 1961.
Hilberg, Raul. *The Destruction of the European Jews*. Chicago, 1961.
Hosbawm, Eric. *Nations and Nationalism Since 1780*. Cambridge, 1990.

Hutchinson, John. "Cultural Nationalism and Moral Regeneration." In *Nationalism*, edited by John Hutchinson and Anthony D. Smith, Oxford. 1994.

Kedourie, Elie, ed. *Nationalism in Asia and Africa*. London, 1971.

Keshles, Haim. *The Annals of Bulgaria's Jews During the Holocaust Period, 1939–1944*. [in Hebrew] Vol. 3. Tel Aviv, 1969.

Keynes, Maynard John. *Activities 1941–1946: Shaping the Post War World: Bretton Woods and Reparations*. London, 1980.

Kochavi, Ariel. *Prelude to Nuremberg, Allied War Crimes Policy and the Question of Punishment*. Chapel Hill, NC and London.

Kubowizki, a. Leon. *Unity In Dispersion: A History of the World Jewish Congress*. New York, 1948.

Lacouture, Jean. *Pierre Mendes France*. New York, 1984.

Lagrou, Pieter. "Return to a Vanished World: European Societies and the Remnants of their Jewish Communities, 1945–1947." In *The Jews Are Coming Back: The Return of the Jews to their Countries of Origin After WWII*, by David Bankier. [in Hebrew] New York and Jerusalem, 2005,1–24.

Lavie, Smadar and Ted Swedenburg, eds. *Displacement, Diaspora, and Geographies of Identity*. London, 1996.

Lazare, Lucien. *La résistance juive: Un combat pour la survie*. Jerusalem, Yad Vashem, 2012.

Levantrosser, F. William, ed. *Harry S. Truman: The Man from Independence*. New York, 1986.

Lewis, A. Mark. "The World Jewish Congress and the Institute of Jewish Affairs at Nuremberg" Ideas, Strategies, and Political Goals, 1942–1946." [in Hebrew],*Yad Vashem Studies* (2008): 181–210

Lipsky, Louis. *Zionist Figures*. [in Hebrew] Jerusalem, 1957.

Lipstadt, D. E. "America and the Memory of the Holocaust, 1950–1965." *Modern Judaism* 16 (1996): 195–214.

Litwak, Yosef. "The Joint's Contribution to the Rehabilitation of Survivors in Poland." In *East European Jewry Between Holocaust and Revival 1944–1948*, [in Hebrew] edited by Binyamin Pinkus, Ben Gurion Heritage Center, Ben Gurion University, 1987,344–388.

Loefler, James. "Between Zionism amd Liberalism: Oscar Janowsky and Diaspora Nationalism in America", *AJS Review* 34 (2010): 289–308.

Louça, Antonio and Ansgar Schäfer "The Lisbon Connection Regarding the Sales of Gold Plundered by the Nazis. [in Hebrew], *Yad Vashem Collected Studies* 27 (1988): 81–94.

Matsas, Michael. *The Illusion of Safety: The Story of the Greek Jews During the Second World War*. New York, 1997.

McCullough, David. *Truman*. New York, 1992.

Medding, Y. Peter. "Segmented Ethnicity and the New Jewish Politics." *Studies in Contemporary Jewry* 3 (1987): 26–48.

Medoff, Rafael. *The Deafening Silence*. New York, 1987.

Milgram, Avraham. "Portugal, its Consuls, and the Jewish Refugees." [in Hebrew], *Yad Vashem Collected Studies* 27 (1988): 95–122

Mints, A. *Popular Culture and the Shaping of Holocaust Memory in America*. Seattle, 2001.

Mittelberg, David. *The Israel Connection and American Jews*. London, 1999.

Molcho, Michael and Yosef Nehama. *The Holocaust of Greek Jews, 1941–1944*. [in Hebrew] Jerusalem, 1965.

Myers, N. David. *Between Jew and Arab the Lost Voice of Simon Rawidowicz*. Waltham MA, 2008.

Neander, Joachim. "The Danzig Soap Case: Facts and Legends Around 'Professor Spanner' and the Danzig Anatomic Institute 1944–1945." *German Studies Review* 29 (2006): 1.
Ne'eman Arad, Gulie. *America, Its Jews, and the Rise of Nazism*. Bloomington, 2000.
— "Cooptation of Elites: American Jewish Reactions to the Nazi Menace, 1933." [in Hebrew], *Yad Vashem Studies* 25 (1996):21–48.
Neumann, Emanuel. *In the Arena of the Zionist Struggle: A Memoir*. [in Hebrew] Jerusalem, 1977.
Nissan, Oren. "A New Perspective on the Rescue of Bulgaria's Jews." [in Hebrew], *Yad Vashem Collected Studies* 7 (1968): 116–177.
Novick, Peter. *The Holocaust in American Life*. Boston and New York, 1999.
Parzen, Herbert. "The Roosevelt Palestine Policy, 1943–1945." *American Jewish Archives* 1 (1974): 31–65
Patterson, T. James. *Mr. Republican: A Biography of Robert A. Taft*. Boston, 1972.
Penkower, Monty Noam. "The World Jewish Congress Confronts the International Red Cross During the Holocaust." *Jewish Social Studies* 41 (1979):229–256.
Pianko, Noam. *Zionism and Roads Not Taken: Rawidowicz, Kaplan, Kohn*. Bloomington Indiana, 2010.
Poznanski, Renee. *Being a Jew in France, 1939–1945*. [in Hebrew] Jerusalem, 1994.
Rabinivitch, Simon, ed. *Jews and Diaspora Nationalism*. Waltham MA, 2012.
Radu, Loanid. *The Holocaust in Romania: The Destruction of Jews and Gypsies Under the Antonescu Regime, 1940–1944*. Chicago, 2000.
Raider, A. Mark, ed. *Nahum Goldmann: Statesman Without a State*. Albany, NY, 2009.
—. *The Emergence of American Zionism*. New York and London, 1998.
Raphael, Mark Lee. *Abba Hillel Silver*. New York, 1989.
Reinharz, Jehuda. *Zionism and the Great Powers: A Century of Foreign Policy*. New York, 1994.
Robinson, Jacob and Oscar Karbach, M. Laserson, Nehemia Robinson, Marc Vichniak. *Were the Minorities Treaties a Failure?* New York, 1943.
Robinson, Nehemia. *The United Nations and the World Jewish Congress*. New York, 1955.
Rojanski, Rachel. "A Foreign and Discordant Language Indeed? On the Question of Ben Gurion's Attitude Toward Yiddish in the Wake of the Holocaust." [in Hebrew], *Iyunim Bitkumat Israel: Studies in Zionism, the Yishuv and State of Israel* 15 (2005): 463–82.
Roper, Trevor Hugh. *Jewish and Other Nationalisms*. London, 1961.
Rosen, Shabtai. "The People of Israel's Great Advocate: In Memory of Jacob Robinson." [in Hebrew], *Gesher* 24 (1978): 91–101.
Rosenman, I. Samuel. *Working with Roosevelt*. New York, 1972.
Rosenman, Samuel and Dorothy. *Presidential Style*. New York, 1976.
Rotem, Stephanie. "Holocaust Remembrance Museums: The Role of Architecture in Constructing the collective Memory of the Holocaust." [in Hebrew] Ph.D. dissertation. Tel Aviv University, 2010.
Sarna, Jonathan. *American Judaism*. [in Hebrew] Jerusalem, 2005.
—. *Ameriican Judaism*. Yale University, 2004.
Schechtman, B. Joseph. *The United States and the Jewish State Movement*. New York, 1969.
Schwarzbart, I. Isaac. *25 Years In the Service of the Jewish People: A Chronicle of Activities of the World Jewish Congress, August 1932–February 1957*. New York, 1957.
Segev, Zohar. "US Zionists in Israel During the Fifties: Political Opposition and a Liberal Alternative." [in Hebrew], *Iyunim Bitkumat Israel: Studies in Zionism, the Yishuv and the State of Israel* 12 (2012): 493–519.
Selter, M. Robert and Norman J. Cohen (eds.). *The Americanization of the Jews*. New York, 1955.

Shapiro, D. Robert. *A Reform Rabbi in the Progressive Era: The Early Career of Stephen S. Wise.* New York, 1988.

Shiff, Ofer. *Integrating Jews: American Reform Universalism vis-a-vis Zionism, Anti-Semitism and Holocaust.* [in Hebrew] Tel Aviv, 2001.

—. *The Defeated Zionist: Abba Hillel Silver and His Attempt to Transcend Jewish Nationalisim.* [in Hebrew] Tel Aviv, 2010.

—. "The Integrative Function of Early American Zionism." *The Journal of Israeli History* 15, no. 1 (1994).

Shpiro, H. David. *From Philanthropy to Activism: The Transformation of American Zionism in the Holocaust Years 1933–1945.* New York, 1994.

Smith, D. Anthony. *The Nation in History: Historiographical Debates about Ethnicity and Nationalism.* Hanover, NH, 2000.

Smith, D. Anthony. "Zionism and Diaspora Nationalism." *Israel Affairs* (1995):1–19.

Sowell, Thomas. *The Economics and Politics of Race.* New York, 1973.

Urofsky, I. Melvin. *A Voice That Spoke For Justice: The Life and Times of Stephen S. Wise.* Albany, 1982.

—. *We Are One: American Jewry and Israel.* New York, 1978.

Vilhjalmsson, Orn Vilhjalmur and Bent Bludnikow. "Rescue, Expulsion, and Collaboration: Denmark's Difficulties with Its World War II Past." *Jewish Political Studies Review*, 18 (2006): 3–29.

Weiss, Yfaat. "The Transfer Agreement and the Boycott Movement: A Jewish Dilemma on the Eve of the Holocaust." [in Hebrew], *Yad Vashem: Collection of Studies* 26 (1997): 129–171.

Weissmann, Yitzhak. *Facing the Colossi of Evil.* [in Hebrew] Tel Aviv, 1968.

Weizmann, Chaim. *The Letters and Papers of Chaim Weizmann.* Vol. 27. 1975.

Welles, Benjamin. *Sumner Welles: F. D. R.'s Global Strategist.* New York, 1997.

Wise, Stephen S. *Challenging Years: The Autobiography of Stephen Wise 1974–1949.* London, 1951.

Wyman, S. David. *The Abandonment of the Jews, America and the Holocaust 1941–1945.* New York, 1984.

Yablonka, Hanna. "The Development of Holocaust Consciousness in Israel: The Nuremberg, Kastner and Eichmann Trials." *Israel Studies* 8 (2003) : 1–24.

—. "Oriental Jewry and the Holocaust: A Three-Generational Perspective," *Israel Studies* 14 1 (2009): 94–122.

Yahil, Leni. *The Rescue of Danish Jewry: Test of Democracy.* Philadelphia, 1969.

Index

Aliyat Ha-Noar 152
American Jewish Committee (AJC) 38, 39, 103, 169, 212
American Jewish community
   and American Jewish Committee 38
   and Holocaust commemoration 201
   and support for Jewish state 22, 43, 98
   and the State of Israel 168
   as a minority 7, 103
   as sponsors 133
   dominance of 22
   power of 5, 104, 224
   standing among world Jewry 225
   studies of 224
American Jewish Congress 1, 6, 37, 41
American Jewish Joint Distribution Committee (JDC) 127, 140, 153, 156, 157
   objections to WJC activity in Portugal 136
American Jewish public
   and Abba Hillel Silver 57, 75
   and Roosevelt 49
   and Yalta Conference 72
   and Zionism 94
   concern for Polish Jews 127
   ethnic activity 95, 96, 103, 215
   objective of 93
   reaction to Holocaust 8, 99
   voting patterns 85
American Jews
   and rescue of Jews 225
American public
   and Abba Hillel Silver 45
Amzelak, Moshe 136
Anglo-American Committee of Inquiry 90
Anielevich, Mordechi 144
Anti-Jewish legislation 199
   anti-Semitism
   American 102
   and Abba Hillel Silver 103
   and Herzl 218
   and Institute of Jewish Affairs 188
   and Poland 126, 127
   and Portugal 139
   and U.S. Congress 40
   fear of 94
   ideology 197, 198
   in Central and Eastern Europe 95
   post-war 215
Antonio Salazar
   ties with Germany 135
Argentina 180, 181
Assimilation 97
Atlantic City declaration 69, 70
Autonomist movement 214
Azaria, Malka 149

Balfour Declaration 1, 2, 19, 77, 82
Barlas, Haim 156, 157, 159
Beck, Jozef 126, 128
Belgium
   rescue of children 25
Benes, Edvard 118
Ben Gurion, David 31, 46, 56, 63, 169
Bergson group 49, 103
Blaustein, Jacob 169
Bloom, Sol 49, 59, 82
Blum, Leon 126
B'nai Brith 16
Boris, King of Bulgaria 162
Brandeis, Louis D. 125
Bretton Woods Agreement 209
Brubaker, Rogers 20, 21
Bulgaria 158
   American involvement 162
   deportation of Jews 161, 162
   opposition to expulsion 162
   support for Germany 161

Catholic 21, 96, 146, 149
Catholic Church 150
Chicago 76, 78, 80, 85, 175
Children
   adoption of 152, 178, 179
   arrests of 27
   care of 138, 149, 152
   condition of 150
   cost to rescue 151
   hiding in Belgium 146

hiding in Holland 146
immigration to America 153
immigration to Palestine 152, 156
post-war needs 177, 179, 180
rescue of 147, 149, 155, 158, 219, 220
smuggling of 121, 148, 150, 157
Claims Conference 186, 207
Cold War 215
Committee of Jewish Delegations 1, 213
Communities, Jewish
   cooperation among 213
   rehabilitation of 176, 178, 225
   restoration of 175, 184, 207
Community, Jewish
   Bulgarian 162
   Danish 163
   Hungarian 165
   in Palestine 182
   in United States 224
   Portuguese 137
   post-WWII 95
Community, Jewish in Palestine 170
Congress Weekly 95, 137, 175, 187, 205
Czechoslovakia 16, 119, 126, 129, 132, 141
   Jewish New Year letter 132
   Jews as national minority 129

De Kauffmann, Hendrich 163
Delbos, Yvon 126
Democratic Party
   and Abba Hillel Silver 81, 84
   and FDR 59, 69, 104
   and pro-Zionist resolutions 87
   and rescue of Jews 97
   Jewish control 100
   platform 81, 86
      and pro-Zionist resolutions 86
      and Zionism 87
Democratic Party Convention 53, 79, 81, 83, 87, 89
Denmark
   and transfer of Jews to Sweden 163
   German invasion of 163
   rescue of Danish Jews 167
   rescue of Jews 219
Dewey, Thomas 53, 54, 74, 77, 78, 80, 81, 84, 85, 86, 101

Dexter, Robert 154, 155
Diaspora
   and Palestine 2
   and the State of Israel 187, 209, 223
   in the post-war world 169, 210
   model 176
   nationalism 4, 168, 169, 171, 188, 201, 212
Displaced persons 97, 116, 148, 169, 176
   and Palestine 184
   resettlement 175, 184
Dovkin, Eliyahu
   and immigration permits 155
   and JDC memorandum 156
   refugee Aliya from France 156
Dual loyalty 13, 92, 213
Dubnov, Shimon 17, 214
Duckwitz, Georg Ferdinand 163
Dulles, John Foster 56, 78, 79, 81, 85

Eden, Anthony 36
Eichmann trial 186, 195
Eisenhower, Dwight 56
Election
   and founding of Jewish State 45
   and pro-Zionist resolutions 58, 76, 86
   and rescue of Jews 99
Emancipation 3
Emergency Council 45
   and pro-Zionist resolution 49
   and Zionism 83
Evian Conference 129, 131
   Extermination 145
   description of 31, 200
   location of camps 194
   reports of 31, 92, 219
   substantiation of 26
   WJC response to 133, 134

Farben, I. G. 207
Fascism 41, 126
Feingold, Henry 7
Feuer, Leon 58
Final Solution 22, 24
Finland
   and rescue of Danish Jews 164
Fish, Hamilton
   and pro-Zionist resolutions 88

Forced labor 199
France
    rescue of children from 138, 146, 147, 150
    support of Polish and Romanian Jews 127
Franco, General Francisco 159
Franco, Nicolas 140, 158
Frankfurter, Felix 54, 61, 62, 80, 90, 125
Free Synagogue 9
Friling, Tuvia 31

Gellner, Ernest 211
Germany
    anti-Semitic propoganda 3, 94
    Jews of 16, 26
    reparations agreement with Israel 186, 207
Globalization 3
Goga-Cuza regime 23
Goldmann, Nahum
    and anti-Semitism 20
    and establishment of Jewish state 43, 92
    and Palestine Question 92, 98
    and policy of restraint 94, 221
    and pro-Zionist resolutions 63, 64
    and WJC ideology 12, 14, 15, 21, 91, 98
    and World Zionist Organization 10, 14
    and Zionist movement 10
    Anglo-American Committee of Inquiry 90
    Atlantic City conference 120, 193, 222
    background 8
    founder of WJC 5, 10
    president of WJC 10
    rescue of Jewish children 147
    rescue of Polish Jews 117, 129
Goldstein, Israel 56, 86
Government-in-exile 133, 149
    Czechoslovakian 118
    Dutch 146
    French 141, 147
    Polish 26, 119, 121, 153
Great Britain 55, 142
Greece
    Athens 156, 158, 159
    Hadari Camp 158, 160
    Thessalonica 159, 160

Grossmann, Kurt 192
Gruenbaum, Yitzhak 35, 36, 37, 3839, 103, 220
Guggenheim, Paul 26, 31

Hadassah 44, 95, 136
Hantke, Arthur 13
Hebrew, study of 152
Hebrew Union College 9
Helman, Jacob 180
Helsinki Conference 12
Herbert Hoover Library 195
Herzl, Theodore 217, 218
Hilman, Sidney 101
Holland 143, 146
Holocaust
    memory 34, 35, 195, 201
    museum Washington DC 199
    reports of 24, 28
Hungary
    Hungarian Jews 165
    rescue efforts 220
Hyman, Joseph 138

Identity, ethnic
    and American Jews 215
    and Holocaust, Museum 200
    and WJC 17, 201, 210, 218
Institute of Jewish Affairs 14, 195, 200, 206, 223
Italy 17, 121, 126, 159

Jackson, Robert 186
Jerusalem 13, 46, 85, 186, 199, 205
Jewish Agency 3
    agreement with Joint Distribution Committee 138
    Aliya department 156
    and trials of war criminals 206
    Executive 56
Jewish identity 203
    and Diaspora nationalism 215
Jewish Institute of Religion 9
Jewish Joint Distribution Committee
    and Portuguese Jewish community 138
Jewish lobby 78

Jewish migration 131
  to Palestine 2, 3, 61, 92, 131, 177, 191
Jewish solidarity 3, 19, 95, 217
Jewish state
  and Diaspora model 211
  and WJC 13, 17, 90
  and WJC policy 178
Jewish tradition 182
Jewish vote 80, 86
  and FDR 54, 68, 87
  political use of 70, 79, 85, 89, 96, 102, 168, 222
Jordana, Count 159
Judenrat 34
Jüdisches Museum, Berlin 199

Kallen, Horace M. 3, 4, 183
Kapo 29, 34, 35
Keren Ha-Yesod 13
Kibbutz Lohamei Ha-Geta'ot 199
Kubowitzki, Leon 115, 116, 166

League of Nations 3, 4, 15, 19, 24, 125, 126, 129, 219
Lemberger, Yehuda 141
Library of Congress 195
Lifshitz, Shlomo 152
Lipsky, Louis 11, 16, 38
Lithuania 115, 185
Long, Breckenridge 164

Macedonia 161
Mack, Julian 11
Mandate 82
Marcus, Robert 208
Marshall, George 63
Masaryk, Jan 118, 129
Masaryk, Thomas 129
Mendes France, Pierre 141
Migration to Palestine 177
Minorities
  ethnic 20, 47, 94, 102, 103, 191
  Jewish 19, 124, 190
  rights of 4, 100, 125, 187, 210
Mizrahi movement 179
Money, fundraising 181
Money, transfer of

  for reparations 207
  from US 120, 123
  to Belgium 121
  to Europe 120, 121, 122
  to France 121, 150
  to Holland 121, 147
  to Poland 121
  to Portugal 136, 151
  to Red Cross 122
  to State of Israel 207
  to Switzerland 122
  to underground activists 166
Monsky, Henry 16
Morgenthau, Henry 94
Munich agreement 132

Nationalism
  and American Jewry 215
  and Warsaw Ghetto Uprising 202
  Diaspora 215
  Jewish 2, 18, 210, 211
Nazi concentration camps 29
  Belzec 27
  Bergen Belsen 160
  Mauthausen 146
  Sobibor 27
  Theresienstadt 164
  Treblinka 29, 31, 33, 34
Neumann, Emanuel
  and pro-Zionist declaration 57
  and pro-Zionist resolutions 51, 69, 74
New Deal 9, 100
New School for Social Research 183
New York Times 32
Niles, David 58, 59, 60, 64, 70, 81, 82, 83, 84, 87, 88, 222
North Africa 196
Nuremburg Trials 186, 194, 195

Opinion 9
Orphans
  in Europe 177
  orphanages 179, 181, 182

Palestine
  as destination for children 153
  as destination for rescued children 152

British involvement 75
immigration to 177
Rescue Committee 220
Peace conference 10
Peshev, Dimitar 161
Philanthropic organizations, Jewish 3, 95, 149
Pilsudski, Jozef 126
Pogroms 17, 26, 31, 32
Poland 16, 25, 26, 27, 119, 128, 144, 207
Politics, ethnic 7, 23, 96, 100
Portugal
    and JDC 138
    Lisbon 119, 121, 135, 136, 138, 158, 220
Post-war rehabilitation 169
Post-war world 190
Procope, Hjalmar 164
Proskauer, Joseph 38, 39, 41
Pro-Zionist resolutions 43, 46, 57, 67, 73, 79, 80

Quakers, American 151

Racism 3, 95, 100, 101
    in American society 100
Radigales, Sebastian Romero 160
Red Cross 145, 180
Reform movement 8
Refugees
    distinction from migrants 130
    from Germany 130
    in United States 94
    non-Jewish 174
    rehabilitation of 173
    status in Portugal 135, 139, 140
    status in Spain 140
Republican Party
    and pro-Zionist resolutions 79, 80, 87
Republican Party Convention 76, 77, 79, 80
    and pro-Zionist resolutions 81
Rescue Committee 156
Rescue of Jews
    and American victory 42
    and policy of restraint 117
    in Portugal 155
Resistance 30
    French 141, 146, 148

Jewish 33, 34, 197, 200, 201
Swedish 165
Riegner, M. Gerhart 24, 25, 117, 118, 123, 135
    telegram 24, 26, 119, 120, 220
Rights
    civil 16, 127
    human 3, 17, 186, 187, 206
    of German Jews 125
Robinson, Jacob 185, 187, 188, 189, 190, 191, 192, 194, 195, 198, 205, 206
    and minorities treaties 186
    and minority rights 187
    and United Nations 14, 185, 186
    and Yad Vashem 186
    letter to Goldmann and Wise 14
    response to UN request 206
Robinson, Nehemia 185
Romania 23, 121, 127
    Jews of 15, 21, 23, 24
Roosevelt, Franklin D. (FDR) 39, 40
    accusations against 82
    and Emergency Council 67
    and pro-Zionist resolutions 64
    and Pro-Zionist Resolutions 63, 65
    and War Refugee Board 151
    and Zionism 66, 75
    and Zionist movement 46, 47, 52, 60, 62, 72, 78
    pro-Zionist declaration 47, 50, 53, 54, 57
    relationship with Abba Hillel Silver 49
    relationship with Stephen Wise 9
    rescue of Jews 36, 42, 220
    Yalta conference 46
Rosenman, Samuel 62
    and Abba Hillel Silver 61
    and pro-Zionist resolutions 61, 63
Roth, Samuel 155
Rotschild, Ida 143

Salomon, Herman 53
Schwarzbart, Isaac I. 205
Shoemaker, Henry W. 162
Silver, Abba Hillel 9, 18, 44, 47, 49, 50, 52, 53, 54, 55, 56, 57, 59, 63, 64, 65, 67, 68, 69, 70, 71, 72, 73, 74, 76, 77, 78, 79, 80, 86, 87, 88, 89, 90, 91, 99, 101, 102, 103, 169, 222

and A. Robert Taft 81, 85, 89
and Emergency Council 46, 58, 101
and Jewish Agency 45
and Jewish vote 79, 101, 102
and pro-Zionist resolutions 45, 51, 58, 75, 83
and threat to withdraw from Republican Party Convention 82
anti-Roosevelt activity 70
position on minorities 100
relationship with FDR 60, 61, 62
relationship with Stephen Wise 46, 82
Slovakia 165
Smith, Anthony 211
Socialists 21
South America 5, 10
and procurement of passports 133
control of donations 13
Soviet Russia 20
Spain
and Jewish refugees 37
and Spanish Jews in Greece 161
and transfer of refugees 135
policy toward Jewish citizens 159
Stettinius, Edward R. 65, 67, 69
and pro-Zionist resolutions 65, 66
and Zionist movement 64
Sweden 163, 166
absorption of Danish Jews 164
accepting refugees 163
Switzerland 10, 27, 121, 180
Szold, Henrietta 152

Taft, Alfonso Robert 52, 55, 76, 77, 81, 88, 89
and pro-Zionist resolution 76
and pro-Zionist resolutions 55
Tartakower, Arieh 6, 121, 122, 145, 147, 173, 192
Taylor, Myron 36
Temple Emanu-El 9
Thrace 161
Tiferet Yisra'el Congregation 44
Training facility, areas of study 175
Truman, Harry S. 9, 46, 58, 93, 97, 98, 168
and support for Jewish state 93
and Zionist movement 56, 74

Unitarian Church 151
United Jewish Appeal 45
United Nations 45, 171, 208
and issues of minorities 208
and Zionist movement 63
Commission on Genocide 208
commission on human rights 206
Relief and Rehabilitation Administration (UNRRA) 174
War Crimes Committee 193
United States
action toward rescue of Jews 40
Defense Department 55, 122, 173
opposition to transfer of food 142
State Department 35, 67, 94, 97, 119, 162, 164, 190
and Jews in Poland and Romania 124
and pro-Zionist resolutions 46
and transfer of money 122, 123
Palestine policy 69
Treasury Department 123, 124
United States Congress 40, 52
United States House of Representatives 59, 67, 74, 100
and pro-Zionist resolutions 43
Foreign Affairs Committee 43, 49
United States Senate 48, 63, 64, 66, 100
and pro-Zionist resolutions 43, 58, 59
Foreign Relations Committee 43, 48, 52, 55, 67, 69, 77
Urofsky, Melvin 13

Vichy 27, 142, 158

Wagner, Robert 54, 59, 73, 81, 94
Wallenberg, Raul 166
War criminals 170, 194, 205, 223
Warsaw Ghetto 25, 27, 29, 32, 34
reports of deportations 27
Warsaw Ghetto Uprising 34, 144
and ethnic identity 205
and Jewish Identity 203
and State of Israel 204
and The Warsaw Ghetto Revolt 205
commemoration 201, 202
in Diaspora 204

in Israel 204
Remembering and Rebuilding 203
role in historical memory 203
role in Holocaust memory 34, 201, 202, 204
Weissmann, Lily 152
Weissmann, Yitzhak 157
   agreement with Portuguese government 135
   and communications network 141
   and French underground 141
   and Haim Barlas 156
   and letter from Robert Dexter 154
   and Nicolas Franco 140
   and Turkish Jews 158
   assistance of Dutch government 147
   background 135
   communications network 141
   envoy to Lisbon 135
   rescue of children 143
   ties with governments-in-exile 140
Weizmann, Chaim 158
   and Abba Hillel Silver 57
   and David Ben Gurion 63
   and pro-Zionist resolutions 63
   and Stephen Wise 10
   and Zionist movement 75
Welles, Sumner 117
White House 56, 64, 70, 85, 86, 93, 97
White paper 1939 47
Wilson, Woodrow 9
Wise, Stephen S.
   1936 convention 14
   1943 address to American Jewish Congress 91
   address at Montreux conference 155, 171
   and American Jewish Congress 6
   and April 1943 press conference 39
   and Democratic Party 1, 8, 9, 69, 79, 85
   and disclosure of Riegner telegram 24
   and Emergency Council 44, 46, 80
   and establishment of Jewish state 43
   and Harry S. Truman 74
   and Jewish vote 70, 97, 98
   and pro-Zionist resolutions 47, 74, 75, 222
   and reelection of FDR 40, 80, 88
   and Republican Party 86
   and support of a Jewish state 98
   and Theodore Herzl 217
   and Zionism 170
   and Zionist movement 8, 69, 170, 208
   as founder of WJC 4, 8
   background 10
   letter to Stettinius 69
   memorandum to United Nations 17
   memorandum to UNRRA 174
   relationship with Abba Hillel Silver 44, 87
   relationship with FDR 42, 56
   relationship with State Department 56
WJC offices 31, 119, 141, 151, 202, 220
   Geneva 118, 123, 151
   Switzerland 26
World Jewish Congress (WJC)
   and Diaspora model 211
   and dissemination of information 119, 120
   and Eastern European migration 131
   and effort on behalf on European Jews 129
   and escape of Mendes France 142
   and food distribution 143, 144, 145
   and fundraising 151
   and memorandum to League of Nations 4
   and philanthropic activity 128
   and policy of restraint 38, 93, 116
   and reports of events in Europe 27
   and rescue of children 148
   and support for Jewish state 221, 223
   and Zionist movement 13
   as a philanthropic body 141
   as a philanthropic organization 149
   as international organization 5
   attitude toward 157
   conference
   Atlantic City 115, 124
   database of names 144
   founding 3
   methods 133
   mode of operation 154
   objectives 12
   objectives of 3, 38
   operation in Portugal 155

      purpose of 217
      transfer of money 154
      World Jewish Congress (WJC)
      and policy of restraint 43
      and reports of events in Europe 35
      and Zionist movement 7, 13
      as an American Jewish body 17
      inaugural convention 1
World War I 15, 185, 197
World War II 100, 121, 133, 135, 185
      refugee problem 36
      War Refugee Board 151, 154, 165

Yad Vashem 199, 200
Yahil, Leni 164, 165
Yale University 195
Yalta Conference 58, 70, 71, 222
Yiddish 182
Yosef, Dov 64
Yugoslavia 161, 165

Zionism 16, 18, 66, 77, 78, 79, 175, 208, 211, 218
      American 17, 43, 44, 57, 67, 73, 75, 81, 83, 84, 87, 89, 96, 169, 170
      and Theodore Herzl 218
Zionist movement 12
      American Zionist movement 46, 47
      and founding of WJC 7, 218
      and Great Britain 95
      and need for WJC 170
      and political parties 101
      Labor Zionist movement 12
      World Zionist movement 43

www.ingramcontent.com/pod-product-compliance
Lightning Source LLC
Chambersburg PA
CBHW050859160426
43194CB00011B/2213